Foreword

This book will hopefully be a useful tool that people in Belfast, and on the Shankill in particular, can use to achieve better living conditions.

My thanks go to all the people on the Shankill with whom I have lived and worked and who when I return ask me what its like to be 'home'. To name individuals would be to do injury to those whose names I never knew.

My appreciation goes to all those who have helped in the preparation of this book by proof-reading it, typing it and providing me with a desk or bed during its production.

Farset Co-operative Press
Farset Co-operative Press is a community publishing group based in Belfast, Northern Ireland. It was founded in 1979 to foster writing in the community and to provide individuals and groups involved in social and community affairs with an opportunity to publish materials on relevant issues.

Already published:
The Shankill: Photographs by Buzz Logan. £2.25
'A collection of superb photographs of the Shankill as it is today.'
(Fortnight Magazine)

The Case for Comprehensives. Published in conjunction with C.A.S.E.

Forthcoming publications:
Citizen's Rights handbook
A practical guide to rights in Northern Ireland intended for anyone who needs information about his/her rights and how to obtain them. Covers Social Security, housing, the workplace, women, children, consumers, the law and courts, prisons and the Emergency Provisions, and contains suggestions on how things might be improved and changed.

Fostering
A book recounting the experience of parents who have fostered children in Northern Ireland.

Chapters

Introduction

This book is a retrospective attempt to understand what was achieved during a three year stint as a community planner in Belfast. I was financed for the work by the Barrow and Geraldine S. Cadbury Trust for the first year and by the Joseph Rowntree Charitable Trust for the last two years. The general theme underlying the research grants was to look for ways in which social scientists might be relevant to working class comunities.

It soon became clear that my own training as a social psychologist was nearly completely irrelevant as the basic problems were not to do with individual difficulties of adjustment (though these did exist) but with social and economic 'solutions' that whole communities were having inflicted on them in the name of progress. Redevelopment schemes and an urban motorway were planned to 'blitzkrieg' through working class Belfast uprooting a quarter of its population on the way. After the 'troubles' these were the biggest issues that confronted local communities in Belfast.

The possible courses of action open to a person such as myself were limited by one's position as an 'outsider' both in national and class terms. As regards the national question, i.e. the fight as to what was to happen internally and externally to the state of Northern Ireland, the sole role that an outsider could play was that of an adviser in terms of knowledge and skills. The one exception was where the 'outsider' operated in the guise of a mediator. Here, behind the mask of 'disinterested neutrality', the mediator attempted to bring opposing factions to the table. However by the fact that he is intervening at some particular stage in a conflict, a mediator implies that a solution is possible at that time. As during a conflict it is usually to one contestant's advantage for a halt to be called (in this case usually Westminster's), a mediator is not in fact being 'objective' but is adopting an ill-defined political position. This position is usually backed by a theoretical analysis which sees conflicts arising through 'miscommunication'. It took a long time for para-military groups in Northern Ireland to work out what was happening and it was only after they had trudged to frequent conferences in Donegal and Scotland that they realised that mediators could also be dangerous.

Excluding the mediator's role, the outsider in terms of the national question can only adopt the role of advisor. This is because taking a political stance involves putting forward a theory of action on the basis of which people get killed. An outsider has no political power base from which to make such statements. Such power can only come from membership of a party, para-military or other political group and it is difficult for an outsider to join such a group because it means taking the decision to surrender one of the few privileges that 'outsiders' have, which is a relative freedom to move about in both Protestant and Catholic areas.

Similarly it is difficult for local people to make an effective contribution without being aligned to a political group. Outsiders who transgressed, i.e. acted as if they were a member of a political party, were

7

soon put in their place as there is no right to criticise without a corresponding commitment to bear the cost.

Many of the same problems emerge in looking at the relationship between middle class 'dealers' and working class communities. What right does a middle class professional have to act in a working class area let alone speak for it? If for example the middle class person advocates a course of action, such as a rent strike, and doesn't live within the community, then he is asking others to bear costs that he doesn't. Even if he lives in the area he is normally cushioned, because of his income, from many of the problems that his clients have to put up with. There is therefore a crucial difference between being a community development worker acting as an adviser to groups and being a community activist, putting forward courses of action.

A community worker has a number of different power bases from which he can operate, based on:

(a) knowledge, either theoretical or practical, about community needs, as evidenced by the holding of a position such as a university lecturer or community development worker;

(b) employment by a government body and thereby having access to funds and control over services;

(c) the support of key groups in the community. The extent of the power in this case will be dependent upon which groups in the community are giving the worker their support;

(d) membership of a political party which has a base in the community.

The power base a community worker chooses to operate from will reflect his own political theory i.e. a local government employee (excluding infiltrators) will normally operate on the premise that social problems are solvable by reforming the system, i.e. a basically social — democratic position, and that the system has the interests of the community at heart.

In terms of my own position I started off with the belief that nine years of the theory and practise of social psychology would enable me to help the less well off. This was soon proved wrong. Social psychology has nothing to offer 'deprived communities', and, as I have argued elsewhere[1], can do nothing but exploit them. Instead of trying to find a use for the knowledge I had, in order to satisfy a feeling that I ought to be doing some good, it became necessary to ask what it was that communities needed. The answer quite clearly was help with planning problems which was how I came to be a community planner.

At first I saw myself as a broker between the wishes of the community and the objectives of the planning and housing authorities. But it became clear, as irreconcilable differences arose, that the interests that the authorities were serving were diametrically opposed to the needs of the working class comunities.

This therefore meant that effective action required a theoretical framework within which the conflicting interests could be understood and the advantages of alternative courses of action assessed. This is what this book attempts to do. From a personal stance as these conflicts of interests emerged, it became increasingly necessary to side with the community's viewpoint as there was no middle ground. This involved handling knowledge and data so that it benefited the community but it still left open the option of whether to be an adviser or an activist. However simply giving advice and not helping groups to find the means to act upon it, could quite rightly be construed as acting against their interests.

Therefore during the course of my time in Belfast I passed from being an academic adviser to an activist basing his position on the support of the community. This produced problems later when community groups no longer proved a sufficiently strong power base from which to fight local authorities. The obvious next step was to move to a political base, but as the basis of political groupings in Northern Ireland was determined by national, not class, issues, the chance of an outsider, even if admitted as a member, to be able to exert influences on social issues was minimal. It was mainly for these reasons that by Easter 1974 I had decided to leave after handing over as much of the work as possible to local community workers who would not face the problems of being an 'outsider'. This decision was subsequently justified by the setting up of a popular front group—the Save the Shankill campaign—which drew on all existing political groups in the area.

The first chapter 'Belfast through the ages' provides a political and economic background up to the 1950's to the subsequent housing and planning issues which dominated community activity in Belfast in the early 1970's. The second chapter, 'The Entry of the Planners' shows how the changing industrial base in Northern Ireland from 1930 onwards led necessarily to the introduction of physical planning. The rate at which the plans were implemented reflected the political struggle taking place between the orange system and the new managerial classes. Chapter 3 examines the development of one of these plans, the transportation plan, and shows how opposition to it grew and eventually killed off its main component, the BUM (the Belfast Urban Motorway).

Chapters 4 and 5 chronicle the effect of these industrial and physical changes on the Shankill Road area of Belfast. It's a horror story which just ran and ran. The next chapter, 'The Repairs that never got done' tells a typical tale of public authority neglect in the face of overwhelming hardship. The chapter on participation looks at the effectiveness of community action while the final chapter draws together the main themes in the book.

Ron Wiener

March, 1975

---

1. 'Community Psychology' The Still Born Child in D. Hawks and R. Wiener (eds.) *The Role of the Psychologist in the Community* Angus and Robertson 1976.

EDITOR'S NOTE

In the second edition the chapters by Ron Wiener are unchanged, but the book includes an additional chapter by Jackie Redpath giving a personal assessment of the major developments on the Shankill during the subsequent six years in which the Save The Shankill Campaign has been in existence. The story of the Campaign illustrates the dilemma of a community faced by a two-fold threat: inner city decline, accelerated by recession and public expenditure cuts on the one hand, and seemingly deliberate and systematic destruction under the guise of redevelopment by the Northern Ireland Office and British Army as a means of solving sectarian strife in Belfast, on the other.
June 1980.

Chapter 1

BELFAST THROUGH THE AGES

The intention of this chapter is to provide the background necessary to understand the origins and development of planning in the Belfast region and how and why regional and local political opposition to the plans arose.

The chapter first examines Belfast's industrial history in order to show how Belfast changed in the space of 25 years from being one of the United Kingdom's leading industrial cities to a city with a quarter of its population unemployed. The effect of this was that to survive economically, Northern Ireland had to attract new industries from abroad. In order for this to happen economic and physical plans were required to make Northern Ireland an attractive site for investors.

The chapter next takes a brief look at the formation of the Northern Ireland state and of the importance of the 'orange system'. This system was instrumental in delaying many of the planners' reforms. It was also the disintegration of this system, due to these economic changes which allowed Protestant working class opposition to make itself heard from 1969 onwards.

The chapter then looks quickly at the political set-up of Belfast corporation as this explains in part Belfast's poor housing record which is the subject of the last section of the chapter. It is the housing issue in particular which has dominated community activity in Belfast since 1969.

THE INDUSTRIAL DEVELOPMENT OF BELFAST

Belfast, which means 'the mouth of the sandbank' is situated near where the River Lagan runs into the sea. In the twelth century Eastern Ulster fell to John de Courcy, a Somerset knight who was part of the Norman invasion of the east coast of Ireland. He and his successors built a number of castles, including one at Belfast.

In 1603 the castle and land around Belfast were granted to Sir Arthur Chichester, who, as Lord Deputy, was responsible for the plantation of Ulster when Scottish and English settlers were brought into the present counties of Armagh, Londonderry, Fermanagh, Tyrone, Cavan and Donegal. By 1641 only 1/7th of the land in the 6 planted counties remained in Catholic hands.

During the seventeenth century and first half of the eighteenth century Belfast was mainly a market town, a passing through place for settlers to the plantation counties and to Antrim and Down which were privately planted by Scottish immigrants. In 1660 its population was 1,000 and this had risen to 2,000 by 1685.

From the early 1700's onwards a linen industry developed in the North. The reason for its development there lay largely in what is known as the Ulster custom where[1]:

11

"The Ulster landlords gave a customary recognition to the right of yearly tenants to remain undisturbed on their holdings so long as they 'acted properly' and paid their rents, and to sell their interest in the holding if they wished to give it up or could no longer pay the rent—the essential point about Ulster tenant right, as it was called, was that it secured the tenant compensation for any improvements he might have made and the goodwill of the farm."

This security permitted the tenant to invest in his land and allowed for the growth of cottage industries such as linen. The growth of this domestic linen industry continued through the eighteenth century and the export of linen cloth rose from 1.7m yards in 1710 to 11.2m yards in 1750 and to 20.6m yards in 1770[2]. Its effect in Northern Ireland was that:—

"you there behold a whole province peopled by weavers; it is they who cultivate or rather beggar the soil, as well as work the looms ... agriculture is there in ruins ... there literally speaking, is not a farmer in a hundred miles of the linen country in Ireland[3]."

The linen industry remained in Protestant hands because Catholics as a result of the religious wars of the seventeenth century "were under such discouragement that they cannot engage in any trade which requires both industry and capital[4]."

Up to this time Belfast remained predominantly a market town with "an export trade in agricultural produce and ancillary industries, such as brewing, distilling and tanning[5]."

"the imports of Belfast consist in rum, brandy, geneva and wines. Till within these two years much grain, since that none; Coals from Britain. Iron, timber, hemp and ashes from the Baltic. Barilla from Spain for the bleach greens. Tea, raw sugar, hops and porter, the principal articles from Great Britain. From North America, wheat, staves, flour and flax-seed ... the exports are beef, butter, pork to the West Indies and France. The great article, linen cloth to London ... Derry, Newry and Belfast, the linen export towns; two-thirds from Belfast ... there are three sugar houses here. The number of ships belonging to Belfast about 50 sail from 20 to 300 tons[6]."

By 1770 the handloom weaving industry was being displaced from Belfast and the Lagan Valley out towards the country areas, as the adoption of power spinning in Britain enabled her to capture the coarse linen market. It was replaced by the cotton industry and with it came the birth of Belfast's industrial history. It started when Robert Joy in 1777 paid a visit to Scotland where he saw the new cotton spinning machinery of Hargreaves and Arkwright and returned to Belfast where he started a small spinning mill on the Falls Road. By 1806, 15 per cent of Belfast's labour force was employed in the cotton mills. The majority of mills were operated by water power and were therefore situated on streams and rivers close to Belfast. The closeness to Belfast was determined by the need to import raw cotton and export finished goods. Belfast's population rose from 8,000 in 1757 to 20,000 in 1800.

However from 1810 onwards the cotton industry began to decline because of competition from Lancashire and after the 1815 depression wages were forced down by a third. Working conditions were not good and weavers worked:

"in small stifling houses; their food was very poor, their working hours from four in the morning to midnight, their average wage in times of depression 4s 6d a week[7]."

The 1825 depression virtually wiped out the cotton industry and the end of protection meant that finer English cottons outsold coarser Irish products while at the same time the invention in England in 1825 of the wet-spinning process undercut the remnants of the old Irish linen industry. The weavers were threatened with starvation and many emigrated to the United States, a practice that had started in the previous century:

"the spirit of emigrating in Ireland appears to be confined to two circumstances, the Presbyterian religion, and the linen manufacture ... the 'passenger' trade as they called it, had long been a regular branch of commerce, which employed several ships and consisted in carrying people to America ... when the linen trade was low, the 'passenger trade' was always high[8]."

Economic salvation came in 1828 when Thomas and Andrew Mulholland decided to rebuild their burnt out cotton mill as a flax spinning mill. The flax industry grew rapidly from one mill containing 15,000 spindles in 1829 to 24 flax mills containing 506,000 spindles in 1852 and already by 1835 over half the total exports from Belfast were linen. As with cotton, the industry required both water power and access to the port, as the industry depended on the importation of raw materials. The population of Belfast grew rapidly from 53,000 in 1831 to 68,000 in 1836 and 115,000 in 1853. Working conditions however were poor. Wages were low, in part because of the large proportion of women and children to men (7:3) who were employed and the hours were long:

". . . it is in the spinning room that little girls are engaged, and here it is that the tender form of childhood is often in danger of being taxed beyond what it is able to bear ... those who have been long in the atmosphere of the spinning room generally become pale and anaemic ... children placed there early and compelled to keep upon their feet the entire day, as the nature of their employment obliges them to do often, suffer from the young and tender bones, which form the arch of the foot, being crushed and flattened[9]."

These bad working conditions, combined with limited health facilities and poor housing conditions meant that in 1852 the average age of death in Belfast was as low as nine years.[10]

The Boom Years

The real industrial boom in Belfast occurred from 1850 onwards with the increasing use of power looms whose introduction was spurred by agricultural wage rises at the end of the famine. From 1861 onwards the industry received a further impetus when because of the American Civil War, the Lancashire mills were starved of raw cotton. The number of such looms rose from 100 in 1850 to 490 in 1862 and the number of employees in the linen industry trebled between 1850 and 1875.

13

The second plank around which Belfast's industrial progress was built was the shipbuilding industry. Because of its original role as a market town and then later because of the reliance of the linen and cotton industry on the import of raw materials and the export of finished goods, Belfast's port was always important. In the period from 1836 to 1852 the number of vessels trading in the port increased from 2,819 to 5,221[11]. A wooden shipbuilding industry had been started as early as 1791 by William Ritchie who transferred his business from Scotland and an iron sailing ship was constructed in 1838. However, the industry did not expand rapidly until 1854 when Harland, a young Glaswegian came in to manage a shipyard. Within 4 years he bought out the owner with money provided by a Liverpool financier. His labour force grew rapidly from 500 in 1861 to 3,000 in 1886 and 9,000 in 1900.

On the basis of these two industries Belfast boomed. Its population grew from 70,447 in 1841 to 349,180 in 1901. Many ancillary industries were established such as marine and textile engineering works and "rope making, vehicle building, heating and ventilation machine making and armaments followed in rapid succession, together with food and drink manufacturing and the service industries[12]."

Belfast therefore in the second half of the nineteenth century shared in the 'success' of Britain's industrial revolution. It had the fastest growth rate of any city in the British Isles. As one speaker against Home Rule put it:

"Belfast had done very well under the Union: her population had quadrupled in 50 years; her wage rates higher than anywhere in Ireland and in some cases up to British standards; as to customs revenue she ranked as the third port in the United Kingdom, being exceeded by only London and Liverpool; she has the largest weaving factory, the largest shipping output, the largest tobacco factory and the largest ropeworks in the world[13]."

By 1912, 70,000 people were employed in the linen, shipbuilding and engineering industries alone and this accounted for more than half of all employment in the manufacturing industries and a further 15,000 were employed in occupations connected with dress.

The End of the Boom Years

By 1925 unemployment in Belfast had reached 25 per cent and it was to remain near this level until after the outbreak of the second world war. The economic bubble burst and it marked the end of Belfast as a viable industrial centre based on the local ownership of wealth.

The industrial collapse was due primarily to the downturn in world trade after the first world war. The linen industry had in fact reached its peak in 1875 after which it entered a period of stagnation. After the war it suffered from competition from mass produced cotton and synthetic fibres and by 1930 there were 20,000 unemployed linen workers in Belfast. The number of employees in the shipbuilding industries dwindled from 20,000 in 1924 to 2,000 in 1933.

14

The situation then at the time of the second world war was grim:

"Northern Ireland was born with a home market too small to support a diversified industry. Her industrial imbalance was of a peculiarly intractable kind. She had only two major industries, linen and shipbuilding, which at the end of the fifties provided about 40 per cent of the total employment in manufacturing industry. These . . . have powerful competitors in Great Britain and produce almost entirely for export. Flax cultivation was virtually abandoned in the nineteen-thirties and both industries became dependent on imported raw materials . . . yet the Government of Northern Ireland has no control over trade with any place outside the six counties. Generally speaking fuel and raw materials are brought from Britain. Here Northern Ireland industry encounters not only monopoly prices but high transport costs[14]."

Furthermore her two main industries, linen and shipbuilding continued to decline and the other old industries became less profitable owing to their low levels of capital investment, smallness of size and because they were so labour intensive. In fact the bulk of Northern Irish capital was not invested locally but in the more profitable English industry with the result that:

"Northern Ireland is starved of capital . . . (because) (a) the limited scope in Northern Ireland for spreading investment risks; (b) the limited scope for profitable industrial development and the lack of faith in Northern Ireland long term economic prospects; (c) the form of business organization—the dominance of the small private company; (d) the limited supply of entrepreneurial ability and enterprise[15]."

For Northern Ireland therefore there was only one answer:

"her economic future clearly depends on the possibility of maintaining and increasing industrial development of new kinds, both by the diversification of the region's new economic resources and by the attraction of new industry from outside (para. 37) . . . the problem is to develop new and viable industries in Northern Ireland in order to absorb the labour which can be expected to become redundant in parts of the economy, to provide the extra jobs which will be needed in view of the increase of the working population and to reduce significantly the existing level of unemployment[16]."

The attempt to attract new industry started in the 1930's with the 1932 and 1937 New Industries Development Acts.

One of the consequences of this industrial situation has been that the ownership of Northern Ireland's industry has passed into British hands.

A second consequence has been an increasing need for Government intervention, firstly to provide the necessary financial incentives to attract industry, and secondly:

"to directly remedy the disadvantages suffered by the area, by building factories, developing communications and access to markets, by moving the labour force to more useful locations[17]."

It was this which led to the need for planning, starting with the local Planning Commission set up at the end of the second world war and later

15

to the invitation to Sir Robert Matthew in 1960 to prepare the Belfast regional plan.

THE ORIGINS OF THE ORANGE SYSTEM

This change in the ownership of Northern Ireland's industrial wealth was reflected in the political struggles that took place, particularly within the Protestant camp from the 1940's onwards. In order to understand these struggles it is necessary to look at the different interests which lined up behind the Unionist party that was formed in 1886 to oppose the introduction of Home Rule.

Foremost were the business and commercial interests. Belfast as we have seen was by 1886 a thriving city which to all intents and purposes was part of industrial Britain. The local industrialists had therefore everything to gain from retaining the link with Britain and with it free trade. This was very important as the markets for linen products were all outside Ireland. As they argued to Gladstone in 1893:

"It was an indisputable thing, and beyond the sphere of argument with those who lived in Belfast, that the condition precedent to their progress was their connection with Great Britain through the legislative union. That again gave the commercial classes a sense of security as absolute as that which existed in London and prior to 1886 no Ulster banker or capitalist ever dreamt of being offered a less valuable security for his investment. As an integral part of the United Kingdom they had shared . . . in all the great progress of industry in the great centres of England which followed the loosening of the shackles of trade they had shared . . . in what proportion would their commercial interests be represented in the legislative assembly in Dublin? They all knew Ireland was an agricultural country[18]." and as one speaker put it a little bit more forcibly they were:

"not prepared to come under the rule of a Dublin Parliament dominated by impoverished small farmers from Munster and Connaught[19]."

Similarly the Protestant landlords threatened by the militant, primarily Catholic, Irish National Land League campaign for rent reductions and state aid for tenants to buy out the land they worked on, saw their interests depending on the maintenance of the Union.

The other main set of interests were represented by the Orange Lodges. The Orange Order had been formed at the end of the eighteenth century when Protestant tenants felt threatened by Catholics who were prepared to pay higher rents and tolerate a lower standard of living. Many Protestant landlords connived in this and a number of organisations were set up by Protestant tenants to protect their position. One of these was the Orange Order.

Similarly in Belfast the Protestant working class was threatened by the rapid increase in the early part of the nineteenth century in the number of Catholics in Belfast. In 1808 Catholics made up 16 per cent of the population and by 1861 this had risen to 34 per cent. This increase was due partly to the increased demand for labour arising from Belfast's rapid industrialisation and partly because of the effects of the famine driving people from the land. Protestants felt their jobs were threatened and

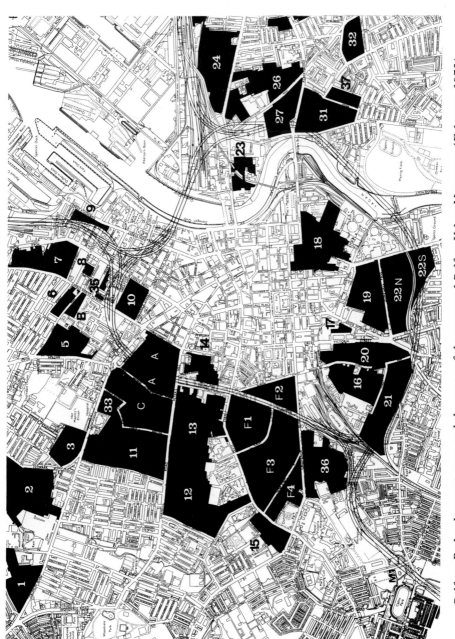

Belfast: Redevelopment areas and the route of the proposed Belfast Urban Motorway (February 1975)

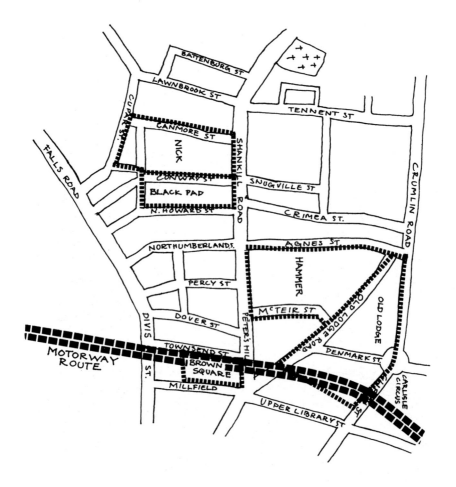

Traditional community areas on the Shankill

The wrecked deck access corridor and maisonettes in the new Shankill. People rejected these 'tombs in the sky'.

The path of the Belfast Urban Motorway at the foot of the Shankill running in front of the 'weetabix' blocks.

"the artisan class in 1800 had been predominately Protestant and since it was clearly too small to defend itself against all the rural unskilled immigrants, it was much more likely to accept the Protestants than the Catholics. So the Protestant artisan class became the skilled workforce in the engineering works and shipyards while the Catholics had to accept the unskilled and more menial jobs. This trend could not automatically change or reverse itself. Indeed it was reinforced by the tendency of people in power to employ those whom they regarded as loyal to their interests[20]."

One result of this were the sectrarian riots which took place in Belfast roughly every 10 years. Thus in 1872 when one policeman was killed, 73 were wounded, 170 civilians were injured and 837 families were forced to leave their homes:

"The mobs . . . on Shankill Road turned their wrath against the Catholic families who lived in that part of the town. They ordered them to clear out or suffer the consequences. And the consequences in every case meant the complete destruction of home, furniture and other effects. Protestants living in Catholic districts got the same warnings and suffered likewise if they failed to obey[21]."

The riots were largely confined to the working class areas of Sandy Row, the Pound (Lower Falls) and Shankill, the same areas which provide the battleground for the present 'troubles'. One effect of the riots was to virtually complete the sectarian divisions in housing in the working class communities in Belfast. Even before 1840, Sandy Row and Peters Hill at the foot of the Shankill were predominately Protestant while Catholics had congregated in the Pound. This probably stemmed from the first Catholic settlement which had developed there, outside the city walls,[22] and also because the first Catholic church was built there and the Falls Road would be the road into the city from the rural west along which Catholics fleeing from the famine would have come. The Shankill similarly became a Protestant stronghold as it was the pathway to the predominately Protestant county of Antrim.

Orange Order parades were often a precipitating factor for these riots. As the Commissioners reporting on the 1857 riots said:

"The Orange system seems to us to have no other practical result than as a means of keeping up the Orange festivals, and celebrating them, leading as they do to violence, outrage, religious anomosities, hatred between classes and, too often, bloodshed and loss of life[23]."

However the marches had a more important purpose than that. They were "at a local level, a means of assessing in symbolic terms an unwritten 'status quo': the local manifestation of the symbols of Protestant power[24]."

It would be wrong to conclude from this that the Protestant working class was consistently a secretarian body subordinate to the interests of the local ruling class. On many occasions their class interests came to the fore. Thus in the late 1860's in Belfast during a period of rising unemployment, the Protestant Working Men's Association was formed which received massive support from working class Orange districts. Again the Land League for a time attracted the support of Protestant tenant farmers and

17

"in January 1881 Davitt addressed a meeting in Armagh chaired by the Grand Master of the local Orange Lodge[25]." Then again in 1906-8 the Independent Orange Order who broke from the Official Order in 1902 "are found taking a leading part in trade union affairs, progressive politics and the Belfast Dock Strike[26]."

However, while class antagonisms existed and were on occasion expressed, the Protestant working class recognised that the protection of their jobs depended upon the exclusion of Catholics from large areas of employment such as the shipyards and the engineering works and Home Rule constituted a threat to this. Much the same was true for Protestant tenants in the countryside who feared that Catholics might recover Protestant occupied land.

Thus the different Protestant groups were bound together by common but hetrogenous economic interests in opposition to Home Rule. But the Home Rule campaign threatened to destroy more than the economic base of Northern Ireland's prosperity. It threatened to engulf Protestants within a Church dominated Catholic state and thus destroy the political and religious liberties of Protestants.

"Popery is something more than a religious system: it is a political system also. It is a religio-political system for the enslavement of the body and soul of man and it cannot be met by any mere religious system or by any mere political system. It must be opposed by such a combination as the Orange Society, based upon religion and carrying over religion into the politics of the day[27]."

The warnings of the Presbyterian ministers during the early part of the century and of the landlords at the time of the Land League were seen to be fulfilled as the Land League campaign merged with the Home Rule movement which the Catholic church was seen to give its tacit support to. Thus Home Rule was not merely a threat to jobs but to the Protestant way of life.

All of these different interests came together to form the basis of the Unionist party which ran Northern Ireland as a one party state from 1921 till direct rule came in 1972. The organization of control, called the 'Orange system' was on a decentralised basis and consisted at the local level of a partnership between the Orange lodges, the Unionist Party, the Protestant churches and local business. The main tasks of the 'Orange system' were to keep the Catholics down and preserve jobs for Protestants. For a variety of factors it was only possible for these tasks to be done successfully if the system was controlled on a local basis. This was because:

(i) unemployment was high and jobs were scarce and therefore local government service became a valuable source of employment. It was therefore important to win control of local government. This worked for both sides:

"Thus we are told that in Londonderry, with a Unionist council, no Catholics are normally employed in senior positions, though some obtain jobs as labourers. In Newry, with a Catholic majority, all the Urban Council's clerical and outdoor staff were said to be Catholic in 1958[28]."

Control of houses was also important at a time when few houses were being built.

However in some cases, such as Londonderry, gerrymandering occurred, to give Protestants control of the council. Here:

"the City Council has a Protestant and Unionist majority of 12 to 8 ruling a population more than half Catholic . . . but the siting of new houses has to be arranged with great care if it is not to upset the Unionist majority[29]."

This was done by forcing Catholics to live in the South ward of the city. This could only be done through the allocation of houses and therefore control of housing became an important issue.

A further advantage that Protestants had in retaining control of local government was that under the franchise for local government elections businessmen had extra votes and sub-tenants, lodgers and servants none. Both of these discriminated against Catholics.

The control of houses and jobs was also necessary to determine the rate of Catholic emigration. Protestants have long feared that Catholics by outbreeding them would gradually gain control of Northern Ireland. Barritt and Carter estimate that without emigration the percentage of Catholics in the population in 1961 would have been 39 per cent instead of 35 per cent and they suggest "that emigration is just about sufficient to drain off the excess births in the Catholic community, and keep the proportions of Protestants and Catholics almost stable[30]." This fear was reinforced by the Protestant attitude of not seeing why he

"should be expected to find capital to build houses for such families, and to subsidise their rents, so that Catholics will live in comfortable idleness on unemployment benefit and family allowance. The Protestants were being asked to subsidise an increase of population which would vote them out of control of their own money[31]."

It was because the proportion of Catholics and Protestants varied from area to area that local control was so important and centralised housing allocation schemes were resisted so fiercely during the 1960's.

(ii) local control was also important on the security front, particularly during IRA campaigns. Northern Ireland emerged during disturbances which lasted from 1920 to 1922 and during which 544 people were killed and many Catholics were forced to flee. In 1920 the Special Constabularly had been established and one of the first efforts of the new Northern Ireland Parliament was the 1922 Special Powers Act. Security from a Protestant viewpoint was more effective when organised on a local level because in each area, the political allegiance of every individual was 'known'. This both permitted, in times of trouble, the easy identification of any strangers and a concentration of resources in 'known rebel' areas. In addition the B Specials provided a valuable source of part-time employment for Protestants.

Underlying the basis for local control was the need for the Unionist party to use the scarce jobs and houses to keep the support of the Protestant working class. The Unionist party, at leadership level, was an amalgamation of business and landed interests: 89 per cent of its M.P.'s at Stormont came from the top two social classes which made up only 12 per cent of the population[32] and it was clearly anti-socialist in its outlook and policies. It was in times of economic depression that available jobs and houses were not sufficient to retain working class support. In 1932 for example non-sectarian riots occurred in Belfast when after a hunger march, the Shankill rioted in support of a Falls crowd which had been baton charged by the police. Again in the late 1950's and early 1960's at a time of rising unemployment, the Northern Ireland Labour Party flourished briefly as an opposition party with the support of Protestant working class voters.

Whenever this happened the Unionist party beat the Orange drum and retained protestant working class allegiance by focussing on the border as an issue and in the short term this worked to the advantage of the Protestant working class especially when unemployment was rife and there was much competition for each job. In 1931 for example the Ulster Protestant League was established to urge Protestants not to employ, work with or deal with Catholics and in 1937 Sir Basil Brooke, the then Minister for Agriculture appealed "to Loyalists, therefore, wherever possible, to employ good Protestant lads and lassies" while Lord Craigavon in 1934 said:

"I am an Orangeman first and a politician and member of this parliament afterwards . . . all I boast is that we are a Protestant parliament and a Protestant state[33]."

The Orange system therefore depended on three things—local wealth, the control of it and the decentralization of power and administration. The local government set up in Northern Ireland was ideally suited to this purpose with:

"two county boroughs, six administrative counties, ten boroughs, twenty-four urban districts and thirty-one rural districts, each with an elected council."[34]

However as we can now see the Unionist party was doomed before the Northern Ireland state was set up. Local wealth disappeared in the post world war 1 depression and control of what was left passed into British hands. This resulted firstly in a shift of power away from the old landed and local business interests to the new Protestant managerial class, as emphasized by the emergence of Faulkner and Bradford to replace O'Neill and Chichester-Clark. A second pattern has been that of increasing government intervention into the running of the economy in order to provide the necessary financial inducements to attract foreign industry. This has led to the increasing centralization of administrative control necessary to properly plan and co-ordinate the restructuring of the Northern Ireland economy. Thirdly it has resulted in the introduction of British ideas about social equality in keeping, as we shall see in the section on housing, with an increasing dependence on the British exchequer to make Northern Ireland viable. Also since 1954 when Southern Ireland abandoned its protectionist policy there has been a coming together of the British, Irish and Northern Ireland's economies as part of the same corporate capital economy. This, in economic terms, made the border an anachronism and the attempt at Sunningdale possible. But it was also these trends which led to the mass of Protestants realising that they were being betrayed and to the rise of Paisley and the eventual break-up of the Unionist party during the 1960's.

BELFAST CORPORATION

As might be expected the political history of Belfast reflects the interests of the Protestant middle classes and it is these interests which account in part for the city's poor housing record. Up to the 1820's Belfast Corporation had been controlled by the Donegal Family:
"The town belongs entirely to his lordship. Rent of it £2,000 a year. His estate extends from Drumbridge (Drumbeg), near Lisburne to Larne, 20 miles in a right line, and is 10 broad. His royalties are great, containing the whole of Loch Neagh which is I suppose the greatest of any subject in Europe . . . The estate is supposed to be £31,000 a year, the greatest at present in Ireland"[35]
Under the Municipal Corporations Ireland Act of 1840 the old Corporation was remodelled along its present lines and the Conservative party won all the seats. The Protestant middle class from then onwards have always ruled Belfast and in fact from 1897 onwards, the Unionist party has always had more than 50 per cent of the seats and has on average held 77 per cent of seats.
"The effect of non-competitive one party rule—control of all offices by one party . . . (has led to) . . . the 'ancient' and 'festering' tradition of municipal corruption"[36]
Throughout its history Belfast Corporation has been under attack for example for, sectarianism. The Commissioners into the 1864 riots concluded:
"The Town Council is, and is likely to continue, of the exclusive character above described i.e. not merely Protestant, but anti-Catholic and anti-Liberal."[37]
Even though in 1911 Catholics made up 24 per cent of the Corporation's employees, the same percentage as in the overall population, they received only 18 per cent of the salaries i.e. they were employed primarily in lower paid jobs.
but more frequently for corruption:
"The report of the committee stated that the 1841 election had been characterised by 'extensive corruption' and 'gross and corrupt personation of voters'."[38]
Yet little had changed by 1973:
"Vote early, vote often, Northern Ireland's most famous political slogan, scrawled on many a gable wall . . . from early morning in little houses on the Falls, the Shankill, Andersonstown, Woodvale, Turf Lodge and the 'Village' the personators were busy."[39]
In 1855 on questions of illegal practise by Belfast Corporation, the Lord Chancellor of Ireland:
"found all the main allegations proved. The Corporation had borrowed in excess, it had misapplied funds, it had borrowed illegally."[40]

In 1926 the Megaw Report on allegations about irregularities in housing contracts

"disclosed considerable negligence in the affairs of the City Housing Department . . . apart from the irregularities of account, other serious charges were sustained . . . 'I believe it to be the truth,' Megaw wrote, 'that there was an undertaking, lubricated with an amount of give and take, between certain members of the Housing Committee, the City Surveyor and (an official) as to the allocation of some of the contracts.' The commissioner also pointed out that the allocation of the sites for the new houses was dictated by the consideration of profit to the vendor and not suitability for working-class housing."[41]

and in 1941 the Dunlop inquiry found the City Treasurer's Department had displayed 'complete laxity' and 'gross neglect' and four councillors were asked to resign.

Not only was the Corporation dominated by one community, it was also dominated by one social class. In 1966 for example, 70 per cent of Belfast's popuation were classified as working class but 83 per cent of Unionist councillors came from non-working class backgrounds. In fact of the last 16 Lord Mayors, 9 have been company directors, 3 estate agents, 3 clothing manufacturers and one coal merchant. Little wonder then that working class housing has not always been to the forefront of their concerns.

BELFAST AND HOUSING

The first house boom in Belfast took place between 1770 and 1825 with the growth of the cotton industry and by 1831 there were 8,526 houses in Belfast with an average occupancy rate of 6.8 persons per house. As there were 42 per cent more families than dwellings, many houses were shared. Houses were built in the low lands near the rivers where the mills were and later in the century near the docks where the shipbuilding boom was occurring.

Before 1845 there were no building or sanitation regulations and the rivers were often no better than open sewers. In 1847 and 1848 there were widespread fever and dysentry outbreaks and in 1849 a cholera epidemic when 3,484 people died. In 1853 a report was drawn up by the Medical Officer of Health[42] which found that of 665 streets in Belfast, more than half were inadequately paved and sewered. The report also found that of 12,902 houses in Belfast, 4,047 had no backyard, 4,326 had no drainage and 6,179 no ashpits and no receptacles for refuse.

Housing conditions were therefore poor.

"The great majority of the poorer classes of houses in this town consist of 4 rooms in two storeys. These are generally occupied by two families. Each room varies from seven to ten foot square, and from six to eight feet high in the lower storey . . . each room, though not always, contains one window, the upper sash of which is almost invariably, in the older houses, made immovable. Such a house is manifestly insufficient to

22

be the domicile of ten individuals, but we have known, and not infrequently, as many as eighteen or even twenty persons sleeping within such limited apartments."[43]

These conditions forced the passing of a number of building and sanitation regulations in the next 25 years. Between 1845 and '47 a series of bye-laws set down minimum standards for buildings including the provision of a backyard with a lavatory and an ash-pit. Many of the houses in the present redevelopment areas were built according to these regulations. Further bye-laws were passed in 1878 compelling builders to allow for a passage between the backs of yards. These bye-laws also stated that each street was to have an intersection every two hundred yards which "led to a change in the street pattern and also broke the monotony of long rows of terrace housing."[44]

Despite the passing of sanitation bye-laws in 1847, it took until the Sanitary Acts of 1865 and 1866 which were concerned with: the paving and sewering of streets, the provision of a water supply to houses and the abatement of nuisances, for anything much to be done to improve the situation. In fact the river Blackstaff remained an open sewer until 1880. This was "allegedly through the opposition of mill owners and iron masters who did not wish to be deprived of their source of water."[45] Not surprisingly sanitation still posed a problem at the turn of the century and despite pressure from Nationalist and Labour councillors the Corporation refused to act. In 1896 it had appointed a special committee to look at the problem:

"However, when the report came up for discussion the combined weight of estate agents and landlord interests on the Council was sufficient to have its main recommendations—more stringent bye-laws—rejected."[46] Another Commission was appointed in 1906 and found that:

"the death rate from typhoid, however, over the previous twenty-five years was such that no other city or town of the United Kingdom equals or even approaches it in this respect, while the annual death rate from tuberculosis was more than double that of England and Wales"[47]

One of the problems that the Commission found was that in houses where two families lived, those in the upper storey had no access to the privy during the day when the family below were away and none during the night which lead to "faecal matter being stored in the upper living rooms until an opportunity occurs to carry it to the yard."[48]

The second building boom in Belfast coincided with the period of the city's greatest industrial growth from 1850 to 1910 when some 51,000 houses were built. The boom was aided by the fact that the second Marquis of Donegal had, through drink and gambling run up debts amounting to £217,000 and was therefore forced in 1822 to reorganise his estates. Before then the majority of leases were for short terms only, 21 years or less, which made people reluctant to build. The 1822 settlement disentailed lease conditions on the property and some tenants were granted longer leases and others were permitted to buy the freehold. The Donegal estate was finally broken up between 1850 and 1858 when much of it passed into the hands of the Commissioners of Encumbered Estates.

The houses were put up by both small scale speculative builders and by larger firms such as Martins who by the 1890's were building between one and two thousand houses a year. However by the end of the nineteenth century the boom was over and there were hundreds of empty houses in Belfast. The slump was due primarily to too many houses being built for rent at levels that only the skilled working and lower middle classes could afford.

The Corporation, as with the provision of new schools, "dominated by estate agents and apprehensive of a possible increase of as much as 30 per cent on the rates did nothing."[49] The exceptions were a number of small slum clearance schemes started just before the first world war including one of some 700 houses in the Falls, Shankill and York Street areas. An old Shankill resident can remember being told, as the houses opposite her fell, that hers was also condemned and would be coming down shortly. It was still there in 1974.

Northern Ireland in general and Belfast in particular were no worse off as regards housing conditions at the turn of the century than many comparable cities in the U.K. What was to put them behind was their building record in the inter-war years when private builders provided 69 times fewer houses than private builders in England and Wales and local authorities 127 times fewer houses.[50] Therefore on 1964 figures only 13 per cent of houses in Northern Ireland were built between 1921 and 1941 compared to 27 per cent of Great Britain's.[51] There were a number of reasons for this.

Firstly that Northern Ireland was, as we have seen, in economic difficulties in this period. By the 1920 constitution, Northern Ireland's financial arrangements with the U.K. were that revenue came from transferred taxes (e.g. motor vehicles duties) collected locally and reserved taxes (e.g. customs) collected nationally and from this was deducted the net cost of reserved services and Ulster's contribution to imperial services. However, the figures arrived at in 1921, in a brief period of post-war prosperity proved inadequate by 1925 when, with industrial depression and high unemployment, Northern Ireland's revenue fell. The Colwyn Committee of 1924 in trying to establish what was legitimate domestic expenditure decided that 1924 would be taken as a base year and after that 'per capita' expenditure in Ulster should increase at the same rate as in Britain. But as the standard of many of Ulster's social service provisions were below those in England this arrangement forced them to remain so. In the period up to 1931 much of government expenditure went on old age pensions and unemployment insurance. The Colwyn formula disappeared after 1932 when to retain it would have meant the British exchequer having to make a contribution, i.e. Northern Ireland was broke. It therefore had to cut expenditure and it was not till 1945 that it was accepted that the British exchequer would lift Ulster's under-developed services to Britain's level and that the province would enjoy the full range of Britain's post-war social security schemes. This, over the years, has involved increasing financial dependence on Westminster so that by 1973/4 the net financial payment from the U.K. Government to Northern Ireland:

"was in the order of £300 millions and made up more or less as follows: Health Services Agreement £16m; Social Services payment £33m; Agricultural Remoteness Grant £2m; Selective Employment premiums £9m; Grant-aid £175m; law and order £10 to £20m; National Insurance funds £28m; agricultural subsidies £28m".[52]

A second reason was the Government's almost complete reliance on private builders to do the necessary building. Altogether 82 per cent of all new housing between the wars was built by private developers, 64 per cent of these with state aid in the form of subsidies.[53] These subsidies, which were withdrawn in England in 1932, continue in Northern Ireland to the present day. The effect of this policy was that new building only kept pace with the increase in the population. There were no slum clearance schemes and no new houses at a price that working class families could afford. This was despite the fact that the maximum size of the house which qualified for subsidy was being continually reduced. Not only were few houses built, but those that were "were generally of lower standard than those built in England."[54]

Many English Housing Acts, those of 1924, 1933 and 1935, which provided for increased local authority involvement in housing and particularly in slum clearance, were not enacted in Northern Ireland. The only legislation to do with slum clearance schemes was passed in Stormont in 1931 but was never acted on.

Another factor was the small size of many of the local authorities which meant that they neither had sufficient income nor competent staff to undertake a building programme.

However national financial difficulties are not sufficient to account for the poor housing record where:

"the failure to accept responsibility, to recognise the scale of the housing problem, to investigate or to plan is evident at every level of Government in Northern Ireland between the wars."[55]

In Belfast itself, of 29,000 houses built between the wars, only 2,562,[56] 8 per cent, were built by Belfast Corporation. Part of this must be because of the same vested interests that prevented the Corporation tackling its housing problem in the pre-war period. In 1941 a report by the Chief Medical Officer of Health of the English Ministry of Health found that

"Belfast fell far short of what might reasonably have been expected in a city of its size and importance . . . the Council were not quite certain what they were doing, whether it was worth doing, or whether they were the people to do it."[57]

From the mid 1930's onwards there were in Northern Ireland, increasing numbers of Unionists who were beginning to complain about the standard of social services that the Unionist government was providing. This eventually culminated in the resignation of the Prime Minister in 1943 as "there was a general feeling that men in office since 1921 lacked the vitality fully to mobilise the country's resources, impress on the United Kingdom the urgency of making complete use of them, and plan for the post-war world."[58]

The second world war, as in England, raised awareness about social problems, got the economy going again and, in Northern Ireland, got recognition that the province had a right to parity in social services. This set in motion a number of inquiries which in the housing field were made more urgent by the effects of bombing which destroyed 3,200 dwellings and damaged 50,000 more.[59] A 1943 survey[60] found that throughout the province, 71 per cent of dwellings required repairs and that in Belfast itself, 23,591 new dwellings were required to replace those which were unfit and reduce overcrowding. This was equivalent to 1/5th of all existing dwellings in Belfast.

In response to such surveys in housing and related areas, a Ministry of Health and Local Government was established in 1944 and in 1945 new legislation was passed which set up the Northern Ireland Housing Trust, a publicly funded body whose task was to build houses to supplement the effort of local authorities. The Act also increased subsidies for working class housing, especially for local authorities. The rate of housing grew from an average of 2,500 dwellings per year in the inter-war period to 7,500 a year for the period from 1946-1971. During this latter period, 191,960 houses were built, 24 per cent by the Northern Ireland Housing Trust, 37 per cent by local authorities and 36 per cent by private enterprise.[61] However this increased building rate has only kept pace with the increase in the number of new households and little inroad has been made into tackling the past years of neglect. The 1956 housing figures[62] show that throughout the province, 95,364 houses were unfit, i.e. 25 per cent of all dwellings and recent Northern Ireland Housing Executive figures reach the same estimate. The 1974 Housing Condition Survey concluded that "in Northern Ireland one in five or 19.6 per cent of the total dwelling stock is statutorily unfit, a total of 89,370 dwellings"[63]

Belfast itself continued its dismal housing record. In the period from 1949-1959 the Corporation built only 6,650 dwellings.[64] By 1960 the Ministry had been worried enough to write a special letter to the Corporation complaining about its building record, pointing out that only a small share of the city rates were going to housing and

"that fundamental changes would be necessary in the Corporation's attitude and approach to the problem of housing in the city."[65]

The problem was vast. Under the 1956 Housing Act, local authorities had two years in which to prepare surveys and plans for dealing with their unfit houses. On the 24 October, 1958[66] the Medical Officer of Health for Belfast reported that in the city, 18,440 out of the stock of 114,995 houses were unfit. In 1960 proposals[67] were put forward for dealing with these unfit houses over a twenty year period by dividing them into 30 redevelopment areas. In 1964[68] a further 8,000 houses and 20 areas were added to the list, though the 20 year time limit remained. Another report in 1962 by the City Architect and the Estates Superintendent concluded that there was a need in Belfast for 58,700 new dwellings over the next twenty years. The Report also pointed out that in the previous year the Corporation had only built 350 flats and houses.

It again becomes necessary to ask why was Belfast's housing record so bad. A number of different factors seem to have played a part. Firstly there was a shortage of land within Belfast's City boundary. The above mentioned 1962 Report for example said that there was only land for 24 per cent of the required dwellings within the city boundary. The Corporation had asked for the county line to be extended, the last such extension had been in 1896, but this had been refused because of the pressure from surrounding authorities. Belfast Council then decided that it wasn't going to build outside the City boundary where they had no control and also they didn't see why "they should have to spend ratepayers' money on building outside the boundary,"[69] especially when that would be to the benefit of other authorities' rate funds. For their part local authorities surrounding Belfast were not keen to take the cities' overspill and numerous disputes broke out between Belfast and the surrounding authorities over such matters as who was responsible for the sewerage which ran from neighbouring authorities into Belfast's system. Eventually the Housing Trust stepped into the breech and took over responsibility for house-building in land between the city boundary and the Matthew stop-line. In fact in the period 1954-59 the Housing Trust housed nearly twice as many people in the Belfast area as did the Corporation. The need to solve the more fundamental dispute, about the area over which the Belfast Corporation should have jurisdiction, and in particular over which land should be allocated for housing Belfast's overspill population was one reason why Matthew was brought in, in 1960 to produce his regional plan for Belfast. Other reasons will be explored in the next chapter.

A second factor lies in the "many allegations about its (Belfast's) neglect in the housing field."[70] While it is difficult to pin down exact causes for this neglect, the best hypothesis is that as in the past, the Corporation was simply reflecting the class interests of the ruling party. This is shown for example by the low expenditure from rates on housing and by its slowness in dealing with slum clearance

This shortage of land for housing in Belfast, coupled with a lack of due concern for the needs of working class people, and a general failure in planning nearly everywhere at that time to take into account social needs. meant that most of the new estates that were built were badly lacking in community facilities. The City Architect for example, in 1964 pointed out to the Housing Committee that the policy on the provision of playspaces in housing developments

"was that use was made of open spaces left naturally by the layout of the housing schemes. No provision was made for formal playgrounds in the housing estates . . . this policy was followed to ensure that the greatest possible use was made of the land available for housing having regard to the scarcity of housing sites within the City boundary."[71]
With the Housing Trust

"financial difficulties also meant that the Trust had little time and money to devote to the development of open spaces."[72]

The effect can be seen on an estate such as Ballymurphy, built in the early 1950's where:

"the amenities, apart from shops and buses, are very poor for an estate of this size. There is a large Catholic intermediate school for boys immediately below the estate but no primary school closer than the Falls Road. Nor are there any churches or buildings for Catholic or non-denominational community activity on or near the estate. There are no proper playgrounds for young children."[73]

Therefore by 1960 Belfast in terms of housing was faced with a situation where; 60 per cent of its dwellings were built before 1919, a quarter of its houses were in need of redevelopment, where there was overcrowding (11.3 per cent of all households in the city were living at a density of over 1.5 persons per room), a shortage of land and a housing authority whose building record was far from good.

It now becomes possible to begin pulling together the main strands of this chapter. From the 1930's onwards the province in order to survive economically had to be able to attract sufficient new industry to compensate for the decline of its traditional industries. The effect was that industrial and, more slowly, political power passed from local hands into those of foreign companies and the Westminster exchequer and the politicians at both Stormont and Westminster who represented these interests.

These changes in themselves forced alterations in the way Ulster was governed. These changes involved a co-ordination of services, the centralization of control and increasing government intervention, all of which led to the end of the decentralised pattern of control by which the Orange system had run the state. It is with a detailed examination of these changes that the next chapter is concerned.

In both economic and social fields, the period from 1945 onwards was a race to try and catch up for the disastrous inter-war period when little money was available to spend on services like housing. However, in housing, as with the problem of the shortage of jobs it had by 1960 only been possible to keep up with the new demand and little had yet been done to tackle the backlog.

In Belfast itself, the Corporation had shown over the years many of the signs of corruption and ineptitude which characterise governments where one party remains in continuous power. The Corporation reflected the interests of the Protestant middle class Unionist party who dominated it. Belfast's legacy by 1960 was a city with a decayed and congested centre, with so many houses suffering from neglect, that only a large scale redevelopment scheme, necessitating the upheaval of a quarter of its population could hope to tackle it.

Chapter 2

THE ENTRY OF THE PLANNERS

Effective planning in Northern Ireland started in 1942 with the setting up of the Planning Commission and the Planning Advisory Boards. This marked the first realisation on the part of the state that if Northern Ireland was to survive economically by attracting industrial development from abroad, then changes were needed throughout the province to make this possible.

PLANNING IN THE 1940's

What these necessary changes were can be seen by looking at the various reports produced under the auspices of the Board.

Firstly housing conditions had to be improved. According to the 1944 Interim Housing Report[1] of 104,470 houses in Belfast only 13 per cent needed no repair work done. The report recommended that there should be large scale slum clearance, new legislation modelled on English lines, as well as an increase in the house building programme.

Also in 1944 there was a report on the location of industry[2] which took as its starting point the lopsidedness of the distribution of population and industry in the province. Two-fifths of the population lived in the Belfast area and on 1935 figures 61 per cent of all jobs in manufacturing employment were in the Belfast County Borough. The report concluded "that the present geographical distribution of industry is unevenly balanced as between Belfast and the rest of the province and that new industries should be attracted, where possible, to provincial towns rather than Belfast."

Among the reasons for arriving at this recommendation were: the difficulty of supplying economically all the desirable amenities in towns with less than 15,000 people; the lack of industrial development outside Belfast and the strategic advantage of decentralisation. For this recommendation to be acted on, the report realised that state intervention was necessary and that this "should be directed towards measures of planning and organisation which will make provincial areas considerably more attractive to industrialists."

The report also pointed out that good transport facilities were necessary to attract industrialists. This point was taken up by a report on the Belfast area[3] produced the following year:

"the importance of a speedy and convenient flow of traffic to and from the city can hardly be overemphasised in the case of Belfast, the capital of the Province, and the business and social centre visited constantly by people from every country and moreover a great port and harbour depending for its prosperity on the efficiency with which great quantities of exports and imports can be handled."

and the following year a separate report on roads was published[4] which reiterated that

"roads are vital to all sections of the community and an adequate road system is alike essential to industrial, commercial and private interests. Industrial and commercial expansion and the changes inseparable from post-war reconstruction require a planned road system."

The report went on to point out that shops and other buildings along main roads destroy or at least impair their traffic carrying efficiency.

The Commission's final report was in 1951[5] and again recommended the dispersal of industry and the need to push ahead with traffic plans. Now none of these plans nor the outline advisory plans which were prepared for many areas from 1946 onwards were statutory plans i.e. they were purely advisory. Nor was there any comprehensive plan for Northern Ireland as a whole around which local plans could be developed even though a report as early as 1944[6] had recommended this.

The reason for going into these reports in so much detail is that the recommendations that they made were almost identical with those produced by the next generation of planners in the 1960's. Matthew[7] for instance in 1962 recommended the setting up of a number of centres of development later called growth centres, in the Belfast region, and key centres in the rest of the province to encourage dispersal of industry from the centre of Belfast. Furthermore according to the 1970-75 Development Programme[8]

"Since 1963, official policy on physical planning has been:

(a) to encourage, the growing concentration of population in towns of economic size and good location, and with good communication lines—the 'growth centre' policy.

(b) to discourage the extension of the Belfast Urban Area, pending the preparation of a comprehensive plan for the Province as a whole . . .

the strategy noted above has been broadly right, as far as it went but some modification and shifts of emphasis are desirable. It now requires to be fully and more vigorously implemented."

The Matthew report bemoans the fact that "adequate machinery for co-ordination of local plans in either a Regional or a National sense does not yet exist" and recommends the setting up of a Ministry to have overall responsibility for planning. Yet as late as 1970 the 1970 Development plan is still pointing out that "statutory powers and administrative machinery are gravely inadequate."

THE DEMISE OF THE 1940 PLANS

The question that needs to be asked and answered then is why plans that were put forward just after the war were to all intents and purposes put on the shelf until 1962. The explanation lies, as the first chapter started to explain, in the economic origins of the Northern Ireland state in 1921, which consisted of a home market too small to support a diversified industrial base and only two major industries, linen and

30

shipbuilding which were already on the decline. At a political level, decisions were made through the decentralised orange system which gave power to local authorities to determine policies in their areas.

The basic economic task that confronted the state was how to overcome the problem of declining employment in linen, shipbuilding and agriculture. According to the Hall Report[9] in 1962.

"the economic future clearly depends on the possibility of maintaining and increasing industrial development of new kinds, both by the diversification of the region's own economic resources and by the attraction of new industry from outside."

As we saw in the last chapter this policy had been followed from the mid-1930's and Greaves estimates[10] that by 1948 foreign, mainly British interests had secured at least 60 per cent of the total investment in public companies. However it wasn't until after the end of the war that this investment really took off and the Northern Ireland economy became dominated by monopoly capital interests. The aim of the 1940's plans was to change the physical and economic base of the Belfast region to further encourage this investment.

These changes involved two main things—firstly physical changes such as redevelopment, an increase in the house building programme and an improved transportation system and secondly increased central government control to co-ordinate the changes. However the new industrial interests and the changes they required threatened the basis of the orange system. The influx of large industrial and commercial concerns would wipe out much of local industry and small scale retail trade, while the centralisation of administation would mean an end of local control and an end therefore of patronage, discrimination and ultimately of the protected position of the Protestant workforce. Therefore while across the water the domination of the economy by an ever decreasing number of large firms was such that the very same plans were being enacted, in Northern Ireland the coalition of Protestant interests was at this stage still strong enough to prevent changes taking place at a political level. The lack of political support was the main reason why nothing much was done with the 1940's plans.

THE CHANGING SITUATION FROM 1950 ONWARDS

However the economic situation continued to get worse. In terms of employment between 1950 and 1973

"in agriculture, forestry and fishing there has been a steady increase in total production but the number employed in 1973 was about 55,000 or 10 per cent of the total in civil employment compared with 101,000 in 1950, a decline of 46,000—during the same period, employment in traditional textiles, mainly linen, has fallen from 65,000 to 19,000, and in shipbuilding from 24,000 to 10,000. Thus since 1950 these 3 industries have seen employment decline by 106,000 or 56 per cent."[11]

Need for Industrial Incentives

The first need was to attract firms to invest in Northern Ireland: in doing this it had to compete not only with Southern Ireland but also

31

with other depressed regions of the United Kingdom. It increased its competitive position by offering more favourable grants than other regions offered and by providing additional services such as advance factories.

According to a Northern Ireland Department of Commerce handout: since 1945:

"Government expenditure on direct assistance to industry totals more than £270 million. For the year 1951/52 the expenditure was about £600,000 and it has grown to over £47 million for the year 1970/71. In addition to expenditure on grants and buildings under the Capital Grants to Industry Acts, the Industrial Investment (General Assistance) Acts, Aid to Industry contributions towards industrial fuel, gas, electricity and contributions towards the cost of employing industrial consultants.

The Government's contribution to industrial activity in Northern Ireland is not measured solely in terms of financial assistance. The Ministry of Commerce pays particular attention to the 'Aftercare' problems of newly established industry, and, in collaboration with the Board of Trade, offers a variety of services for the information and assistance of exporters."

This policy had some success and by 1966 217 new industries had been established, 117 of these in advance factories[12]. The decline of employment in traditional industries was to some extent offset in engineering by new firms in mechanical and electrical engineering such as Rolls Royce and an expansion of employment in the construction industry. In textiles the decline in linen was compensated for by the new synthetic textile plants such as Courtaulds and I.C.I. These new firms in comparison to the old linen mills were highly capital intensive and highly productive. Thus while output per head in the linen industry only increased from £290 to £681 between 1949 and 1966, in the textile industry the increase was from £365 to £1,181[13]. Finally between 1951 and 1973 employment in the service industries went up from 201,000 to 277,000.

In addition to lower wages, Northern Ireland was able to offer green field sites for industrial expansion which is what the new firms were looking for. However, as in Belfast itself, there was a shortage of land, with industry and housing competing for what there was, it made sense to locate new industries outside Belfast where land was freely available and cheap. It was this which lay behind the growth centre policy, despite what the planners said about the need for dispersal of job opportunities throughout the whole province. If one looks at Matthew's[14] projected employment figures one finds that in between 1961 and 1981 the percentage of jobs in the Belfast region (i.e. within 30 miles of Belfast) instead of decreasing, will slightly increase from 61 per cent to 64 per cent of all jobs in the province. The main shift is clearly intended to be from the centre of Belfast to surrounding areas. Whereas in 1961, 86 per cent of the jobs in the Belfast region were in the Belfast Urban Area, by 1981 this was expected to drop to 76 per cent.

32

Outside the Belfast region according to Matthew and subsequent reports, industrial development was to be concentrated in the key centres which would provide employment opportunities for those forced off the land. In both the key and growth centres, the given reasons for their development were:

"it is held that the less prosperous parts of the country can be developed more effectively by some concentration of effort on towns that are relatively well located. The second proposition is that the cost per head of providing public services for the people and for industry will decline for a time as a town grows in size. The third consideration is that a town of some size is often needed for modern industry. The availability of manpower for service industry and the desirability of diversity of manufacturing employment must be taken into account in determining the minimum size of a developing urban centre."[15]

In order to make sure that the land in the growth towns was cheap enough to attract industry, the necessary land was compulsorily purchased, at or near to, existing use value. For the new town of Craigavon the Government acquired 6,250 acres of land. The fact that it was able to do so reflected both the decline of the agricultural interests in the Unionist party set-up and the increasing importance of central government as a financial backer safeguarding industrial development.

Then the necessary infrastructure needed to be set up. Industrial sites had to be developed, services laid on and roads built. This necessitated pushing ahead with the Belfast transportation plan, as the only way exports and imports could reach the growth towns from the docks was by driving across Belfast. This explains why when planning consultants were called in, in 1965, to produce a development plan for Belfast, not only were separate transport consultants appointed, but they were appointed before the main team of consultants—Building Design Partnership. The brief for the traffic consultants, Travers Morgan, clearly specified that an urban motorway should be part of their design thus making sure that industrial needs would be protected.

Labour Mobility

The next thing that was necessary to make both the key and growth centre policy a success was to make sure that sufficient people moved there to provide the waiting labour force that would make them attractive to industrialists. Firstly people in rural areas had to be persuaded to move to the key centres.

"in the past there has been however a certain unwillingness to move on the part of the unemployed in rural areas. One of the aims of the mobility proposals is to try and overcome this inertia and to persuade the more energetic unemployed in remote areas to move to new housing and to employment . . . "[16]

The second aim was to get people to move from the Belfast Urban Area to the growth towns in the Belfast region. Altogether this overspill would involve about 100,000 people who would otherwise have settled in the Belfast Urban Area. Now the planners did not think this movement of population was an unfair burden:

"we do not regard some movement of population within Northern Ireland as involving in itself an unendurable social hardship. On the contrary, we consider that it is essential: to provide employment . . . to provide labour for firms in urban areas and not least, to allow the much needed redevelopment of Belfast."[17]

Matthew solved the problem of how to persuade people to leave Belfast by putting a stop-line around it, thereby restricting the amount of land available for future development. The stop-line left a fixed amount of land to be divided between housing and industrial needs and once that was used up people would have no option but to move to growth towns. This can be shown by Building Design Partnership's housing need calculations for their redevelopment areas programme. They estimated that 74,500 new homes were going to be needed in the Belfast Urban Area by 1981. This figure was made up of:

31,000 families affected by redevelopment
30,000 new households
3,500 families affected by land clearance for the urban motorway
9,000 houses needed to clear the waiting list
1,000 to allow for vacancies

However there were only sites for 47,500 houses within the stop-line. Hence 27,000 families would have to move to the growth centres.

The normal argument put forward to justify the stop-line is "to correct the unbalanced growth of the Belfast Urban Area in relation to the remainder of Northern Ireland."[18] However as we have already seen that while the plan might have diminished slightly the role of the Belfast Urban Area it did not affect the predominance of the Belfast region as a whole.

| | Percentage of Population in each area[19] | |
	1961	1981
Belfast Urban Area	39	36
Rest of Belfast region	25	30
Rest of Province	36	34

Out of 80,000 new jobs Matthew forecast would be needed, 10,000 were to be in the Belfast Urban Area, 40,000 in the rest of the Belfast region and 30,000 in the rest of the province, roughly maintaining the existing distribution. Now this could be justified on the grounds that it was in the Belfast region that the greatest decline in traditional jobs was taking place or because of the importance of the Belfast docks. Both of these are valid reasons, though Londonderry and Warrenpoint could easily have been developed as alternative harbours. Nevertheless the most important reason was that since the Protestant population was concentrated in the Eastern part of the province a dispersal of jobs to west of the Bann would have meant in fact taking away jobs from Protestants and giving them to Catholics. This would have threatened one of the links by which the Protestant working class was bound to the Orange coalition.

Training and Education

It wasn't however only enough to move 100,000 people to the new towns—they also had to be the right sort of people.

"Modern industry (so much of which has been attracted to the Province in recent years) requires a greater proportion of skilled workers, unlike its nineteenth century counterpart"[20]

In order to meet this need the Government set up a number of training programmes and the 1964 Industrial Training Act enabled the Government to set up a number of training boards and training centres which increased the number of places from 500 in 1964 to 2,200 in 1969. But a more basic change in the education system was required because

"the educational systems of most industrial societies, by early selection procedures, severely limit the numbers receiving higher education and able to fill skilled, managerial and technocratic jobs . . . the education system (in Northern Ireland), though of a high standard in comparison with many of the regions of Great Britain, has not as yet responded sufficiently to the changing demands of industry."[21]

The education system in Northern Ireland, which operated under the 1947 Act which was based on the 1944 Butler Education Act, permitted some 22 per cent of pupils to enter grammar schools while the majority of the rest were condemned by the 11+ exam to secondary intermediate schools, though well off parents, whose children failed the exam, could still purchase their entry into the grammar school. The result was that in 1970-71 of all school leavers in Northern Ireland only 9 per cent went on to university and of these 94 per cent came from the grammar schools. Seventy-nine per cent of secondary intermediate pupils left school at the lowest possible leaving age of 15, compared with 8 per cent of grammar school children.[22]

Now this system is highly functional when the dominant industries are labour-intensive and need primarily unskilled labour. But with the switch to capital intensive industries and the rise in white collar service jobs, the system requires a more highly skilled workforce. It therefore needs to liberalise its selection procedures i.e. go comprehensive so that more pupils have the opportunity to learn skills. It should be noted that it doesn't really matter if this results in a slight drop in the quality of education that those in the former grammar school streams received, as the aim is to raise overall standards. The true elite are not affected as they still receive their education at public schools.

The beginnings of the necessary change came in 1969 when the Advisory Council for Education were asked to look at the whole question of the eleven plus. The Report when it came out in 1973 duly recommended that

"the Minister of State make now a declaration of intent to eliminate selection as soon as possible through a re-structuring of the educational system."[23]

The second necessary step was to remove education from the control of the local councils where dominant petty bourgeoise interests were all in favour of selection. This happened in 1973 when in line with the overall re-organisation of local government, 5 Education Area Boards, under the control of the Ministry of Education were set up to take over supervision of education from the local authorities.

Immediately they started to do their job. Within three weeks of becoming operational the South Eastern Education and Library Board had at a special meeting

"passed a motion endorsing the recommendation made by the Burgess Report that selection at 11-plus be abolished and the education system restructured accordingly."[24]

Systematic planning

None of these changes could take place unless there were comprehensive plans to lay down how all the different services should be co-ordinated

"a combined operation covering industry, housing, transport and the consequential services necessary to support new or enlarged communities . . . it is likely to require special legislation . . . in addition the administrative burden of organising an operation of this kind, involving thousands of families, many industrial concerns, a variety of land interests and public authorities requires preparatory work of a high order."[25]

The post-war plans needed to be brought up-to-date. Therefore at an economic and regional level there were reports by Isles and Cuthbert in 1957, the Hall Report of 1962, the 1965 Wilson plan and finally the 1970-1975 Development plan. From the Hall Report onwards the message was the same:

"we have emphasised the urgent necessity—that is even more pointed, in view of recent events—to make Northern Ireland more favourable in this age of intense international competition, for the expansion of employment opportunities.

Every available means must be used to this end. In general terms, this means that labour, land and services must be found in the right places for new industrial projects and these must have ample opportunity to enlarge the scale of their initial operations."[26]

At a more localised level since 1963 planning progress was just as rapid:

"Area plans have been published for Antrim, Ballymena, Londonderry and the Coleraine-Portrush-Portstewart triangle.

A comprehensive and imaginative plan for the Belfast Urban Area has been prepared by Building Design Partnership and Travers Morgan covering all aspects of physical planning, including transport, redevelopment and housing, giving the blueprint for action necessary to make the city and its immediate environment more attractive and allow it to function more efficiently.

Plans are being prepared for Newry, North Down, West Tyrone and East Antrim . . . The Amenity Lands Act, the New Towns Act and the

Land Development Values (Compensation) Act are all useful beginnings of the control of development . . .

A regional roads policy has been worked out . . . The Belfast Harbours Commission have plans for development. The new airport at Aldergrove is functioning . . . the new regional centre of Craigavon is in being, and Development Commissions have been set up and are at work in Craigavon, Londonderry and Antrim/Ballymena."[27]

Reorganisation of Local Government begins

The implication of these changes was that the whole of the Belfast region needed to be treated as a single political, planning and administrative area. But the situation in 1961 was that in this region there were 34 local authorities, 19 of which were planning authorities; 30 were responsible for the provision of housing and 22 had responsibility for roads. Matthew's recommendations included a general review of administrative boundaries and "the creation of a Ministry of Planning and Development."[28]

This, as we have seen simply repeated suggestions made in the planning reports of the 1940's. But by now the economic and political balance of power was beginning to swing in favour of those elements within the Unionist party who represented the new industrial interests as shown by O'Neill becoming Prime Minister in 1963. But progress was still very slow.

In 1964 the Government published a White Paper on Town and Country Planning which proposed a central planning authority. In 1965 the recommended Ministry of Development came into being with responsibility for planning, housing, roads, transport, water, sewerage and local government. But each local authority still retained control of planning strategy and land resources in its area. In its 1969 report, Building Design Partnership noted that the growth centre policy had been disappointingly slow in producing effects and recommended yet again the

"early establishment of overall Government responsibility for planning strategy, control of land development and conservation, with appropriate delegation."[29]

Political Opposition to these Reforms

The reason of course why progress was so slow was that the further increase in central government powers meant dismantling the existing local government system. But the role of central government was increasing all the time.

This was for a number of reasons. Firstly central government financial support was necessary if the new industrial policy were to succeed. Not only were there the direct grants, tax concessions etc. to attract new industries but money had also to be found to lay on the necessary infrastructure such as an improved transportation system. In between 1961 and 1969, public investment as a percentage of gross domestic product rose from 9.9 per cent to an estimated 15 per cent.[30]

Hence Stormont was forced to play an increasingly important role in the running of the economy.

Secondly the fact that Northern Ireland had to rely increasingly on Westminster financial assistance meant that Stormont was forced to pass similar social welfare legislation to that enacted in England in the post war years. This forced Stormont to lay down province wide legislation in education, housing and other fields which threatened the autonomy of local authorities. Furthermore the social welfare legislation threatened to upset the balance of Protestants and Catholics in the community. As the number of new jobs created never quite matched the number lost in declining industries, the difference was made up by emigration and high rates of unemployment. As it was important for the Unionist party to make sure that the majority of available jobs were reserved for Protestants, Catholics made up a disproportionate number of those on the dole and boat queues. From a Protestant point of view this reduced the risk of Catholics becoming the majority party simply by having the faster population growth. However social welfare benefits and changing economic circumstances began to change this. Whereas between 1951 and 1961 net emigration from Northern Ireland averaged about 9,000 persons per annum; between 1961 and 1966 the average had fallen to 6,900.

The final reason for the growing importance of central government was that the complexity of financial, social and economic changes that were taking place required increased civil servant intervention to understand and co-ordinate them. In general the capability of the civil service to act as an innovatory force in Northern Ireland has been limited both by the political necessities of maintaining the orange system and the consequences of one party rule at both central and local government level. This has meant that there have been few discussions on the social merits of different policies with the result that much legislation is simply copied directly from Westminster Acts without being adapted to take account of regional variations.

The history of the Unionist party through the 1960's is the attempt by those in it who represented the new economic interests—O'Neill, Faulkner, Bradford, etc., to force through the necessary centralisation measures. The opposition came from the amaglamation of local capital, small businessmen and skilled Protestant workers whose economic livelihoods were threatened by the changes. These elements exercised their power through the decentralised local government structure and were thus virulently opposed to its dismantlement

But the changes in the ownership of Northern Ireland's industrial wealth meant these interests were no longer able to prevent these plans going ahead as they had done in the 1940's and early 1950's.

Who the new industrial masters are is shown by the fact that "of all the manufacturing firms in Northern Ireland employing 500 or more workers, Great Britain is the country of control of about 45 per cent; Northern Ireland of about 22 per cent; the USA of about 20 per cent and EEC countries of about 10 per cent.[31]

38

The consequence was that:

"by the middle of the 1960's the expanding sections of Northern industry were no longer in the hands of local businessmen. The tough minded, self-made Northern Protestant businessman who had been 'the backbone of Ulster' and who controlled the Unionist party and the Orange Order no longer wielded decisive economic influence."[32]

This is further shown by the fact that in the period from 1950 to 1970 the proportion of income derived from self-employment fell by 10 per cent which "reflects the decline of locally owned producing and trading establishments."[33]

But these businessmen and small traders and others such as those whose power and/or employment lay in the existence of so many local authorities were not prepared to give up without a struggle. At this stage in the early 1960's the Protestant working class was not important as part of the opposition to these changes. While new jobs were being provided for them locally to replace those lost in the declining industries they had little to fear. In the early 1960's in fact they gave significant support to the Northern Ireland Labour Party who were one of the groups pressing for the reform of the state. It was only after 1969 that the Protestant working class realised the full implication of these reforms.

Reform of Local Government Completed

The Government first publicly announced that it was tackling the thorny subject of local government reorganisation in March 1966 and in 1967 it published a White Paper. In 1969 the MaCrory Commission was set up to examine the whole matter and suggest how the re-organisation should be carried out. While it was slowly proceeding in this field; the Government to speed up the growth centres, set up Development Commissions for Craigavon in 1965 and later for Antrim/Ballymena and Londonderry. The 1971 Resettlement Services Act (N.I.) gave the Ministry of Development power to provide services and assistance for the resettlement of people and businesses from the Belfast Urban Area to the towns of Bangor, Newtownards, Carrickfergus, Craigavon and Antrim. In 1971 the Ministry set up a Development Advice Centre and people from redevelopment areas were offered financial inducements to move to the above growth towns.

The Report of the MaCrory Commission[34] came out in 1970 and duly recommended the centralisation of all essential government services with the Ministries taking overall control for planning, education, etc. The local authorities were reorganised into 26 district councils and left with responsibility for community facilities, environmental health, etc. The reorganisation didn't take effect until 1st October 1973 when the Ministry of Development some 29 years after it was first recommended, became the planning authority for the whole of Northern Ireland.

It now becomes possible to answer the question raised at the beginning of the section as to why similar sets of plans were produced in both the 1940's and the 1960's. The answer is that both sets of plans had the same function—to help transform the Northern Ireland economy so as to make it attractive to monopoly capital interests—but that whereas in the 1940's and 1950's the interests which were threatened by these changes were strong enough to thwart them, by the 1960's further penetration of the economy had weakened their power base. The 1960's planners main task was to up-date the earlier plans and provide them with the added credibility which expensive, foreign, experts bring with them.

THE GROWTH CENTRE POLICY AND LABOUR MOBILITY

The success of the growth centres depending on people being prepared to move from the Belfast Urban Area (the area within Matthew's stop line) to the centres.

However despite all the plans, people were reluctant to move where industry said they ought to go to. For example in the 18 month period from April 1965 to October 1966, 16,556 people according to BDP,[35] left the centre of Belfast but 75 per cent of these moved to the outer suburbs, still within the Belfast Urban Area. Of the 2,877 who moved to the rest of the Belfast region, only 132 moved to the Craigavon Area, 579 to the Antrim/Ballymena Area and 673 to Bangor. In 1971/72 according to figures supplied by the Development Advice Centre, 3,343 moved to growth towns under statutory and emergency housing schemes. In the next year the figure dropped to 2,775. Few of these came from redevelopment areas. This is borne out from further figures given by the local Northern Ireland Housing Executive office which shows that out of 154 families who left the Shankill Redevelopment Areas between February and April 1974 only 7 went to growth centres.

The actual movement of people followed a two step process. People moved first from the inner city areas to the new housing estates being built around the edge of Belfast by both the Northern Ireland Housing Trust and occasionally by Belfast Corporation or to the growth centres closest to Belfast—Carrickfergus, Bangor and Newtownards.

One of the reasons why people were reluctant to move further away was that the majority of those who moved still retained jobs in the Belfast Urban Area to which they commuted daily. According to the Development Advice Centre over two thirds of those who moved to Antrim, Bangor, Craigavon and Newtownards in 1972/73 were employed in the BUA.

A second reason is that it remains possible to maintain old family and friendship ties when the move is to the inner growth centres while a move further out means at best a once a week visit to old haunts.

Those who moved first from the inner city areas tended to be the skilled manual and non-manual workers with young families and higher than average incomes. Among the reasons why they were the first to leave were: having too few points to qualify for a house closer in; wanting to make a better life for themselves and less attachment to traditional community norms. The effect of this trend was to leave the centre of Belfast with an ever increasing proportion of elderly people.

The next step in the process was for people to move from the outer estates to the growth centres. According to Building Design Partnership[36] "there is a greater movement among people in outer areas, 10-20 per cent have taken steps to move house. Four in ten families on Northern Ireland Housing Trust or private estates are prepared to move further from Belfast."

To put it more bluntly, once a family from a traditional working class area has moved away from the area, then it is more likely to move again. The reasons for this will be explored during later chapters but in essence the initial move represents a break with traditional communal values to a more material set of values where getting ahead is seen as the goal and success is judged by the accumulation of private possessions.

One piece of evidence for this is that approximately one third of those who moved to Bangor, Carrickfergus and Newtownards, became a house owner for the first time.

Those who made the second move tended to be those whom the industries were keenest to attract i.e. the more skilled workers. One controlled study[37] found that those who moved to growth towns tended to be young married couples who came from higher social groups with higher incomes than non-movers. They were also more likely to have a car and less likely to have had members of their family living close to them in their previous house. The main reason for moving was because of a better job being offered to them.

Hence at both stages it was both the location and availability of jobs and closeness of community and family ties which were crucial to the pace and distance that people were prepared to move.

In recent years the situation has been further complicated by the 'troubles'. First of all Belfast's population has, against all expectations, actually started to fall. Even though no one, including the Ministry of Development, is quite sure why this fall has taken place, it is hypothesised that it is due to a combination of: people wanting to leave Belfast to get away from the violence; the carrots of the growth centre policy beginning to take effect (except in Craigavon where the removal grant was raised in 1974 to £500 to persuade more people to go there) and redevelopment. A lot of people though are leaving Northern Ireland altogether. On latest government estimates, January 1975, the annual emigration rate has more than doubled to over 18,000 per year.

However the crucial difficulty is that owing to the 'troubles', the greatest housing need is for Catholics who have suffered most from the intimidation and general violence which has forced over 60,000 people in Belfast alone to move house. The Catholics are all crowding into the area where they feel safest—i.e. West Belfast while the area in the Belfast region where most houses are available is Craigavon. But the people's refusal to move has forced the authorities to consider bending the stop-line at West Belfast to make room for the number of people crowding in.

RECENT HOUSING AND REDEVELOPMENT POLICIES

As we saw in the last chapter, Northern Ireland's house building record during the inter-war period was abysmal. However if industrial development was to come then new houses had to be built in the right place and Belfast turned into an attractive city.

Most plans from the 1940's onwards have recommended that house building must be speeded up and redevelopment started if the growth town policy were to be a success. As local authorities either couldn't; because of smallness of size or lack of income; or wouldn't either because of the cost involved to the ratepayers or because house building requirements were subordinate to political needs; do the job themselves, new agencies had to be created. The first of these was the Northern Ireland Housing Trust set up in 1946 to be superseded in 1971 by the Northern Ireland Housing Executive. Before examining its record it is worth looking at the problem with which it was confronted in the Belfast redevelopment areas which had the greatest concentration of 'unfit' houses in the province.

Local arguments for and against redevelopment

According to the 1944 Housing Report[38], 87 per cent of houses in Belfast needed repairs.

"The Committee would like to point out . . . that the only way to get rid of slum property is to pull it down . . . it may be taken, therefore, that in Belfast important central areas require clearance and redevelopment."

The Committee went on to recommend that new slum clearance legislation, along English lines, should be implemented. This did not happen until 1956 and the first redevelopment scheme didn't begin for another three years. The question that needs to be asked here is why redevelopment began in 1960, and then at a very slow rate, rather than in 1944 when the extent of the problem was first documented.

One of the reasons was given in the last chapter when it was shown that Belfast Corporation because of a desire to keep down rate expenditure declined to build outside the city boundary and there were few suitable sites left within the boundary.

However there were some people on the Council who saw that redevelopment and road improvements provided business opportunities for the larger shopkeepers and estate agents who were well represented on the Council:

"A former Lord Mayor of Belfast, Alderman Sir Cecil McKee, who appeared before the Belfast Corporation inquiry last year, is found in the report of that inquiry, which was presented to the Northern Ireland Parliament yesterday, to have taken part in proceedings in which he had a pecuniary interest and to have influenced decisions on the redevelopment of Bridge Street in Belfast, where he owned property . . . The Report revealed many cases of members of the Council being present without dissociating themselves from the proceedings while decisions were taken in which they had a pecuniary interest."[39]

While at this time such actions were not strictly against the law, as the Minister for Health and Local Government, Mr. Morgan pointed out.

"conduct by members of the Council which showed little or no awareness of the care, which those entrusted with the privilege of governing the city should have to keep their personal interests and duties quite separate and distinct from their public responsibilities."[40]

But it was not only as individuals that some members of the Council saw the advantages of redeveloping Belfast. The middle class ruling Unionist party saw part of its duty to lie in keeping down the rates of its property owning members.

"Councillor Brown drew attention particularly in the rateable value of the City which had improved the product of a 1d. rate by £350 from £19,750 in 1963/4 to £20,100 next year . . . the increase was mainly attributable to the development of commercial sites . . . this showed how the city benefited materially by new development and redevelopment was, therefore to be encouraged and inspired. It was, however, of the utmost importance to see that planning observed the fundamental law that the most desirable sites were reserved for rate-paying developments. There was everything to be gained by confining non rate-paying development to sites off main thoroughfares, for instance hospitals, schools etc."[41]

It was therefore in the interests of the city to get rid of housing to the suburbs and new towns and encourage industrial and other commercial development within its boundaries. On this point it was not particularly successful as it was faced with pressure from other quarters to maximise the number of people who remained in the areas after redevelopment.

There was another factor which encouraged the Council to pull down old houses and erect new houses for which they got government subsidies. This was that the rateable value of a new house was approximately four times that of an old house. Therefore even if only half as many houses were rebuilt, the Corporation would still get twice as much money in rates as it did from the old property.

There were those though on the Council who stood to lose by redevelopment. In particular there were the small traders whose businesses would be swept away and the local councillors whose power base would be threatened or destroyed by the removal of population.

These differences of interest reflected a split within the Orange system between those who stood to gain by the entry of new capital and those who stood to lose. It was in the former's interests to make an alliance with central government forces pushing for reform and it was this which explains why the two major planning teams for Belfast, Travers Morgan and Building Design Partnership came to be jointly appointed by both Belfast Corporation and the Ministry of Development.

Tied in with the above factors was the fact that by the end of the 1950's houses in the redevelopment areas were no longer profitable for anyone. At the end of the nineteenth century and in the early part of the twentieth century many people bought houses in the redevelopment areas as an investment. Thus in 1894 four houses close to Percy Street in the Shankill Road were advertised for sale for £300[42]. They brought in £33:16:0 in rent per annum, less £7 ground rent so that the initial investment was recovered within 11 years. Now from about 1950 onwards the situation changed. Rents had been frozen for the majority of houses at 1914 levels with only minor increases allowed in 1920, 1951 and 1956. As late as 1966 the rent for many houses in the Shankill was still under 50p per week. Income no longer matched outgoings in rates and maintenance and some landlords even stopped collecting rents to try and avoid responsibility for repairs. Therefore landlords were not opposed any longer to their property being compulsorily purchased.

Finally even though the majority of tenants were reluctant to move, old communities began to be broken up as the younger people moved to the new estates and towns. Once redevelopment actually started, the opposition of most tenants began to crumble as with blight setting in, living conditions deteriorated rapidly.

Redevelopment and Monopoly Capital

A different set of factors pushing for the redevelopment of Belfast in the past 1950 period were tied up with the need to attract foreign investment.

Firstly there was concern with the outward appearance of the city:

"the total image presented to the modern industrialist has many facets, but outward appearances are becoming more and more important. The old adage—where there's muck there's money—is now seen as the shortest of short term principles—dust or mess, dilapidation, physical confusion, these are rightly not held any longer as symptoms of business acumen and success. A down-at-heel atmosphere is the worst enemy of industrial progress, in spite of its great natural advantages, the dilapidated towns, the slums and congestion of central Belfast—all these are liabilities that the economy of the country cannot afford in this critical stage of its history."[43]

A further factor was the need to build an urban motorway which was seen to be necessary for the movement of industrial goods. As the City Surveyor argued:

"a considerable part of the Ring Road passes through areas of bad layout and obsolete development including several redevelopment areas."[44]

This land had the advantage of being much cheaper and of course the working class areas would protest less than middle class areas. In fact the central government was so keen for the road plan to go ahead that:

"the Ministry will offer every possible assistance to the Corporation . . . the net cost of the scheme will attract Road Fund Grant at the rate appropriate to new Class 1 Roads (at present 90 per cent)"[45]

Redevelopment was also necessary if 100,000 people were to move to the growth centres. According to Building Design Partnership, redevelopment was going to destroy 27,000 properties and replace only two thirds of them. The rest of the people according to the plan, would have little option but to move to the new centres.

Finally redevelopment by wiping out small traders served to guarantee the retail stores the large markets they needed if they were to be persuaded to set up shop in the city. This policy was successful as:

"locally owned distributors and retailers were hit by the operations of British Home Stores (from 1965), Boots (from 1966), Marks and Spencer (from 1967) and the expanded activities of the Mace and Spar chains (since 1968)"[46]

One of the largest chain of local supermarkets, Stewarts, had

"joined up with George Weston Ltd. way back in 1935. Weston's is a North American based company (which had retained earnings of $132m in 1972). Through one of its main subsidiaries in the U.K. Associated British Foods (profit after tax in 1972 £13m) it controls 80 other companies including the Fine Fare chain which has 538 shops of which 471 are supermarkets. Stewarts in 1969 . . . had net profits of £252,364 . . . also owned the following three bakeries, Tip Top, Thompson's and Reids."[47]

This increasing concentration in fewer and fewer hands was simply another aspect of the general trend in modern capitalism for the market to be dominated by a small number of firms heavily dependent upon state aid. In the case of shopping, one part of this aid was to give the stores a guarenteed consumer market. Building Design Partnership saw the creation in Belfast of 12 such centres as being one of their principle tasks:

"As the trend to larger units and rationalisation of shopping in Redevelopment Areas takes effect, the number of shops will be reduced . . . greater personal mobility, and a much wider range of leisure opportunities, will lead to less frequent shopping trips . . . increased mobility, the need to supplement existing local shopping, and substantial movement of population to outer areas suggest the need for large local centres. In England the 'Woolco' developments (large suburban stores with a wide range of goods and ample car parking) exemplify present trends."[48]

The Northern Ireland Housing Executive:

In the period from 1944-1962 about 5,500 houses were built on average per annum in Northern Ireland. The Wilson Plan recommended that on average over 10,000 houses per year should be built between 1964 and 1969. However as the Ministry of Development was estimating that something like 100,000 houses were ultimately needed to replace those who were unfit, the 1970-75 Development Plan recommended the target should be raised to 15,000 per year. It was this need for more houses which was one factor leading to the setting up of the Northern Ireland Housing Executive as the sole housing agency for the whole province in 1969. The perceived advantages of such a body according to the communique which announced its arrival on 10/10/69 were: [49]

"a common public authority rent structure throughout Northern Ireland; improved mobility which is the key to regional development; an end to allegations about sectarian discrimination in housing allocations; the attraction of more high quality professional and administrative staff to housing work and the opportunity to use modern efficient management techniques; economies of scale; the organisation of contracts to ensure a steady demand on housing contractors and thus more efficient building; the elimination of unnecessary variation coupled with greater opportunities for research and experiments; the introduction of advanced estate management—but above all, a new opportunity to solve Northern Ireland's housing problems in the foreseeable future."

The second factor which led to the formation of one centrally run housing authority was the need to remove housing control from local authorities owing to the increased outcry by those involved in the civil rights movement over discriminatory policies in housing allocation towards Catholics.

The Housing Executive came into being in October 1971 and between then and July 1973 took over the housing functions of 61 local authorities, 3 development commissions and the Housing Trust. It was headed by Harry Simpson, who had made a name for himself in the housing field in Lambeth in London, who brought over Rae Evans as his Director of Development.

By the end of 1974 both Simpson and Evans had returned across the water as the Housing Executive slipped further behind its house building target. The failure can be seen from the following table.[50]

	NIHE new houses completed	Private new houses with subsidy built	NIHE new houses started	NIHE approved but not started
1971	9,102	4,220	9,093	5,307
1972	7,203	4,003	6,087	3,137
1973	5,966	4,017	4,196	2,833

Each year the number of new houses has fallen. In 1973 in the city of Belfast the NIHE built only 435 houses.[51] In fact since redevelopment started the rate of clearance of unfit houses has averaged 721 per annum for the City of Belfast with an average rate of rebuilding of 178 houses per annum.[52] Even including private housebuilding total completions have fallen from 13,916 in 1971 to 10,557 in 1973, way below the annual target of 15,000 houses per year laid down in the 1970-1975 Development Programme.

46

A large part of the problem can be laid on the 'troubles' as the Housing Executive has had to cope with rent strikes (17,183 tenants on strike in March 1973), robberies of staff (44 in 1972/73); intimidation, vandalism, squatting (affected 5,184 dwellings in March 1973) and bomb damage to buildings it owns. (In Belfast 14,000 dwellings were affected by 284 explosions in 1972/3). In addition the Executive had difficulty in getting professional staff—less than two thirds of positions at this level have been filled and suffered from a high turnover rate when in the year 1972/3 18 per cent of its employees resigned.

Furthermore intimidation and assassinations caused delays on building sites; the centralisation of housing control created vast bureaucratic problems and the reorganisation of local government led to procedural difficulties between the Housing Executive and the various Ministries with responsibility for housing.

However it would be wrong to lay all the blame on the troubles. As can be seen from the above table, the number of approvals was down which means that the Housing Executive wasn't getting as many houses off the drawing boards as before. Also in its first three years of operation not a single General Improvement Area was created. Yet way back in 1944 the Housing Report had recommended:

"It is essential that property owners and local authorities, either by grants or by purchase and subsequent reconditioning, should be urged and enabled to carry out an extensive repair and reconditioning programme at the earliest possible date."[53]

Finally as will be seen in subsequent chapters housing management left a lot to be desired. This was perhaps not surprising when one of the reasons for the setting up of the NIHE was the inability of the previous authorities to build enough houses. It might therefore have been thought that with reorganisation the opportunity would have been taken to weed out all those whose work was unsatisfactory. This was not done because it was not politically possible. The centralisation of housing control was a sufficient threat to the Orange coalition without the added risk of alienating those whose jobs would have been lost if open competition had been encouraged for all positions.

CONCLUSION

From a physical planning point of view the battle during the 1960's in Belfast was largely over land use. How could land in the Belfast region be used most profitably by whom. One of the factors that delayed planning progress for a long while was the interpretation of the 1920 Government of Ireland Act which laid down that planning restrictions might be viewed as the taking of property and could therefore carry compensation. In England this problem had disappeared with the Town and Country Planning Act of 1947 which nationalised development value. However in Northern Ireland this Act never became law and local authorities were therefore reluctant to carry out any planning as they could always be sued for planning compensation. In order to get round this the Ministry of Development from February 1963 compensated

47

any local authority so sued on an extra-statutory basis. This arrangement was made official by the 1965 Land Development Values Act. This meant that one way to make money was to get planning permission refused. Under this arrangement for example the Ministry of Development paid out £125,700 in 1965[54] and £233,064 the following year.[55] The fact that it took until the end of the 1960's to change this state of affairs shows just again how slow the battle was for the progressive elements within the Unionist party to emerge and gain control.

However by 1973 the necessary changes had been made to the structure of the province. Local government had been reformed, the economic and physical plans produced and all that was required was the political power to enforce them. But in 1968 came the 'troubles' and with them the end of being able to use the Unionist party and Stormont as the political base to represent monopoly capital interests. The logical next set up was Sunningdale—an attempt to create an alliance between the progressive Unionists and middle class Catholics as part of the political rationalisation for the whole of Ireland, north and south, in terms of the changing economic conditions. With the collapse of the Assembly in June 1974 at the hands of the Ulster Workers Council this political avenue came to a halt.

The reforms also wound down. The growth centre policy picked up slowly at first as people began to leave Belfast but they didn't necessarily go to the towns where they were most needed. New industrial investment which is what it was all about began to fall off. House building failed to meet its target. As the next chapter will show the Belfast transportation plan also ran into political and economic difficulties.

Chapter 3

ROADS RUN RIOT

THE HISTORY OF BELFAST'S ROAD PROGRAMME

The need to develop an improved transportation system for the Belfast region was, as the last chapter showed, closely linked in with the need to attract new industry to the province:

"Since one of Northern Ireland's main problems in encouraging industrial growth is its remoteness from the major centres of population in Great Britain, the transport links with Great Britain are of crucial importance in the creation of the necessary condition for the attraction of new industry. Firms located in Northern Ireland must be able to bring in raw materials easily and cheaply from Great Britain and abroad and must be able to ship manufactured goods out to markets in Great Britain and throughout the world on services which satisfy the industrialist's requirements on speed, frequency, reliability and cost."[1]

The new industries, as far as the plans for the East of the province were concerned, were, to be concentrated in a number of growth centres around the Belfast region. It was therefore essential that there should be good transport connections between these towns and the docks. The main ports in Northern Ireland are Belfast, which "handles over 60 per cent of Northern Ireland's seaport tonnage of imports and exports, over 50 per cent by value"[2] and where in 1972 the value of the imports passing through Belfast docks was £441 million[3]; and Larne, which is also in the Belfast region, some 21 miles north of Belfast. The value of imports passing through Larne docks in 1972 was £302 million. This can be compared with £27 million at Londonderry, £17 million at Newry and £10 million at Warrenpoint"[4], indicating again the dominance of the Belfast region in the economic life of the province.

The precise need therefore from the Unionist's party viewpoint was for an upgraded road system to carry goods in between the growth towns of Craigavon, Antrim/Ballymena, Newtownards etc. and Belfast and Larne harbours.

The importance of speedy traffic flows had been mentioned in 1945[5] in a report on the Belfast area which proposed a ring road system for the city. A separate report on road communications[6] in the following year:

"expressed the opinion that the existing road system was inadequate to deal efficiently with future traffic needs and recommended that two new classes of roads, arterial (trunk) and motorway, be added and be the responsibility of Government. It expressed the view that further centralization in roads administration was not only desirable but essential . . . The Report specified desirable minimum standards of construction, recommended the speedy provision of a motorway between Belfast and Portadown and the construction of by-pass roads for 22 specified towns."[7]

While some progress was made in the following fifteen years on the main roads between towns which were the responsibility of central government, much less was done to implement the programme within cities. Part of this was due to the number of different authorities which were involved:

"in the Belfast region responsibility for the main road system is shared between the Ministry of Commerce, Belfast County Borough, Antrim and Down County Councils, seven Municipal Boroughs and five urban districts."[8]

Part was due to:

"the high cost of modern roads—dual carriageway or motorway—(which) will, even with Government grant, make some local authorities reluctant to undertake new works."[9]

and part was due to the delay in centralising responsibility for all roads in one government department. The reason for this, as with other plans produced in the 1940's, was the political opposition of the decentralised Orange system.

In Belfast itself, for the above reasons, little progress had been made by 1961 in implementing the 1945 ring road plan for the city with its inner, intermediate and outer ring roads. In 1961 the City Surveyor produced a report which argued that the 1945 plan was out-of-date because of increased traffic flows and what was now needed was a Grade Separated Road system which included an elevated central ring road linking the main radials into the city centre. The importance of getting this road plan implemented was stressed in the report for the Belfast region which Matthew produced the following year in which he argued:[10]

"the urban motorway system inside Belfast is essential to link the main roads feeding traffic into the central area of the City and the port facilities. It is essential that it should be completed at the earliest possible moment."

As with the location of industry planning reports considered in the last chapter, the 1960 road plans simply up-dated those produced two decades before. But by this time not only had the need to attract new industry intensified but control of the economy was shifting to the new industrialists and those who represented their interests at Westminster and Stormont. At Belfast Council the same forces which were in favour of redevelopment also supported a road plan seen as necessary to attract profitable industries to the city. The plan also appealed to the car owning middle classes who dominated the Unionist party and hence the council.

In 1964 the City Surveyor came up with a further version of the urban motorway scheme. Arguing in support of his plan, he pointed out that the road would pass through areas of "bad layout and obsloete development including several redevelopment areas"[11], areas where land would be cheaper to purchase and that in addition the scheme would receive a 90 per cent grant from central government. This financial and political support at both local and central government level indicated, as with redevelopment, a coming together of political and industrial interests behind the urban motorway programme. The industrial interests included both overseas and local firms who saw the road building programme as a long term source of profitable contracts. In addition to Sir Alfred McAlpine & Sons who were the main contractors for much of the M2 motorway running north from Belfast[12], the following are some of the other firms who worked on the scheme:

"John Finlay (Concrete Pipes) Ltd;
H. R. Holfeld (Belfast) Ltd.;
Clarke Engineering & Construction Co. Ltd.
Road Signs Ltd.;
Sterling Cable Co. Ltd.;
Ready Mixed Concrete (Ulster) Ltd.;
Samuel McCourt (Plant) Ltd.;
Colvilles McKinney Ltd.;
R. Cullen;
B. Begley (Fencing) Ltd.;
James Boyd & Sons (Carnmoney) Ltd.;
John McCourt & Son;
Cassels & Reid Ltd.;
W. J. Kane.
Charles Hurst (Commercials) Ltd.;
P. J. Lagan (Contracts) Ltd.;
Moore Bros. (Quarries) Ltd.;
Plant & Marine Engineering Co. Ltd.;
Cementation (Northern Ireland) Ltd.;
Murphy Contractors and Plant Hire.;
B.W.D. (Hydraulic seeding) Ltd.;
Balfour Kilpatrick Northern Ireland."[13]

One result of this coalition of interests was the joint appointment by Belfast Corporation and the Ministry of Development in 1965 of the firm of R. Travers Morgan & Partners (N.I.) to produce a transportation plan for Belfast.

The task that Travers Morgan were given was not to produce an entirely new road plan. Instead, according to them their job involved the:

"development of a transportation system incorporating past planning decisions, notably the Urban Motorway system (and) the creation of public confidence in the continued efficient operation of the City in the future in so far as this has a bearing on the attractiveness of Belfast as a place in which to live, work and carry out business".[14]

The road plan was therefore to be an up-dated, more detailed version of the 1945 plan. There was no need for it to be radically different from the earlier plan as the industrial needs that it was to serve had not changed significantly in the meantime. It was therefore not surprising that Travers Morgan's transportation plan ended up being based on three ring roads as well as a central area distributor box linking primary and district distributor roads. The inner ring road was to be an elevated motorway, six lanes wide and thirty feet high which was to link together the motorway radials running to the growth centres. This motorway was the core of the system which would "enable traffic from outer parts of the study area and the province to travel to and from the Central Area and the Docks quickly and efficiently."[15] Among its short term road building priorities, which were due to be completed by 1976, the Report recommended the construction of the first leg of the urban motorway which was to run through West Belfast linking the M1 (running south-west to Craigavon) and M2 (running north-west to Antrim/Ballymena) motorways which stopped abruptly at the southern and northern edges of the city.

The importance that Stormont gave to implementing the road transportation plan can be seen from the amount of money allocated to road building in the province which, from 1965-1970 worked out at roughly $1\frac{1}{2}$ times as much per head as was spent in Great Britain.[16] Expenditure on new road building in Northern Ireland rose from some £2 million in 1956 to £15 million in 1967 and the Ministry of Development estimated[17] that it would remain at this level (at 1967 prices) until 1986 with half of the money being spent in the Belfast Urban Area. In 1973/4 public expenditure on roads in Northern Ireland totalled £30 million, some 4 per cent of all public expenditure.

ROAD BUILDING IN NORTHERN IRELAND WITHIN A TOTAL UNITED KINGDOM CONTEXT

So far we have considered the importance of a road programme in the context of Northern Ireland's industrial development. But transport planning in Belfast was little different from that in many cities in the United Kingdom such as Leeds, Glasgow, Birmingham etc. which ended up with urban motorway ring road solutions. It is therefore necessary to look at the more general factors which pushed transport planning towards this type of solution if one is to fully understand Belfast's transportation policy.

The greatest single factor which led to a rapid growth in road building in the post-war period was the increase in the number of cars produced which changed motoring from a minority pursuit of the middle classes to something in the reach of most people. In Great Britain the number of private cars and vans currently licensed rose from 2.5 million in 1952 to 12.7 million in 1972[18] while in Northern Ireland the number of private cars rose from 47,618 in 1949 to 304,144 in 1972[19]. By 1972 45.3 per cent of all households in the United Kingdom owned one car and a further 8 per cent, 2 cars; in Northern Ireland the respective figures were 42.7 per cent and 5.3 per cent[20].

This increase in car ownership changed the whole pattern of transportation. In 1953 cars and taxis accounted for less than 30 per cent of personal milage travelled, by 1971 this had risen to 77 per cent[21]. The increased importance of the car in determining how people move from A to B can be seen from the following table:[22]

Table: Growth of Personal Travel in Great Britain
(units: thousand million passenger miles)

		1953	1971
Rail	... ...	24.1	22.1
Road:	pedal cycle	12.9	2.6
	motor cycle	4.8	2.7
	car and taxi	37.3	208.6
	bus, coach and trolly bus	50.7	34.0

which shows that all other ways of travelling have actually declined since 1953.

This pattern in personal travel is similar to that which has taken place as regards the movement of goods. Between 1953 and 1971 goods transport increased by 57 per cent[23] and "this increase was entirely accounted for by road goods transport, which increased by 260 per cent". In the period (1955-1971) the capacity of British Rail freight wagons declined by 65 per cent.

This increase in car ownership has been aided by a number of factors. The first of these has been the Government policy towards public transport where, before 1968 "the accepted philosophy was that public transport should be a commercial undertaking and should not be subsidised or helped by the state."[24] This was also the policy of the Northern Ireland government where the Ulster Transport Authority, which was set up in 1948 to bring all rail and road transport under the one Authority, was expected to balance its books.

The overall effect of this policy has been to force transport bodies to cut unprofitable services. In Northern Ireland for example the number of miles of railroad fell from 824 in 1949 to about 200 in 1972. Not only have services been cut, but fares have had to be raised. In between 1961 and 1971 while the cost of purchasing a motor vehicle in Great Britain rose by about 12 per cent and the cost of running it by 52 per cent, rail fares went up by over 80 per cent and bus and coach fares over 100 per cent[25]. It is little wonder that people switch from public to private transport.

A further factor encouraging road use has been the government's policy towards road building. In Great Britain the amount of public roadway available for motoring between 1953 and 1971 increased by 12 per cent. The road building programme has received a powerful impetus from the activities of the road lobby:

"the road lobby is a vast and complicated network which draws financial and moral support from a variety of industrial, commercial and other interests. Six major areas of support may be identified:

   (i)   the Motor industry
   (ii) the Bus Operators
  (iii) Road Haulage Firms
  (iv) The Motorists' Organizations
   (v) The Road Construction Industry
  (vi) The Oil Industry

Support also comes from other sources, such as the steel industry, insurance companies and farmers."[26]

In Northern Ireland a similar, though less well co-ordinated road lobby exists, with the added support of industrialists in general. Thus in the debate over whether the first leg of Belfast's urban motorway should be scrapped or not, the C.B.I.'s Northern Ireland Regional Council described the road as being:

"absolutely essential for the continued growth of the province and to safeguard jobs . . . it was important that goods should move freely. Most of industry's raw materials had to be imported and it was essential that there should be a quick and free movement."[27]

The road lobby's position in Great Britain is strengthened by the dominant place that the motor industry has in the countries' industrial structure:

"In 1971 the country's 700,000 motor and component workers produced 7.2 per cent of the country's G.D.P.; but 11 per cent of visible exports, and the industry earned a bigger surplus on the balance of trade in that year than did the economy as a whole."[28]

The First Compromise

By the late 1950's and early 1960's people were beginning to question whether the policy of adapting urban life to cope with the increase in car ownership might not have unacceptably high costs. These costs included the destruction of the environment, traffic congestion (in the 1950's the volume of London traffic doubled with the effect that by 1958 London traffic speeds were the lowest ever recorded)[29] and road accidents. In the space of 10 years from 1953 to 1963 the number of people killed and injured on British roads rose from 226,000 to 356,179. The time was clearly coming for some sort of a compromise between these costs and the increasing demands for road space made by the road lobby.

The Buchanan report on Traffic in Towns[30] spelled out what such a compromise might look like. The Report pointed out that the increase in the number of motor vehicles resulted in cities in the grossly inefficient circulation of traffic and adverse effects on human life and surroundings. It was therefore clear that "there are absolute limits to the amount of traffic that can be accepted in towns, depending upon their size and density."[31]

The Report still thought "that the motor vehicle is a beneficial invention with an assured future" but that changes were needed in the design of transportation schemes if large number of vehicles were to be accommodated without undue costs. Among the changes that were required were that: different traffic uses should be separated from each other (i.e. through city traffic from local traffic) by for example the "canalisation of longer movements onto properly designed networks." These networks involved hierarchies of road for the different kinds of traffic and the creation of traffic free, environmental areas to cut down accidents and environmental costs.

These conclusions provided the groundwork for the Belfast Transportation Plan which:

"followed the principal expounded in the Buchanan report that given great increase in the use of cars it is necessary to choose a hierarchy of roads for moving traffic around rather than through environmental areas."[32]

The roads in the hierarchy included:

"the motorways which include the Urban Motorway and the radial motorways (which) are to accommodate the longer movements into and out of the city and from one side of it to the other. The primary distributors are intended to give access to the central areas of the city. The intermediate ring road will provide inter-city connection between radial roads and will serve traffic from one city area to another. The outer ring road will serve long distance movements between outer areas."[33]

Below the ring roads there were the primary distributors for carrying through from one district to another, then district distributors for moving traffic about within districts and finally local roads such as access roads to buildings and land.

The Travers Morgan transportation plan was not therefore much better or worse, according to the then accepted criteria, than similar plans being prepared for other cities in the United Kingdom. If it hadn't been for the 'troubles' it is quite likely that the short-term priority roads in the plan, including the first leg of the urban motorway, would have been built. At the public inquiry into the first leg in 1969 there were few objectors.

The Compromise Breaks Down

But after 1970 things changed both locally and nationally. At the latter level it was becoming clear that a large number of people were no longer satisified with the transportation compromises of the 1960's. It was no longer accepted without question that the car was a universal benefit whose everpresent growth could be accommodated by careful transportation planning.

A number of criticisms were made of the existing compromise. It was argued firstly that transportation planning was too concerned with simply designing roads to take account of projected increases in traffic flows. It did not for example take sufficiently into account the dynamics of increased car ownership as a function of the decline in the quality and an increase in the cost of public transport. This dynamic has been described in one report in terms of increasing car ownership leading to a decline in the use of public transport so that "operators are obliged to reduce services in order to balance their books in conventional terms. This leads to a further fall in usage and further cuts in services, resulting in even greater car usage."[34] This increasing car usage then leads to more congestion and environmental damage and then to increased use of other roads as cars, trying to by-pass the jammed through roads, look for short-cuts.

Travers Morgan themselves admit that the decline in the use of public transport in Belfast was due in a large part to increased fares and poorer services.[35] According to their figures while the use of public transport in

55

Belfast declined by 40 per cent between 1951 and 1966, only 15 per cent of this drop could be explained by increasing car ownership. The rest was due to increases in fares and a decline in the quality of service. This deterioration of service coincided with the onset of redevelopment and the dispersal of population and the centralisation of shopping, leisure and community facilities. This meant that people had further to travel to go either to work or to the local community centre. It is not surprising that car ownership went up. However, as the car is needed both for travel to work and to go shopping; shopping, instead of being a daily activity becomes a once a week trip to the supermarket. Supermarkets are then in a position to justify their existence by showing that the trend is for greater mobility and less frequent shopping trips and that therefore what people clearly want are large, centralised district centres with ample car parking space.

One cannot therefore assume that an increase in car ownership means that all the people who buy cars wanted to do so. The evidence is that a number of them were forced to do so. If that is the case it then becomes difficult to predict what the increase would have been if better public transport facilities were available.

Furthermore predictions such as that by Travers Morgan, that the number of cars in the Belfast area would treble between 1966 and 1983 make a number of assumptions. The first is that past trends in the cost of public transport, vis a vis the cost of buying and running a car will remain similar. The second is that road building will continue at a sufficient rate to prevent road congestion getting appreciably worse and thirdly that there will not be an increase in transport policies, such as control of parking spaces, aimed at restricting the accessibility of cars to key areas. In Belfast, as elsewhere, these assumptions in times of: an energy crisis and more recently and perhaps temporarily in terms of a shortage of oil; an economic depression and rampant inflation are no longer tenable. An example of how inflation can affect the cost of a project is shown by the Belfast Urban Motorway scheme. In 1961 according to the City Surveyor it was going to cost £10 million and in 1964 between £25 and £30 million. By 1967 according to Travers Morgan's figures the cost had risen to £77 million and by 1972 according to objectors at the public inquiry into the Belfast Development Plans it had risen to over £100 million. Finally by 1973 the Belfast Urban Study Group estimated that the full cost would amount to £300 million. It was this rapid escalation in cost that was one of the factors that was to sink the scheme.

A second set of criticisms about the 1960's compromise was that it still paid too little attention to environmental and social costs. The following for example are some of the costs raised by different objectors to the Belfast transportation plan.

Cost of the Belfast Transportation Plan

One cost was the amount of land and the number of houses that would have to be cleared to accomodate the motorway. Altogether the motorway was estimated to take up 300 acres of land which previously held 7,000 houses. Of these 5,700 were in scheduled redevelopment areas. The other 1,300 houses would not have had to be demolished if it were not for the motorway. Given that housing authorities were aiming to get back 62 per cent of dwellings after redevelopment, this meant that going ahead with the motorway entailed the loss of land that could have been used to house over 4,000 families close to the city centre. This was at a time when the waiting list for houses had 9,000 families on it.

A related cost to the destruction of houses, was the break-up of communities. In the case of Sandy Row for example, which was a small Protestant working class community near the city centre, and which was particularly badly hit by the road scheme, the original plan would have meant that of the 2,400 houses in the community, 790 would have been demolished and a further 500 rendered uninhabitable because of 'noise' shadow.[36] Uncertainty about the motorway's future led to blight affecting communities in its path[37] and also to house building delays. For example one of the first redevelopment schemes, that in Upper Library Street, got further and further behind schedule because of the "urban motorway" (1964); pending a decision "as to the exact form of the motorway (1966); progress disappointing "pending a decision on the Urban Motorway (1967).[38]

Not only did the motorway knock down existing houses, but it determined the design of the dwelling to replace them. This was because:

" to avoid noise spread from the Urban Motorway to housing in the Shankill it is necessary that deck access type housing should be erected adjacent to it. These should be constructed with the main living areas facing West and the deck access kitchens and bathrooms facing East."[39]

Yet what people wanted to live in were terrace houses, not six storey blocks of flats and maisonettes. Furthermore these were so badly constructed that they were unlikely ever to be effective as sound barriers. Also contrary to the original plans the Shankill flats were built with some of the bedrooms facing towards the motorway. People in the Cullingtree estate on the Lower Falls were in even a worse position as some of the flats there were within 75 feet of the first leg of the motorway and their living room faced directly onto it. The Belfast Urban Study Group calculated that:

"the only way that the noise levels in these flats could be brought down to the recommended levels would be if the Motorway had a noise screen at the edge and all the flats had sealed double glazed windows with $\frac{1}{4}$" glass, 8" apart, insulated with heavy walling and mechanical ventilation. To build new dwellings to this standard would increase costs by 20 per cent and the conversion of the existing flats, none of which are built to this standard would be virtually impossible."[40]

But even more than the type of dwelling, the road plan determined the whole way that estates were to be laid out. In order to cope with the expected 192 per cent increase in the number of cars over the next 20 years, the Travers Morgan report recommended that many of the existing radial roads, which functioned as community shopping centres, be turned into primary and district distributors. This, on safety grounds, made them less viable as shopping streets. With the shops gone, other buildings, such as maisonettes, were needed as noise barriers. But without the shops the roads lost their function as community focal points and this reduced local people's sense of identity with their area.

Another lot of social costs can be measured in terms of the increase in road accidents that can be expected to accompany the increase in the volume of cars using the roads. Between 1959 and 1972 in Northern Ireland the number of road accident casualties rose by 60 per cent. According to a Department of Environment report[41] during the three year period 1970-72 there were in Northern Ireland 884 fatal accidents resulting in 948 deaths at an approximate total cost of £17.1 million. While it is true that in recent years car accident rates have not risen as fast as the increase in the number of cars this is in part due to the decrease in the number of pedal and motor cyclists who used to make up a high proportion of casualties. Also it is clear that casualty rates are higher for road compared to other forms of transport. Therefore a policy based on accommodating an increase in car usage will lead to higher accident rates than policies emphasizing alternative means of transport. Thus in Britain "in 1971, the number of casualties amongst car drivers and their passengers was 24 times larger than amongst bus drivers and passengers".[42]

A further aspect of the social costing of road schemes is that the working class areas bear the brunt of them. The Belfast Urban Motorway scheme was no exception in this case. The working class had, for example, fewer opportunities to make use of the road schemes. In 1966 in the Belfast region while professional and non-manual workers owned 7 cars for each 10 households, among semi-skilled and unskilled manual workers this dropped to three cars per 10 households.[43]

Not only could they make less use of the improved roads, but the motorways were planned to run primarily through working class areas. There were two reasons for this. Firstly because the land was occupied by slum housing it was cheaper to purchase than land elsewhere and secondly it was possible to use the more widespread powers available under the housing legislation to get possession of the land. While this might have made economic sense it meant that it was the working class who had to move elsewhere, see their communities broken up and suffer from noise and lead pollution. Those forced to move further away were confronted with a poor and expensive bus service. Some were therefore forced to buy a car which would involve them in even more expense. The road scheme in terms of private motoring therefore benefited the car owning middle classes who gained by having improved access to the inner city areas without having to bear many of the environmental and social costs which the road system entailed.

It is not only the working class as such that is discriminated against in a transportation policy geared to the motor car. Other groups are equally badly hit. These include all of those who can't afford a car—old age pensioners, one parent families and the unemployed—as well as those who

58

through physical or mental handicap can't drive. Also in those families who own a car and where it is used for travel to and from work, the housewife suffers.

The argument put by the objectors to road plans in Belfast, as that done by others elsewhere was that when the full social and environmental costs are taken into account:

"from the point of view of the community as a whole, a system which relies increasingly on cars for the journey to work is almost certainly more expensive, even in purely economic terms, than that which makes greater use of public transport."[44]

Therefore by 1970 the compromise reached a decade before, between the perceived needs of road users and the cost to the environment was breaking down. The original premise of the compromise, that the car was a beneficial invention with an assured future was no longer taken as given. In some cities such as Leeds this reassessment arrived too late to prevent inner city areas being torn up to make way for urban motorways. In other cities such as London a long debate ensued as to whether existing road plans should go ahead while in Nottingham in 1972 the new Labour council went a step further and abandoned a £100 million road building programme. Its new transport policy, which indicated the outlines of a new compromise, was:

"designed to strike a balance between the environment, the pedestrian, public transport, the commercial vehicle and the private car, so as to obtain the maximum freedom of movement for everyone that is compatible with a civilised way of life.

Public transport shall be greatly expanded and improved so as to provide a really attractive alternative to the private motor car despite the consequential need for very substantial public subsidies and severe restrictions in the use of private motor cars at peak traffic periods. The community cost of supporting public transport will be much less than the alternative cost of attempting to provide for much freer use of the motor car."[45]

In Belfast, by 1970, the first phase of the motorway ring road had been submitted to public inquiry and approved, much of the land for the road had already been cleared and tenders were out for basic piling work. It was then decided, because of the number of objectors to hold a public inquiry into the rest of the Travers Morgan Transportation Plan as well as Building Design Partnership's plan for Belfast. This inquiry was held in February 1972 and it gave a chance for all of those who were opposed to the transportation plan to make their objections known.

Thus the churches were worried that people were going to be forced into fixed moulds by the physical constrictions of the road plan. Others raised the problems of: scarce energy resources, the effect of the road plan on community life and pollution. Other people doubted the accuracy of the figures relating to projected increases in car ownership and claimed that the report paid insufficient attention to public transport alternatives.

Objectors also raised points about particular aspects of the plan; the most comprehensive of these, being those put by the Sandy Row Redevelopment Association. The Association attacked virtually every aspect of the plan ranging from:

"there was an underlying defect in the plan proposals in that there was a prior assumption that a ring road should be the central feature of the replanned Belfast . . . (to fears) . . . that their community will be destroyed if the main shopping street is replaced by the proposed road."[46]

All of this was of little avail. Though in particular cases such as Sandy Row some concessions as to the alignment of roads was made, the overall Transportation Plan, according to the Inspector's report was to go ahead. As he said:

"it is regrettable but inevitable that some people will have to be adversely affected for the benefit of the community at large" and "I do not consider that the matters raised . . . justify my acceptance of his request to recommend the abandonment of motorway construction in Belfast, the use of the available land for house and office building and the transfer of available funds from motorway construction to the improvement and subsidy of public transport."[47]

HOW THE BELFAST URBAN MOTORWAY WAS STOPPED

Yet just two years later it looked like these very things would happen. Part of the reason why this turnabout occurred was to do with the breakdown of the 1960's compromise. But this would have had little effect if construction of the motorway had already begun. In order to understand why this had not happened it is necessary to look briefly at the political changes that took place in Northern Ireland from 1969 onwards.

The crucial component of the motorway ring road or B.U.M. (Belfast Urban Motorway) the shortened name that it came to be called by, was the first leg. By 1973 even though most of the land was cleared no contract had yet been signed. The explanation for this lies in the 'troubles' which began in 1968. The construction work involved in building the motorway was beyond the capability of any local firm to handle which meant that the main work had to be done by a firm from across the water. The catch was that the line of the motorway ran right through the Lower Falls and Lower Shankill areas which were the scene of much of the violence. Firms were therefore reluctant to commit men and materials to these areas especially as the scheme was bitterly opposed by local residents. The Official IRA from the beginning, and later parts of the Ulster Defence Association, made it clear that they were prepared to take more direct action to stop the road going through. As this was clearly not a bluff and it was something well within the capabilities of the organizations to arrange, the contracts remained out to tender, despite the Ministry of Development's attempts at a:

"a somewhat unorthodox contractural idea. A £4m 'pay as you go' piling contract will be let as soon as politically possible . . . tenders were asked to quote for setting up a base and then for the cost per foot of pile driven."[48]

Therefore the direct and indirect threats associated with the 'troubles' were sufficient to mount a holding operation. The threats could stop the motorway being built but they could not prevent: the rest of the road plan slowly being implemented; the spread of blight to areas through which the motorway was due to run and money which could have been used for much needed housing remaining tied up for when the road actually began.

For this to change, three things had to happen. Firstly the case for the motorway and the road plan itself, had to be called into question; secondly an alternative plan had to be produced and thirdly it was necessary to show that the alternative plan had popular support.

The case against the motorway passed through a number of stages. The first opposition to the scheme came in 1964 when the Urban Renewal Society, a group of concerned middle class, mainly professional people, opposed the idea of there being a separate transportation plan for Belfast. They argued that what was required was:

"a master plan for Belfast of the future, with the roads balanced against the traffic, housing and environmental needs of the city . . . (instead) we have a road plan being foisted on the city irrespective of what it needs."[49]

Though there was limited support within the council and wider community for this viewpoint such basically liberal sentiments were not to be allowed to stand in the way of a road plan which was seen as essential for the province's economic prosperity and which on top of that would bring money and jobs to local firms.

The next major case against the motorway wasn't mounted until the 1972 public inquiry into the development plan, when, as we saw earlier, a number of objectors put forward comprehensive arguments attacking the way the plan was produced and showing the social and environmental costs that would be caused if the plan went ahead.

In the following year the Belfast Urban Study Group was set up. It consisted of an ad hoc group of people centred around Queen's University who were concerned about the effects of the various plans that existed in redevelopment, transportation, shopping and other fields. The idea behind BUS was, to provide some of the research necessary to back up the case against the motorway being put by community groups and to lobby politicians. It produced two booklets[50,51] which summarised the case against the motorway, listing the social and environmental costs. Furthermore BUS claimed that Travers Morgan had failed to show any need for the motorway because of the volume of industrial traffic. BUS went on to claim that there were two alternative routes bypassing the centre of Belfast which could carry this traffic to the docks. Thus there was no special argument in terms of the province's precarious economic position which could be used to justify the motorway.

The first report by BUS recommended:

"politicians of all parties to: abandon the present Travers Morgan road plans; halt all road building in Belfast and to commission one or two teams of consultants to produce alternative plans based on a commitment to public transport."[52]

The main advantages of a policy based on public transport (in the case of Belfast this would primarily mean an improved and subsidised bus system as well as traffic restraint schemes) were that it was: cheaper; more socially equitable; less environmentally polluting; quicker to implement and more flexible (bus routes can be easily altered to meet changing demands, motorways can't). Also that it would free more land for housing and prevent fit houses and for that matter communities being demolished and would stop people being forced to buy cars that they did not want.

The model for such a programme was provided by Nottingham and BUS arranged a teach-in where Frank Higgins, then chairman of Nottingham transport committee, outlined what had been achieved there in terms of free bus services, traffic collars, car parking and so on. Shortly afterwards the Republican Clubs brought out a pamphlet on the Ring Road[53] putting the case against it within a socialist context, questioning some of the data that Travers Morgan had used to arrive at their conclusions and indicating in detail how the Nottingham scheme could be applied in Belfast.

Therefore the first two parts of the package had been completed. The arguments put forward by Travers Morgan to justify the motorway scheme had been seriously questioned and an outline of an alternative policy had been prepared. What was left, was to show that the alternative plans commanded popular support. This was necessary if politicians were to be persuaded to vote to scrap the existing transportation plan.

The task of rousing public concern was made easier by a number of developments. There was the rapid growth in the number of community groups in Belfast after 1971 and by 1973 there were some 300 operational groups in the city. This growth can be traced to a number of factors. The violence in the province led to many social problems such as intimidation and squatting which traditional government services were unable to cope adequately with. In addition the people themselves had lost faith in the government institutions being able to help them. Of course from a Catholic point of view the whole role of government had been to oppress them. A further factor leading to community agitation was the setting up of a Community Relations Commission and its adoption of a community development strategy. Also as one effect of the violence was to politicise people and to make them aware of their power to effect events this made it easier to involve them in social problems. These ranged from housing conditions to agitation arising from the activities of the British army.

Housing was one of the key social problems. The redevelopment programme was at last beginning to get under way and communities were confronted with: blight (rats, lack of housing repairs etc.) in the old areas; badly built, mixed rise housing development schemes which few wanted and the threat of a motorway running by their front doors. The opposition of the community groups to the first leg of the motorway was primarily channelled through the Greater West Belfast Community Association (GWBCA) an umbrella body which represented many of the groups in the area on problems that they had in common.

Other working class and more politically based groupings were also involved in their opposition to the motorway. Foremost on the Catholic side were the Republican Clubs. Though they saw such community action as being of secondary importance compared to a solution of the national question, they nevertheless argued that social problems should not be:

"forgotten or not discussed. If this happens, working class communities will find they have gained little from the present conflict and that the only people to suffer are themselves as unemployment increases, new slums take the place of old ones and monster roads carve up the city."[54]

On the specific issue of the motorway the Republican Clubs produced a booklet, organised demonstrations and ran educational classes. Even though they hoped that joint Protestant and Catholic working class opposition to the motorway would emerge this never happened at any meaningful level.

As far as the Protestant working class were concerned the issue never aroused much widespread concern except in the case of Sandy Row which was directly threatened by the road plan. In other districts such as the Shankill, there were a number of reasons why it was difficult to arouse much popular concern.

Firstly opposition to the road plan focussed on the first leg of the motorway. This only affected a small part of the Shankill area, while it was the general upgrading of all roads, to carry the predicted increases in traffic, which was to threaten the viability of the Shankill Road as a shopping street. In fact some Protestants at first saw the motorway as being a useful military barrier between themselves and the Catholic Unity Flats.

Secondly Protestants did not see the motorway as yet another arm of British imperialism out to exploit the Irish, but instead along with the Unionist party as part of the changes to the state necessary to protect their jobs. As such it was a different issue from housing where the civil rights campaign brought home to the Protestant working class how much they had suffered at the hands of the Unionist party.

Thirdly it was difficult for Protestant areas to align themselves with a campaign which they saw as being dominated by Catholics when it was the IRA with the support of the Catholic population which was daily attempting to destroy the state of Northern Ireland.

It was only at a much later state that progressive elements within the Protestant working class saw that the motorway and transportation plan was an attack on their class interests. This happened on the Shankill when people began to see what the effects on the ground would be in terms of community destruction if the plan went ahead. The plan also began to be seen as part of the British package for the province, a package supported by the Faulkner led wing of the Unionist party which was negotiating them into a United Ireland. The Unionist party had therefore broken its part of the Orange contract. Protestant working class and petty bourgeoise interests were to be sacrificed on the twin alters of monopoly capitalism and civil rights for Catholics and Paisley was proved right—the price of rapprochement was to be domination by the Catholic south. Because it was the Unionist party which was betraying the Orange coalition it now became possible for local people to attack them without being accused of disloyalty. As a local Protestant para-military paper put it:

"But the working class Loyalist—by far the largest section of the community which has consistently for over 50 years given their individual support to the Unionist party must have their voice heard .

As was said previously the Unionist party has jailed them, failed them and flailed them . . . Who have the principal sufferers really been in this conflict? Again the working class Loyalist! Who has suffered all along the line from deprivation and want? Not only the working class Republicans— but again the working class Loyalist."[55]

It was only once this attitude had emerged that a parallel but separate Protestant working class opposition movement to the motorway could begin.

Gradually therefore, the third part of the plan, that of showing popular support for a cessation of road building and a switching of resources to public transport, fell into place. The popular opposition was dominated by community groups, including a few Protestant groups attached to the GWBCA who associated themselves with the campaign because of their solidarity with other groups on the more important problems related to housing. It received support from the Republican Clubs, from professional bodies such as BUS and from the Alliance party. Though the Alliance party basically represented progressive professional and business interests and strongly supported the economic changes taking place to the province, it used local issues, as the Liberals across the water did, to win popular support. Therefore the Alliance party on Belfast Council took up the cause of the motorway objectors as:

"it was urgently brought to the notice of councillors both by people who are suffering through 'blight' and uncertainty, and by expert planners who did not think an urban motorway is the right solution to Belfast's traffic problems."[56]

However, while the Belfast Council section of the party remained committed in its opposition to the plan, the main body of the Alliance party, as might be expected given the interests it represented, at its 1974 party conference: "decided that Belfast needs its urban motorway, despite the fact that one of the party's Belfast councillors has been instrumental in getting the scheme delayed."[57]

There were still those who defended the need for the motorway to go ahead as originally planned. These included the industrialists who felt that it was necessary for the movement of goods, and the politicans, particularly within the Unionist party, who had committed themselves to a policy of attracting industrial investment and saw the road plan as being an important plank in terms of what they had to offer. Thus:

"the Belfast Urban Motorway or an equivalent was a necessity, the Minister of the Environment, Mr. Bradford, told the Institute of Highway Engineers . . . Phase one of the Motorway would take four to five years to build, the Minister said, but was needed now to deal with Belfast's choking traffic."[58]

By now the once monolithic Unionist party had begun to come apart at the seams with the setting up of the Vanguard and Democratic Unionist

Parties. Both were opposed to the Unionist Party's attempt to make a political settlement along the lines dictated by the new owners of Northern Ireland's industrial wealth. They draw their support from those who suffered both economically from the advance of monopoly capital i.e. local business interests, small shopkeepers etc., and from those who saw the political settlement as a betrayal of the Protestant way of life. However, on the case of the Urban Motorway the interests in particular of the Vanguard party, which represented the remaining local independent business concerns, coincided with those of the Unionist party, as the motorway meant jobs for local contractors. Vanguard were therefore prepared to give the scheme at least tacit support.

Also supporting the road plan were the civil servants in the fairly powerful roads section of the Ministry of Development. When the House of Commons Committee on Urban Transport tried to find out why road schemes designed years before were still in existence:

"various suggestions were made explaining this situation. Mr. Foster spoke of the wish to build highways still being strong, and that this was largely because there were a very large number of people who had devoted their life to thinking about highways, and were not easily dissuaded. Professor Hall indicated administrative inertia as a relevant factor in the situation."[59]

It is easy to see why this might be the case in Northern Ireland especially where the deadening effects of one party rule would have meant less discussion about the different social goals that alternative plans might have aimed to achieve. Also the transportation plan had been in existence in one form or other since 1945 and all subsequent planning in Belfast was undertaken on the basis that there would be an upgraded road system. This had affected the planning of shops, the layout of communities, the siting of industrial estates etc. Therefore an alternative plan would have involved the replanning of the whole of Belfast and the scrapping of much of the work that the roads section had been engaged on since it was first set up. It is little wonder that the Department's policy was always to try and find an amendment to the existing plan rather than to think of redrawing it.

What was now needed from the objector's viewpoint was a decision by politicians to reverse their earlier stand on the motorway. The first step in this process was to get the support of Belfast Council. With the reorganization of local government, which became effective in 1973, the new district council lost control of road and planning services to the Ministry of Development. Therefore any decision reached by the council could only be a recommendation to the then Westminster Minister of State responsible for development, Mr. D. Howell. But the objectors argued that if the Council came out against the motorway this would show that the Belfast people were against the scheme and made it that much more difficult for the Ministry to steam roller it through.

The situation was made easier for the objectors, because with the break-up of the Unionist party, the result of the elections to the new council meant that for the first time, the Unionist party were no longer in an overall majority. However because: the two Republican councillors were not taking their seats; some of the Protestants who were not associated with the Unionist party were for the motorway and because of the political situation some Protestant councillors were hesitant about being seen to vote alongside Catholics, it meant that if the Unionist party voted as a block it could not be defeated.

The motorway came up at the first full council meeting of the new council. A motion was proposed jointly by a Unionist and an Alliance councillor calling on the Government to reconsider the need for the ring road. The Unionist councillor who supported it, Harry Fletcher, represented Sandy Row the area most badly hit if the ring road were to go through. As other Unionist councillors also felt pressured on the issue because of the degree of working class protest, the Unionist party split, with many abstaining and the motion was carried by 27 votes to 8.

This therefore meant that central government could either accept this decision or move to have it altered. It could hardly proceed with both the community groups and the elected representatives united against them. As it wasn't prepared to drop the scheme, it left the government with the task of getting the Council's decision changed. It took them 6 months to do it and they used five different tactical approaches.

The first and least successful was to embark on a public participation exercise where the community groups and bodies such as BUS were invited up to Stormont to meet the Minister for the Environment in the newly constituted Assembly, Roy Bradford, plus civil servants and representatives from Travers Morgan. This attempt at persuasion failed miserably:

"The Belfast Urban Study Group yesterday met the Minister of the Environment, Mr. Roy Bradford and his senior advisors to discuss the proposed urban motorway.

The delegation pressed the Minister to abandon the scheme in preference to an outer ring-road, by-passing most of the city. They argued that the outer ring-road is preferably socially and economically as the main conduit of traffic entering the city.

Mr. Bradford told them that he felt that noise levels in flats bordering the first phase of the motorway could be brought down to acceptable levels, and if this could not be done, then alternative uses for these buildings would be considered. He also stressed that he wanted freedom of choice for car owners.

The Study Group said afterwards that they remain convinced that spending two-to-three hundred million pounds on a road transport solution for Belfast, which by 1986 would simply replicate 1966 conditions was a waste of men, money, materials and land which could be better used in other fields such as housing. They also argued that no case had been made out for spending £49 million on the first phase of the motorway."[60]

The participation exercise was also aimed at Assembly men and at the city councillors. The second approach was to persuade the key councillors who supported the motion to change their minds. The three councillors

66

who mattered in this context were part of a delegation elected by the Council to put their case to Howell. The first of these members was Tom Donnolly from the Catholic SDLP party. His attitude to the motorway up till then had been:

"People are looking forward to the rebuilding of a city fit to live in and close study has convinced them that the motorway would be a monstrosity. Areas like the Cullingtree Road-Divis Flats complex in the Lower Falls and Sandy Row and the Shankill Road would be greatly affected by increased noise and exhaust pollution . . . the elevated motorway would separate the Protestant and Catholic communities in West Belfast permanently . . . the people of the areas are completely opposed to the motorway plan."[61]

Fred Proctor was from the Democratic Unionist Party and represented the Protestant working class upper Shankill area. His influence was important in persuading other Loyalist councillors of the case against the motorway and at this stage he was strongly opposed to B.U.M. The final member of the trio was Harry Fletcher, a Unionist, but who through his membership of the Sandy Row Association had been one of the earliest opponents of the scheme. His view was that if it went ahead "Sandy Row will be annihilated . . . But Sandy Row is a famous community, a real community, a loyal community. We won't go."[62]

By July 1974 all three had changed their mind. At the council meeting held then Proctor voted against any further delay to the motorway, as did Donnolly who went as far as to recommend that all three phases of the motorway should go ahead while Fletcher abstained.

How did this come about? Earlier in 1974 a delegation of councillors, assemblymen and civil servants had gone to see Glasgow's motorway system and Nottingham's public transport policy in operation. The visit to Glasgow seemed to have impressed Donnolly in particular and this was the main factor persuading him to change his mind. Proctor was also impressed by what he saw there and also believed that significant concessions had been made to his objections as to how the road would affect the Shankill Road. For example, he claimed that he was told by the Ministry of Development that if noise levels were too high in the Shankill flats facing the motorway, then they would be turned into warehouses. A totally unrealistic suggestion given the shortage of dwellings in Belfast. Also he was reassured that the scheme would not mean any widening of the Shankill road even though plans existed in the local road planning office to turn the lower part of the Shankill from a two lane to a four lane road. Finally, in the case of Fletcher, the Ministry made significant concessions as to how the road plans would affect Sandy Row following the recommendations of the public inquiry.

Fletcher would also have been affected by the third tactic which was to reassert Unionist control within the council. This was made easier by a by-election which a Unionist won and which put them back with an overall majority.

The fourth tactic was simply to delay matters until the steam had gone out of the situation. Therefore the original council vote on the motorway in October 1973 was followed by a meeting of the General Purposes Committee in November at which the Ministry and Travers Morgan put their case. As a result of this meeting the Committee asked the Ministry for further information on a number of points. This didn't come till February 1974. In the meantime some councillors demanded that they should hear both sides of the case so a further meeting of the General Purposes Committee was called in March to which the Belfast Urban Study Group and the Greater West Belfast Community Association were invited to give their side of the case. They had been led to believe that the Council would make a final decision on the motorway at the end of this meeting so considerable effort had gone into a campaign to lobby councillors. However, against all expectations no vote was taken. Instead it was learnt that two trips to Glasgow and Nottingham had been arranged, the latter not taking place to June thereby postponing the final vote until the July meeting of the council.

By then the Ministry had played its last card in the form of a compromise solution. This was that; the first leg of the motorway should go ahead (as well as a river crossing that no one objected to) while phases 2 and 3 would be postponed until the affects of phase 1 could be seen; some adjustments would be made to the line of roads, particularly as regards Sandy Row and full consideration would be given as to how environmental factors could best be mitigated.

The media came out in full support of this "sensible compromise" and so in July when a similar motion was put before the council it was lost this time by 25 votes to 12.

But it was a hollow victory. With 'law and order' not yet returned to the province there was no way of stopping the groups using direct action to prevent the motorway being built. But more important was the downturn in the United Kingdom economy and the need to cut government expenditure. This together with the rapid increase in oil prices called into question the viability of expensive urban road schemes. In the province itself it was clear that there just wasn't sufficient money to cope with both the housing problem and the urban motorway. So just four months after the council vote, the latest Westminster Minister in charge of Development and the Environment, Mr. Concannon announced that there was to be a review of the whole transportation plan.

Concannon was able to justify his decision in terms of the changes in thinking that had taken place in the past few years:

"since the Transportation Plan was prepared there have been important changes in thinking about transportation planning in urban areas with particular reference to the role of public transport. The consultant's brief takes full account of this, they have been instructed to place greater emphasis on improvements to public transport and among the alternatives I have specifically requested is the examination of a non motorway solution."[63]

Thus exactly thirty years after it was first conceived it looks like the Belfast road plan is dead and buried, though given that the same consultants,

Travers Morgan, have been re-appointed to carry out the review, there might well be a resurrection.

The 1960 compromise was dead. In Nottingham and then in other cities a new compromise with greater emphasis on public transport was being worked out. The cities which suffered most were those who had pushed ahead and got their road schemes built before the re-apprisal started. Belfast too would have suffered the same fate if the 'troubles' hadn't given the people the power to stop it. They held out until the need for a new look at the earlier plans was accepted, especially when it was clear that it need not have catastrophic effects for industrialists. Even though the case for a new compromise had been made it took the economic crisis to remove the props from under those who were still holding out for the motorway to be built.

Just what the effects would have been if the plans had gone through will be looked at in the next chapter.

Chapter 4

THE RAPE OF THE SHANKILL

The next three chapters are concerned with the Shankill Road area of Belfast. They show how the plans produced for the Belfast region, themselves a product of changing economic circumstances, were, along with the process of redevelopment, responsible for the rape and plunder of the Shankill. This chapter tells of the rape, which according to the dictionary,[1] is defined as to "rob, strip, plunder (a place)". Part of the definition of "plunder" is "to take (goods, valuables etc.) with illegal force, as an enemy; to embezzle; to take by robbery, steal." The next chapter will show how this was done throughout the act of redevelopment. Finally chapter six will describe local community efforts to get unfit houses repaired.

BACKGROUND

The Shankill Road is a Protestant working class district of some 200 acres starting half a mile from the city centre on the western side of the city. It takes its name from an ancient church built in the fourteenth century. In the sixteenth century the Shankill became a route for travellers passing between Antrim and Belfast. The subsequent history of the Shankill is closely tied up with the industrial development of Belfast. Its importance stemmed from the two rivers which ran through it and which were used as a source of power for the linen industry. As early as 1770 there were 2 rubing mills, 2 corn mills and 2 bleach mills in the area. However the period of greatest growth was between 1850 and 1900 when linen factories, brick works, foundries, and engineering works were erected.

It was during this period that the Shankill Road became an important shopping street and this was due both to the increase in population in the district and because the Shankill was a main thoroughfare with trams running along it from 1880 onwards.

The growth of housing closely follows the industrial development in the area. At the end of the eighteenth century the foot of the Shankill, Peters Hill, was one of the fashionable parts of the city for rich merchants to live in. With the spread of industry into the area they moved elsewhere and their houses were taken over by handloom weavers. From 1832 onwards rows of tightly packed terraced houses spread up along the Shankill with densities of over 200 persons per acre (net). These houses were often owned by nearby mills:

"Hence the Charters family who owned three mills and occupied two others also owned one hundred and thirty-five dwellings which were situated close to their factories."[2]

Most of the houses in the present redevelopment areas were built before 1878 and the most common design was where:

"the ground floor consisted of a parlour with a scullery attached. At the rear was the 10 foot square enclosed yard which houses the privy and the ashpit. The first floor had three bedrooms, the largest of which measured twelve and a half feet by ten feet. Refuge and waste from the privy and the ashpit had, therefore, to be carried through the scullery and the parlour before it could be disposed of. The outward appearance of the houses was also similar, being all built of red brick . . ."[3]

As described in the first chapter, living conditions were grim during the second part of the nineteenth century, sanitation was poor, work hours were long and wages often low. From the turn of the century, the Shankill, like the rest of Belfast, has suffered from the downturn in the fortunes of the shipbuilding and linen industries and "due to this long history of decline there has been very little investment in either industrial or residential premises until recently"[4]. However Protestant control of key industries has meant that unemployment has never been the major problem in the area that it is in Catholic estates such as Ballymurphy and Turf Lodge where for example a survey found in 1973 that 38 per cent of the economically active population were unemployed[5]. Housing conditions on the Shankill have, with the years, continued to get worse and as long ago as 1930 the Peters Hill area for example was considered unfit[6]. However, because of the financial and political reasons discussed in the first chapter, except for one or two small schemes, no concentrated attempt was made to redevelop the houses until 1960.

LIFE ON THE SHANKILL BEFORE REDEVELOPMENT
The Extended Family
The basic living unit was the extended family and "it is usual for married members of a family to try and obtain housing near their parent's home"[7]. This can be best illustrated by taking one set of 4 streets in the Hammer community on the Shankill and looking at five families.

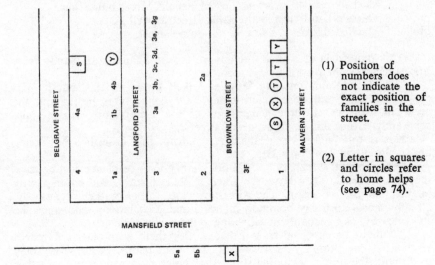

(1) Position of numbers does not indicate the exact position of families in the street.

(2) Letter in squares and circles refer to home helps (see page 74).

Family 1

1:      Mother who has lived in Malvern Street for over 50 years
1a: Married daughter 2 streets away
1b: Married daughter 2 streets away
In addition two married sons live within the same community.

Family 2

2:      Mother lived for over 50 years in same house in Brownlow St.
2a: Son lives in the same street
Has another married daughter living elsewhere in the same community.

Family 3

3:      Mother has lived in Langford Street for over 50 years
3a, b, Married daughter, 2 nephews and a niece all living in the same
 c, d: street as well as
3e: her sister-in-law who herself has
3g: a grand-daughter living in the same street as well as
3f: a married daughter living one street away
and another daughter a few streets further away in the same community.

Family 4

4:      Mother over forty years in her Belgrave Street house has
4a: One married son living in the same street and
4b: another living one street away
as well as another one living 3 streets further away.

Family 5

5:      Mother over 40 years in her Mansfield Street house has
5a: Married son living in the same street as well as
5b: Married daughter living in the same street.

    This pattern is of course not unique to the Shankill. In Sandy Row another Protestant working class area:
    "Streets contain not only families linked by social ties, but by ties of kinship also, and once again many have connections throughout the area. In some cases three generations of the same family reside quite separately within this small group of streets."[8]
    Nor is this pattern basically different from that described by Young and Willmott in London's East end:[9]
    "The Bethnal Greeners . . . did not change their residence just because they got married. They have remained in their district, and consequently in their families, of origin. The wife stays close to her mother because she already shares so many common interests and associations, and since she stays nearby, she keeps them alive and renews them.'
    As might be expected from Bott's work[10] there were clear differences as to what constituted women's work and what man's. Hence everything to do with the home, including often the choice of a new house, together

with child rearing and education, were women's work. The men went off to their job and supported the family financially. Thus redevelopment associations tended to be dominated by women.

The basic reason for the continuation of the extended family system up to the 1950's was that until then there were few economic advantages to be gained from moving which would have compensated for the communal benefits of life in a close-knit community. It was the influx of new industry, the setting up of growth centres, the continuing deterioration of living conditions in inner city areas and the onset of redevelopment which was to change this.

The Neighbourhood

The living unit above the extended family was the neighbourhood which consisted of one or a small number of streets joined together through interlocking families. Therefore Malvern and Langford streets could be classified as a neighbourhood quite separate from the more self-contained Brownlow Street which looked on the others as a clannish lot. This neighbourhood was described by one local resident as

"a very close-knit community made up to a large extent of families whose children when they married, tried to get a house near their parent's home. The community spirit in this district showed itself in many ways and the word 'neighbour' really meant something more than people living nearby. No matter what trouble a family may have had, whether it was, sickness, death or financial difficulties, there was no shortage of people willing to help out, If for example a mother with young children should have taken ill, there was no need for the husband to take time off work. because the neighbours would all play their part to make sure that the family was well looked after. This for them was the natural thing to do because any help they gave was out of genuine concern for the family in need of their help. This attitude probably stems from the fact that for them it was a natural thing to go in next door for a chat and a cup of tea and through time it was as if the people in a street were part of a large family. Living so closely together, arguments and fights, usually over children, were easily started, but quickly forgotten."

Within the neighbourhood there would normally be at least one corner shop which would be; a meeting place for the women, the store for necessities and the communal fridge, which as it stayed open until near midnight could be raided when necessary. The younger children would play in the streets which were in Newman's[11] terms a 'highly defensible area', an extension of the house, where all felt they had the right to accost strangers and would take on a collective responsibility to look after the children. Therefore over time a whole set of complex co-operative relationships were built up, centered on the family but including most people in the neighbourhood. According to one local resident:

"everybody was, as they say, 'in the same boat' so everybody helped everybody. Neighbour knew neighbour and one's families' sickness or good fortune was everybody's. A death in the street was a personal bereavement to all. After school us kids completed our homework then out onto the street to play football, with a home-made ball, 'piggy' or rounders, marbles or 'Fut the bucket' with an empty can. When the older members came home from work they joined in the games until dark, and sometimes after dark but 10.30 p.m. was very late. Friday night was bath night. The girls helped to clean the house and it was a common sight to see a semi-circle outside each door scrubbed clean. Brass work on each door gleaming after polishing with brasso. Then one by one the family were called in to bath in a zinc bath in front of the kitchen fire."

One dominant feature of the relationships within the neighbourhood was that they were vertically integrated. That is that through the family structures and long standing friendships, people of different ages were joined together. One way this has happened was through the role that old people in the neighbourhood played:

"the 'grannie' of Sandy Row not only baby sits and helps out with the younger children, but often it is she who collects the older ones from school when the mother is at work. There are cases where one child from a large family will actually live with its grandmother and be cared for by her."[12]

and within the neighbourhood itself:

"if elderly people needed any help it was usually given willingly by her neighbours. Anyone who was ill and lived alone nearly always gave the key of the house to someone who would call and make sure that all was well. Neighbours arranged for meals. If painting or decorating was needed by a person who was not able, or had no family nearby then neighbours would help out .This help to them was not one way traffic for they in turn would help neighbours by looking after children at different times. If, for example, someone did work for a pensioner and refused payment then the pensioner would find some way of making payment i.e. by buying sweets or toys for their children or even at times buying the children clothes or footwear, which with their income they could not really afford. Most pensioners in this area have lived here most of their life and have developed close friendships with the families living around them."[13]

A particularly important relationship was that between old age pensioners and their home helps. If one looks at the map on page 71 (home help is the letter in the circle; the old age pensioner the same letter in brackets) one can see that:

"the elderly and infirm of the district, with home helps who were paid for by the Belfast Welfare Authority, nearly always had someone who lived near their home and this had the advantage of having someone who knew them well and was usually quite willing to tend to their needs outside the person's allotted hours."[14]

Therefore the local neighbourhood was based on the extended family and friendships built up over time with neighbours in the same or nearby streets. Building Design Partnership in a local survey found that 68 per cent of households in the Shankill had at least one close relative in the district and 79 per cent visited these relatives daily.[15]

There were however, exceptions to this feeling of neighbourliness. In the Shankill area for example, there were isolated cases of individuals and families who, with redevelopment, were discovered to be living in filth and suffering from malnutrition. Often people living on either side would, because of the stench, know that something was wrong and yet would not intervene. This was because these people were isolated in so far as they had no immediate family living in the area and neighbourliness was dependent on it being asked for. On the other hand there were cases of individuals with a history of mental illness who were cared for by the neighbourhood. This included everything from washing them to tolerating their eccentricities. This required a neighbourhood where most people were known to each other and which could therefore protect defenseless individuals from others.

The Community

The basic neighbourhood unit consisted of around 200-750 people. The next level in the community consisted of a collection of such neighbourhoods. In the Shankill area there were a number of clearly designated communities such as 'the Hammer', 'the Nick', 'the Pad', the little Hammer', and 'the Banjo'. These each consisted of some 30-50 acres and contained some 2,000-4,000 people. Originally the boundary of the area was determined by the size of the farmer's fields on which each new group of terraced houses was put up in the nineteenth century. Over time each community took on a character of its own. Originally these were probably to do with the place of employment and differences in employment skills, though by now within the redevelopment areas many of these differences will have disappeared with the changing employment patterns.

The Hammer community which is centred around the Hammer playground is said to have got its name from the days when street battles took place between the different communities. The 'Nick' who were traditional Hammer enemies used hatchets as their favourite weapon and the Hammer got its name because the weapon it favoured was the hammer.

"as the years passed the Saturday matinee was replaced by football in the morning and a senior league game in the afternoon. This was the time when I first became aware of the 'gangs'—because to travel from the Shankill to Windsor Park we soon learned it was safer to travel with a gang . . . the chief gangs of the road at that time were the Nick, the Hammer and the Pad. Each of these covered an area next to the Shankill. These gangs fought each other as well as the common enemy from the Falls."[16]

Each community had its known fighting heroes whom it would take a squad of policemen to subdue. One such person was said to have kept a lion for a pet; another was famous for having thrown his wife through a window and a third for having stuffed a policeman up his chimney.

The Pad, or 'Black Pad' to give it its full title, got its name from the time when the main street in the community, North Howard Street was covered with a mixture of cinders and sand and beaten hard. The 'Nick' on the other hand derived its name from Nixon Street which served as a small social centre for the community, consisting of three pubs and three corner shops, one of which stayed open all night.

The community tended to be the main living area for people in the Shankill. It contained pubs, shops, small businesses, churches and meeting halls. The Hammer community for example contained three primary schools, a playground, a Unionist hall, 2 band rehearsal rooms as well as 70 shops and small businesses (excluding those on the front of the Shankill Road), 4 public houses, three churches and three mission halls, all in an area with some 3,000 people. For many people therefore the community met all their needs and except for going on to the Shankill Road itself, they would rarely leave it. It was not uncommon to find people who couldn't place streets which were no more than a quarter of a mile from where they lived but which were outside their communities' boundary.

The size of the community in addition to the previously mentioned reasons was also determined by the defensive need to be able to recognise everyone who lived in it and therefore in times of conflict to immediately recognise strangers. Within each community the churches played an important role in providing minimum social welfare facilities so that

"any communal outings for children were confined to what were known as 'Sunday school trips' because the outings were arranged by the churches in the district."[17]

The Shankill Road

Not all parts of the Shankill were grouped into easily identifiable communities. These other parts were usually known by the main streets in the area such as the 'numbered streets'. However, all the different parts and communities were joined together by the Shankill Road itself which has always been one of the main shopping streets in Belfast. It was where, particularly on Saturdays, that people from all over the Shankill, as well as from other parts of Belfast, would meet to shop and talk and look:

"Saturday was looked forward to eagerly. Mother did her shopping during the morning, then we were given a penny each to go to the pictures. Then after tea everyone was washed and dressed and all out on to the Shankill where we walked down one side of the 'Road' down North Street to Bridge Street and up the other side. All the shops were open. Street traders at every corner, also hand-carts lined one beside the other, down both sides of Lower North Street. During this weekly trip we met and chatted with neighbours, workmates, schoolmates and friends from all districts of Belfast. The shops remained open until 11.00 to 11.30 p.m."[18]

As far as the people were concerned:

"to me, the Shankill was a great shopping centre and the people on it were so friendly and happy" and "I have lived on the Shankill Road nearly sixty years. To me it has always been the brightest and friendliest road in the city. The people come from different parts of the city to shop."[19]

It was through the Shankill Road that all the communities gained a common identity and sense of purpose which was celebrated in particular on occasions like the 'Glorious Twelfth':

76

"The Shankill really blossoms out in the month of July, when thousands of houses on the road receive special treatment . . . the 'Eleventh Night' bonfires of the Shankill Road are known all over Ireland and thousands of visitors usually make the trip . . . to see how the fires are burning, and to admire the artistry in the famous arches which span scores and scores of streets. Then on the 'Twelfth day' the famous No. 9 District of the Belfast County Grand Orange Lodge steps it out smartly, headed by bands from West Belfast Orange Hall at the top of the road."[20]

Another way in which different communities were joined together was through membership of bodies such as the Orange Order which embraced the whole area. For example, in Sandy Row, 33 per cent of the people belonged to the Orange Order while only 20 per cent belonged to a church group.[21] But the key to the area was the Shankill Road which was its heart:

"The Shankill Road is the place of my birth. I was born in Matchett Street on 10th August 1894 and am now going into my eightieth year. So through all my life I have found the Shankill Road a great place to live in . . . the Shankill is a cheap shopping centre and I have been shown kindness and good respect always. After 67 years in the same place you get to know everybody around you."

The Shankill then was based on the neighbourhood which itself was dependant upon the extended family and friendships built up over long years. Neighbourhoods combined to form communities and communities to form the Shankill area. Above the Shankill there was the regional level of West Belfast but this was more an administrative area which had little meaning for most people and further above that was the whole city of Belfast many parts of which were entirely foreign to Shankill residents.

It was this which the redevelopment destroyed and the destruction lay in years of housing neglect; declining industries and the promise of a better life in new towns. The destruction was not based on ignorace but, communities had to be altered to fit in with the new economic needs of the province. Building Design Partnership understood full well how the old Shankill operated.

"close kinship ties characterise the district; in one survey area four in five families had at least one relative at hand whom they visited daily. Shankill shopping is well known, attracting many customers from distant areas . . . and the Road constitutes a meeting place for the exchange of news and views which in one of the assets of living there. Other factors have contributed to the strength and length of Shankill roots. Small business enterprise permeate the district . . . a wealth of social facilities exist centring to some extent in religious groups . . . all this indicates an old established community with limited mobility and little desire to change the pattern of their lives . . . so the Shankill emerges as more than a geographical living area—it is a living and lively community wherein the majority have strong family ties and share similar political and religious beliefs."[22]

THE BEGINNING OF THE END

The beginning of the end for the Shankill Road started as long ago as the turn of the century with the decline in the linen and shipbuilding industries and the consequent need to attract foreign investment to guarantee industrial survival. This as was seen in the second chapter led, from 1944 onwards, to the growth centre policy. It followed that if the new industrial estates in the growth towns around Belfast were to be successful, young skilled workers had to be attracted there. This is what happened. A study of labour mobility in Northern Ireland[24] has shown that those who moved to new towns: are young married couples whose parents are better educated; have better aspirations and who have higher incomes than those who do not move. A further study of newcomers to one of the Craigavon estates[25] found that the intake population tended to consist of young married couples with children of school age, of whom 65 per cent were semi-skilled and where 49 per cent owned a car.

There were of course reasons why the younger families moved first. Probably the simplest was that there were a shortage of houses in Belfast where there was a waiting list of over 9,000 families. As young couples had few points and were therefore at the bottom of the waiting list, they had to be prepared to move to new estates if they wanted to get a house. A second reason was the increasing desire by young people to improve themselves and to give their children more opportunities in life than they had had. As one young person on the Shankill put it to me: "for community feeling, what is better than the Shankill? But the Shankill isn't the whole world. One must be able to stand up anywhere."

These changes in attitudes were a result of a better education; more opportunities; the influence of television; the delapidation of the redevelopment areas and so on. The strength of the community was most important in times of poverty. With increasing economic affluence and more opportunities to get ahead, these considerations became more important than the nature of the community in which one lived.

The effect of this movement by young families on a redevelopment area such as the Shankill can be seen by comparing the number of people per house in phase 1 of areas 12/13 in 1966 compared to 1973.

Number of people per house	1973[26]	1966[27]
1	25%	20%
2	32%	25%
3	21%	19%
4	8%	15%
4+	14%	21%
average family size	2.66	3.15

Similarly in areas 11/33 the average family size in 1966 was 3.25[28], by February 1973 this had dropped to 2.7[29]. This population movement had a number of effects. It meant firstly that it hastened the onset of blight in redevelopment areas and removed from the areas some of the people who might have been experted to have opposed the plans for the area. Also as can be seen from the figures it meant there was an increasing percentage of 1 and 2 person households, many of which consisted of old age pensioners. These required assistance and help to cope with the problems associated with redevelopment just at the time when the traditional family and neighbourhood supports were being broken up. Finally it spelt the end of the old type of community. With the need of modern capital to continually rationalise production in the search for profits, labour is expected to move to where it is most needed. Labour mobility requires a family structure that is easily transportable i.e. the compact nuclear family rather than the three generation extended family.

Already in 1966 Building Design Partnership had found on new estates around Belfast that:

"ten to 20 per cent of the families had taken steps to move house in the first year of a tenancy in order to obtain an improvement in housing; to live in a better area with different neighbours; and also because of a wish to move to a better job, to better shopping and other facilities."[30]

Therefore with the extended family broken and with increased mobility the two basic planks of the old type of community were finished. Once the attraction and strength of the old community had been broken then criteria such as type of job and the amount of money it paid became more important in determining life styles than the nature of the social relations within the community within which one lived.

The Shankill and the Transportation Plan

One plank in Northern Ireland's attempt to attract new industry was the creation of a road building programme which was discussed at length in the last chapter. Its final form, the Travers Morgan Transportation plan for Belfast, had serious consequences for the Shankill Road. First of all the Shankill was to be compartmentalised by a series of main roads—a six lane elevated motorway was to be the eastern boundary to the area; part of the intermediate ring road, 4-6 lanes wide, the western boundary; a six lane primary distributor road the northern boundary and a four lane primary distributor road and industrial estate the southern boundary. There was to be a two lane local distributor road running through the middle of the area, north to south and the Shankill Road itself which ran through the middle of the area, east to west, was to stop being a shopping street:

"Corporation proposals to withdraw ribbon shopping from the Shankill Road into a new shopping centre, thereby relieving the road of parking and other problems, and allowing for its upgrading as a traffic route, have created a need for the new housing itself to be designed to screen the site from the effects of an increase in the adjacent traffic load."[31]

The Shankill Road was therefore to become simply a main traffic artery and with no shops the increased flow of traffic led to the Housing Executive claiming that it had to build six storey blocks of flats that no local people wanted along the front of the Shankill road in order to block off the traffic noise.

The transportation plan not only physically divided the Shankill but meant that in designing housing layouts, planners had to allow for an expected 4 fold increase in car ownership. This not only reduced the amount of land available for housing but given the need for cars to be parked as close to houses as possible (a maximum of 150' from the dwelling[32]) determined how parts of the estate were laid out. Altogether through the need for land to be allocated for car parking and roads, as well as for open spaces, the amount of land available for housing in the Shankill fell from 113.08 acres pre-development to 99.23 in Building Design Partnership's post-redevelopment plans.[33] This reduction was another argument used by architects to justify building high rise flats if they were to get back as many people as possible after redevelopment.

The Shankill and Building Design Partnership

Perhaps even more critical for the Shankill were Building Design Partnership's plans for the Belfast urban area. In particular that there should be in Belfast the:

"establishment of 12 district centres to include shopping and substantial car parking, with recreation, leisure, social and community facilities and possibly, housing, offices, hotels, warehousing and other services."[34]

One of these was to be on the Shankill. The shopping was due to be removed from the road itself and placed in a centre on the north side of the road while opposite there was to be a leisure centre. The intended catchment area of the centres was some 82,000 people i.e. it was not only to serve the Shankill area but was to be the centre for the whole West Belfast district. In looking at why the centres have to be so big, Building Design Partnership provide the answer as they argue that one needs "to have a minimum catchment population of about 30.000 as this is an important threshold at which the attraction of stores such as Woolworths and other multiples becomes feasible."[35] The creation of 12 centres, each dominated by one or two multiples, meant in practise as we have seen the wiping out of much of the local competition and a virtual monopoly for the multiples.

In looking at the old Shankill it was seen that the basic living units progressed upwards from the extended family as far as the Shankill area with the regional level of West Belfast or city wide considerations having little importance. The Planners however, started from the other end. The crucial planning determinants were the economic needs of the whole of the Belfast urban area and these extended down to a consideration of their implication at a regional level. Concern for the area, community or neighbourhood only appeared once the plans for the city had been drawn up. An example of how decisions made at a regional level produced odd results at a more local level can be seen by examining how Building Design Partnership arrives at its post-redevelopment population standards for the Shankill. As an article by John Greer shows[36] Building Design Partnership's targets that 62 per cent of the houses and of the population in all redevelopment areas should be replaced were totally arbitrary figures. The effect of taking these figures as the crucial standards was that the occupancy rate, the number of people living in each house, became a

Shankill old and new. Left hand side shows the row of shops which fronted the old Shankill. On right are the 6 storey blocks of flats and maisonettes to replace them.

The new Shankill estate. Note the wrecked drying yards – an example of undefinable open space and the car park given priority over play space.

The old Shankill. The street was an extension of the house and belonged to everyone in the neighbourhood.

The noise barrier flats on the Shankill — shortly to be demolished.

purely residual figure. The result was that when these standards were applied to the Shankill, the resultant post redevelopment occupancy rate was estimated to be 3.6 persons per house. Yet in 1966, the average household size in the Shankill which, like elsewhere, had been falling consistently for years; was only 3.08. Therefore because the Shankill had to conform to the norms produced for the whole of Belfast, new houses were being built to accommodate on average larger families than those wanting to be rehoused in the area.

THE NEW SHANKILL

The pattern of life in the new Shankill then was determined largely by the two master plans for Belfast. The new centre of the Shankill was quite fittingly to be a shopping centre, put up by private developers. The old centre, the Shankill road; "part of the Ulster way of life"[37] was therefore to go. Instead of being a thriving shopping street and the historical centre of the area, it was to become a main traffic route blocked in by 4-6 storey blocks of flats and maisonettes. These dwellings, built as noise barriers, had, as it were, their backs to the Road itself and people were therefore to be encouraged to face inward into the estates and not on to the Road. This was reinforced by the pattern of pedestrian paths which were planned to run through the estates linking each with the new district centre.

According to the plans the Shankill redevelopment areas were to be divided roughly by the roads into 4 communities, each of about 2,500 people.[38] Each of these communities were, in terms of numbers ,about the same size as the old Shankill communities but covered an area two to three times as big. Each community was to have its own community hall, couple of pubs, nursery/primary school and corner shops.

The planners and architects saw their task basically as a physical one. Their prime concern was that the numbers of people returned matched up with the standards laid down by Building Design Partnership. Thus:

"Redevelopment targets and social proposals:
4.1 General: If the Building Design Partnership's forecast of 4,000 dwellings in the total Shankill area by 1986 is to be realised, a return of 1800 dwellings must be the minimum target for this redevelopment area (area 12/13).
The basic design principle of the development plan will be to create within this total, two main sub-communities, each with its own service amenity buildings."[39]

Houses or Flats?

The importance of physical over social criteria in design was most apparent in the debate over the proportion of houses to flats that there should be in the Shankill area. At the beginning of redevelopment in 1960 planners argued that given: shortage of land for building within the Belfast area; the reduction of the amount of land available for housing; the desire by people to be rehoused in the same area after redevelopment; a belief that many of the objections to living in flats would fade away when people moved into them; studies which showed that groups of people such as childless couples were suitable for living in high rise blocks and the lack of knowledge about low rise building schemes available at that time; the only solution was to builds flats. This was despite the fact that few people wanted flats, a point clearly accepted by the planners.

"Q: Would you accept it now that the overwhelming majority of the people have expressed themselves as being opposed to the idea of living in flats?

A: (Walsh: Town Planning Officer) I accept that:"[40]

The people gave reasons for their opposition. Stairs would be too difficult, mothers with young children would have problems with flat life and so on. Fourteen years later when further up the Shankill road six storey blocks of flats were built in Upper Townsend Street, a study found that:

"difficulties included the noise from people walking up the stairs, the worry about fire, the fact of not having a 'proper' front door, not being able to keep a close eye on one's car and not being able to make much noise . . . lifts so rarely work . . . even when it works it is often dirty and foul-smelling . . . the stairs constitute a major difficulty for a large group of people. There are those who are not well and find climbing the stairs very hard. There are mothers who have small babies and for various reasons cannot use the pram sheds and have to take the prams upstairs with immense difficulty . . . many of the small children hardly ever get out as their mothers are afraid to let them down the stairs on their own."[41]

The people fought hard to get rid of the flats. By 1971 the 15 storey blocks had been scrapped. By 1974 all flats or maisonettes over 4 stories had gone. Finally in 1975 the first phase plan was produced which did away with flats altogether. On one level it was simply a fight where the strength of the people coincided with: increased building costs and reduced Government subsidies for high rise flats; increased awareness of the social costs associated with flat life; more knowledge about low rise high density building schemes and a realisation by all concerned that not as many people were going to get back after redevelopment as had been originally planned for. Though throughout the fight the planners had always claimed that in order to get back everyone who wanted to return, i.e. according to nearly all the surveys[42] about two thirds of the population in redevelopment areas, it would be necessary to build flats. However, this assumed that all those who had said they wanted to would, after vesting, actually return. This could only have happened if a leapfrogging programme of clearance had been implemented where there were houses waiting in another part of the area for those in the next houses due to be demolished. This rarely happened and it meant for most people that they had to move out of the area. Now even though most of these people thought at first this move was only temporary, experience over time, according to the minutes of the Housing Committee "had shown that only a small proportion of displaced families were anxious to return to

82

their original district."[43] Therefore it should have been clear from the beginning that the two-thirds return rate was never on and if the people themselves had realised this, it would have greatly strengthened their negotiating hand.

On a more basic level the fight over houses and flats was a last ditch attempt by people to preserve their way of life. They realised that flats were the preserve of the nuclear family and if there was to be any chance of retaining their old way of life then houses were necessary. In June 1974 there were, according to the local Housing Executive office, some 500-700 flats lying empty in West Belfast which were perfectly usable. These were not on the edges of troubled areas, and therefore vacant because of the disturbances, but simply reflected the fact that people preferred to remain living in houses, which had long since been condemned rather than move to flats. In the lower Shankill estate one fifth of the brand new maisonettes were lying empty and vandalised. Even when people moved into flats they only saw this as a temporary step until houses became available. This was shown by what happened when intimidation started and many people were forced to leave their houses. In places such as New Barnsley, those who remained and were living in flats, left them and took over the houses.

Though planners themselves as Building Design Partnership's various reports show recognised people's desire to live in houses rather than flats, this was for them rarely as important a goal as achieving set numerical targets. It was only when people started to refuse flats that a change in policy occurred as it was an increasingly costly endeavour to put up buildings which were immediately vandalised. This becomes clear when one looks at the reasons the Ministry of Development gave at the end of 1973 to justify its switch to a policy of low rise housing:

"High-rise accommodation, that is, above 5 storeys . . . has in general not proved popular in the Belfast Urban Area . . . experience elsewhere has shown that high-rise development can pose considerable social problems both for the elderly and persons with young families. The cost of high-rise buildings is higher than for low-rise building considered not only in terms of money but also in terms of lost amenities and the social well-being of families."[44]

Building New Communities

As redevelopment broke up the old communities the extended family could no longer be used as a basis for bringing people together. The neighbourhood unit too was lost and with the decline of the Shankill road as a shopping street there was no area focus to draw people together. Instead for planners the main basis was now to be the community, this being the level at which it was most economic and convient to provide the necessary social facilities. The planner was then faced with the task of how to create a sense of community. The answer was to base it on common interests and as people of different ages have different interests this was reflected in the type of facilities offered. There were to be old persons' clubs for the old age pensioners and then community centres for the middle-aged:

"two groups of meeting rooms for the use of residents' associations, women's groups or informal gatherings are provided for social and community events."[45]

youth clubs for the teenagers where

"organised youth clubs will exist in several church halls, in addition to which a thriving branch of the YMCA will be relocated with comprehensive facilities for sport and leisure. The Corporation's District Leisure Centre will provide even larger indoor recreational facilities."[46]

Further down the age scale:

"play space for the seven to twelve age group, mainly hard surfaced kickabout pitches, to be dispersed throughout the housing zones. Play space for the two to seven age group will be provided adjacent to shops and other facilities as well as incidental small areas convient to individual housing groups."[47]

In the old Shankill, particularly at the neighbourhood level, estates as we saw were integrated vertically. That is, through family and friendship links people of different ages were joined together. In the new estates where integration is on the basis of interest such links are horizontal with no links across age barriers. This was one of the factors which led to the outbreak of vandalism on the new estate in the Lower Shankill which earned it the title in some quarters of 'Apache territory'. In practice, despite, or rather because, of what the housing authorities provided in the way of facilities, the main interest in most new estates in Belfast and elsewhere, that existed to bring people together, was the need to do something about the deplorable housing and social conditions on the estate.

Old People

Of all the groups that suffered from the loss of neighbourhood, the worst off were the old people. In looking at the old Shankill, it was shown that old people had a number of useful roles that they could play. These were however dependent on the neighbourhood. Once that, and the extended family were gone, not only was there no one left to look after the old people but there was nothing left for the old people to do. This was clearly recognised by the planners and architects who provided old persons' homes, sheltered dwellings and blocks of one bed flats for old people with different degrees of infirmity. Each group of old persons' dwellings were set on their own. These were at least provided within the confines of the redevelopment area instead of being isolated out in the country but they were still isolated physically and psychologically from the surrounding community. The consequence of this was that whereas the occupants knew most other people within their set of dwellings they knew few other people on the estate and worst of all, few people on the estate knew anyone in any of the old persons' dwellings.[48]

Therefore instead of an old person being 'Mrs. Brown who lives next door and looks after Billy when he comes home from school' they become one of the indistinguishable 'oldies' who live in that block over there who are therefore no longer part of the community so you might as well go and throw stones through their windows. In reply to this line of argument, the authorities would argue that old people wanted to live alone. This was tested in a community survey and it was found[49] that "two-thirds of those who answered the question said they wanted the latter (rehoused in the middle of everybody else) and only one-third wanted to be rehoused together with other old age pensioners". On further questioning it became clear that those who wanted to be rehoused with others, were mainly those whose families had moved away and who were therefore feeling lonely and isolated and therefore saw little advantage in being rehoused in the centre of the community. The noise which is made by children you don't know is annoying and a little frightening but if they're part of your family then it's friendly and reassuring. The situation was made even worse for old people by the fact that there were too few houses being built for them. This appeared to be because of the laying down of unrealistic proportions of different house sizes which underestimated the number of one bed units needed.

	House Sizes				
	O.P.D's	1 Bed	2 Bed	3 Bed	4 Bed
a) Building design Partnership's[50] recommendations for the Shankill area.	21%		40%	30%	9%
b) Families in Shankill Redevelopment areas in 1974 wanting rehousing in the Shankill area[51]	27%	23%	28%	17%	5%
c) Size of all dwellings being built in Shankill redevelopment areas.	10%	12%	26%	42%	9%

As far as could be calculated on 1974 figures based on occupancy rates at the time of vesting of areas 11/33, 12/13; 817 one bed units of accommodation were required in the new Shankill estates. However there were only plans to build 508. This means that some 300 small person families, of whom, according to Housing Executive figures, at least half would be seeking old person's dwellings will be forced to leave the redevelopment areas. The short term problem was even worse with some 200, one and two person households, wanting new accommodation in the new Shankill estate when only 90 one bed units were planned to be built.

85

Old people were therefore low on the priority list for housing consideration. They had little political power and less economic value. The more important and more general problem though and this is one which needs to be faced by all sections in the community is what to do with the elderly who are becoming an increasingly high proportion of the population. In Northern Ireland according to census figures, people over 65 made up 6.1 per cent of the population in 1901 and 10.5 per cent in 1966. It is estimated that by 1990 this will have risen to 11.3 per cent[52]. It is not only a problem of increased financial cost to the rest of society in terms of health and social welfare but is as much a problem of what to do with people thrown on to the economic scrapheap. What was envisaged for the Shankill residents seemed to be small colonies of elderly people with no useful role to play who will fill out their remaining years talking to other people in the same condition. It is difficult to see in the short term what can be done as a willingness by most people to accept responsibility for looking after old people irrespective of what small acts they can perform in return, and especially when there are no family obligations, is dependent on a sense of being joined together as a part of some community unit. However as the neighbourhood as a unit of social living now seems to have no place and is anyway dependent on its survival on a stability of population which no longer exists, the sharing and concerned community is likely to remain for most old people very much a pipe-dream. In fact they might well be better off in the American dream of the sun cities reserved solely for the retired. At lease these recognise the uselessness of old age for what it is and that if the rest of society has nothing left to offer you, then you are better off without it. It then becomes possible to try and create the fantasy that the purpose of work is to retire well so that one can do all of those things that were always dreamed of but which there was never time to do. In the Shankill there was only a token attempt to reintegrate the old people into the community and so they ended up half way in between, neither as a member of a caring community or as part of their own separate world.

The Reduction of Social Facilities

As we saw in the old Shankill the comunity as a unit met the living needs of most of its people. There were numerous shops and small businesses and many different meeting places such as pubs and halls. With redevelopment however, not only did the physical area that a community covered increase, thus making it much more difficult for people to identify with it as an area, but the number of social and economic units were greatly reduced.

Take the case of shops and small businesses. Before redevelopment in the Hammer area there were 70 of these in a community of some 3,000 people. In each of the 2 planned new communities in 12/13 for approximately the same size population there will be about 12 shops.[53] There is no room for small businesses though other communities[54] in the area are having 2 yards which will each have room for 4 small businesses. It was recognised that the loss of shops would be to the detriment of communal life:

"Isn't it a fact that there has been a loss of communal feeling and this has been a growing problem?

A. Booth (City Planning Officer): Inevitably there is a loss of communal feeling . . .

Q. Isn't it important to retain, as far as possible, the character of the district?

A. Yes.

Q. And that one of the best ways is to retain the existing shopkeepers who have connections for years with residents?

A. It is, in theory, but to replace the same number of shops with the same number of shops doesn't work."[55]

Not only were the number of shops to be drastically diminished but there was to be a change in their ownership. In area A the first part of the Shankill to be redeveloped for example only 5 out of the previous 108 traders tendered for the 25 new shops and only 2 obtained them. The basic reason for this pattern is the increase in the rent charged for a corner shop in the new estate compared to what shopkeepers paid in the old redevelopment areas. In 1973 shop rents in the Hammer community averaged about £327 per year. The rent of a new corner shop was estimated to be £750 p.a.[56] The new community shops therefore are branches of chain stores, such as the Spar shop in area C. Such shops become commercial concerns opening from 9.00 a.m. to 5.00 p.m. and this means a loss of their social role as an evening meeting place for the neighbourhood.

The reduction in the number of shops was necessary if the success of the district shopping centre was to be guaranteed and there had to be such a guarantee because otherwise no property developer would ever think it worth his while to develop them. The driving out of the small shopkeeper while it reflected economic trends towards larger units in the retail trade, also reflected the dominant interests within the Unionist party at Belfast Council and Stormont level. For example if subsidies for small shopkeepers; as Building Design Partnership had recommended as a possible policy to be followed by the Council; had been accepted then this would have enabled the small shopkeepers to compete with larger firms at both community and district shopping levels.

In addition to the shops there was to be a reduction in the number of small businesses in the area. The economic costs of this will be considered in the next chapter but as Building Design Partnership themselves pointed out there were many social advantages in these local employment sources, such as their contribution to "the strength and length of Shankill roots."[57]

However in Area C:

"there are a number of small businesses, 34 in all, including coal merchants, scrap dealers, wholesalers and manufacturers in the area. It is proposed that 8 of these should be replaced in courts of 4 each, specially constructed for them".

The reasons for this reduction are tied up with an economic strategy based on the needs of large industrial corporations. This saw only a limited long term role for small businesses in the face of competition from larger bodies and that the labour tied up in these small concerns could be more profitably utilised as a work force for the new industries.

However these same economic forces were also at work in other areas. In areas 12/13 there were 17 public houses before redevelopment. On the advice of the Licensed Vintner's Association the Housing Executive was only planning to provide 5 new ones. Therefore while the drop in population was to be only one third,[59] the number of pubs were to be reduced by two thirds. This decision is particularly surprising given that the percentage of household expenditure spent on alcohol continues to rise, from 3.1 per cent in 1968 to 3.7 per cent in 1972[60]. The explanation lies partly in the fact that the Vintner's Association represents the interests of the larger breweries who will obviously do better if the competition is reduced and partly in the fact that new buildings mean increased rents and rates which existing pub keepers can't afford. Again the number of pubs is being decided by economic interests with little regard to the role that pubs played as centres for community and neighbourhood life.

The same pattern of a reduction in the number of social facilities is repeated the whole way through the redevelopment plans. It is therefore more economic to have one multi-purpose community centre which can be shared by different community associations rather than building a number of smaller centres which would belong to these associations or neighbourhood groups. Similarly with the leisure and youth facilities. These are all now grouped into centres ignoring the demand of teenage gangs for a piece of turf they can claim their own. Again with the provision of health facilities, G.P's instead of being scattered throughout the area were being given a health centre. This was fine from the point of view of their efficiency, but it necessitated a much longer walk for most people in the community if they wanted to see the doctor. This was particularly trying for the more elderly people.

Therefore the quantitative reduction in facilities at a community level played an important part in limiting the social cohesiveness that the new estates could attain at a local level below the community.

The Neighbourhood

Even though the main focus, as far as the planners were concerned in the new estates, was the community, there was some attempt to create smaller neighbourhood areas. Plans for example talked of "major pedestrian routes sub-dividing each of these two main sectors into smaller community groupings of three to four hundred dwellings each."[61]

It is worth looking at the first detailed plans produced for one of these groupings in areas 12/13[62]:

A = Rows of 3 bed 5 person houses. Total number 48.
B = Rows of 4 bed 6 person houses. Total number 21.
C = Blocks of 3 storey flats/1 bed ground floor/2 bed 1st and 2nd floors. Total number 40.
D = Corner shop.

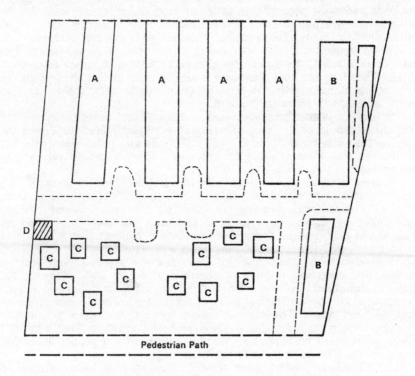

Pedestrian Path

One of the crucial things which helped create the sense of neighbourhood in the old Shankill was that family units of different size: childless couples, old age pensioners, young families etc. lived side by side. This enabled a series of functional relationships to be built up where, for example, old people could look after the children. As can be seen, in the above plan there is no possibility of this happening. Families with young children living in the houses are separated by a road from smaller family groups living in the flats. It is in fact a three fold separation, by; family type; physically by the road; and thirdly by type of dwelling, houses as against flats.

Therefore functional relationships can't be used to create a sense of neighbourhood. The extended family has been broken up and can't be used and even where people within the same family want to be housed next to each other, because they will consist of households of different family sizes it will not be possible to do this. A few friendships might have survived the move but Lawrence's study[63] suggested that this only

89

happened in a minority of cases. There is one corner shop situated on the edge of the area. But as we have seen this is unlikely to open in the evenings and most probably, in order to keep down labour costs will be self service. Because of the centralisation of social facilities there is no other meeting place—no community hall, no laundrette and no pub. Given the general difficulty that flat dwellers have to communicate with each other it would be unrealistic to expect there to be much interaction there. Therefore the only basis on which people in this area might be expected to come together is through the common interest that families in the houses will share in children.

The point is that neighbourhood as a social unit never really entered into the planning of the area. There was a physical need to divide the area up into smaller units on the basis of roads and pedestrian paths but no thought was given at all as to how a feeling of neighbourhood was to be created.

During a series of meetings with the architect for the area, it was argued that a start would be made in making a neighbourhood if areas were so planned that dwellings of different sizes were placed next to each other e.g. a two storey house next to two one bed flats and so on. This would enable those friendship and family patterns that still existed to be transferred intact to the new areas and would provide a basis on which new patterns could develop. This idea was rejected both because of increased costs and because of shortage of design staff. However the architect did admit that over time as family members grew up and moved the result would be that family units of different sizes would end up living next to each other. The obvious retort to this, was that if this was expected to happen and if this was seen to be a good thing, then why wait fifteen years for it to happen by wastage, when with a proper allocation policy it could be built in from the beginning.

As numerous studies have shown[64] designing an estate around a neighbourhood base does not necessarily mean that people will establish relationships with those living near them. This will be dependent on them having common interests. Many planners now argue that in days of increased affluence and car ownership such interests will no longer be tied to a specific local geographical base and that a neighbourhood dimension is therefore irrelevant: the squash player will travel to the district leisure centre and the bingo player to the local cinema. This thinking is all very well for those who are mobile but in days of increased public transport costs and poorer services it discriminates against the old; the handicapped and women with children who do not have a car at their disposal. For these people a neighbourhood base can increase the ease with which they can come together.

Also it is important to think not only in terms of the quantity of relationships that people might have but also their quality. There is a difference between a sports companion and someone with whom one can confide. It is at this latter level that the disappearance of the extended family and the neighbourhood as living units can be such a loss.

Again the above studies have shown that often it takes a number of years before social networks emerge on new estates. However this is no

90

justification for not making it as easy as possible from the beginning for such friendships to be established. High rise flat blocks for example make it extremely difficult for people to get to know each other. Also as the pressure for profits will continue to concentrate industrial production in those factories and areas where profits are highest, the need for workers to move from job to job is likely to increase. This will make it more difficult for friendships based on a time dimension to develop.

Vandalism

The main issue in the Shankill around which the argument about the need for neighbourhoods centred was vandalism. Before redevelopment started, vandalism as such was never a major problem. There were a number of reasons for this. Firstly there was little open space which didn't belong to anyone. The main play area was the street and the street was seen to be an extension of the house which belonged to everyone in the neighbourhood. Therefore all had a right to control what went on in it. In addition everybody in the neighbourhood, and for that matter in the community knew each other, so that it was impossible for anyone to commit delinquent actions behind the cloak of anonymity.

With redevelopment all of this changed. It started when the onset of blight forced people to leave and with this the social control in the area gradually disappeared. It didn't re-appear on the new estates for a number of reasons. Firstly there was much more open space. A lot of this was however at the end of a row of houses, or next to roads, or surrounded by factories. In Newman's terms it was space that could not be defended because it did not belong to anyone. Therefore open space which is surrounded by houses and flats and on which the children of householders play will be seen to belong to the householders and they will patrol and protect it. Open space which is situated away from houses or even close to high rise flats, where there is no possibility of direct physical supervision of what goes on, is no-one's responsibility. Even though planners will say that it belongs to the community or the neighbourhood it cannot belong to something which only exists in a physical and not a social sense.

It was not only space outside dwellings which was seen as belonging to no-one. The same problem applied to the staircases and deck access corridors in the six storey blocks of flats. These were not only full of rubbish and dog shit but became free play areas for young people. They began, for example, throwing objects over the edge including a jack handle which fell on a woman's head and she had to be rushed to hospital.

Another change in the open space from before was that the street no longer belonged to the neighbourhood. Not only was there no sense of neighbourhood but with front gardens and housing alcoves, few houses fronted directly onto the streets and the street was therefore no longer an extension of the house.

A second factor which contributed to vandalism was the lack of facilities for young people in the area. It was of course common wisdom that these should be provided. As far back as 1944 a report recommended:

91

"everything should be done to make new housing estates real communities . . . the Committee recommend therefore that, in laying out estates in future, it should be accepted as normal policy that sites should be earmarked for churches, community centres, schools, post offices, shops, inns, open spaces, amusements and other similar facilities where these do not already exist near at hand."[65]

Of course as estates like Ballymurphy, Rathcoole, Springmartin and others testify, such good intentions, because they cost money and used up valuable housing space, were rarely acted on. Yet even as late as 1973 it was stated that:

"the Housing Executive will never build large areas of public housing but instead this will be in small units, so people can feel they belong to a community. Future planning will allow for adequate amenities as not only did Mr. Simpson feel they should be there but they should be there at the beginning."[66]

Yet a year after residents began moving onto the Lower Shankill estate and a year after the Housing Executive took over responsibility, a report found that:

"Play areas

a) . . . the area is at present being surfaced and its completion is 'imminent'. It will be an unsupervised area and is the only play area of any significance which will exist in the area in the immediate future.

b) . . . this area is in a very early stage of planning . . . it is unlikely to be provided for some time but it is the only potentially worthwhile play space in the whole area.

c) . . . these are various pocket sized toddler and play areas . . . there appears little likelihood of these areas being completed for some time and they are unlikely to be of much use anyway . . .

Community Centre

. . . A centre should eventually be built just above the Old People's Centre. This vitally important facility appears likely to be built fairly soon."[67]

A third reason for the outbreak of vandalism is to do with increased anonymity. This was a function both of the break-up of the old networks and of the fact that the estate was now based on the community and that as this covers a vastly increased area it became difficult for people to be able to place and identify all young people. Therefore because of their mobility young people by going to parts of the estate away from where they live had a fair chance of remaining unknown.

A fourth reason had nothing to do with housing at all and was due simply to the breakdown of conventional law and order processes because of the 'troubles' and the condoning of much behaviour, which normally would have been frowned on, because it was seen to be part of the defence of the area.

Therefore what was happening in the new estate was that there was a breakdown in the ties which kept a community together while the design of the new estate hindered the development of alternative social control mechanisms. The solutions were therefore quite clear. They involved doing something about the physical design. Therefore tenants in the flats wanted entrance doors installed, the deck access corridors blocked off by gates and the lifts manned by local residents. In addition they wanted an adventure playground and asked for other open space areas to be better sited so they could be more easily supervised. Another suggested solution was to create real neighbourhoods of about 500 people encompassing a block of flats or a small group of houses, by having in each neighbourhood one flexibly designed house or flat which could be used as a meeting place/pre-school centre etc. In addition to social problems, the other things that people in a neighbourhood have in common are basic needs such as washing clothes, shopping etc. It therefore made sense for there to be communal laundries and corner shops situated in the centre of each area. The second way of attempting to make a neighbourhood work that was suggested was to give it responsibility for the physical and social management of the area. If the 'caring community' had been destroyed by redevelopment such that it could not be recreated in its original form then the alternative was to have a committee of those who 'felt most responsible' elected by members of the neighbourhood taking over this role. The tenant's association is therefore the successor to the old neighbourhood and its power is dependent on its ability to solve problems.

The formation of tenant's associations on new estates is made more difficult by the increasing individualization of families. If there are no immediate links to bring people together to cope wth problems then each family has little recourse but to turn to social welfare workers for assistance. Thus the caring community and the home help is replaced by the professional warden of the sheltered dwellings as the custodian of the aged.

The third suggested solution was an increase in police patrols. This is related to the above point. If the local community can no longer control what is happening then it needs to call in outside forces to enforce control. The difficulty is that what constitutes 'law and order' and more particularly appropriate punishment in the eyes of the police, is not necessarily identical with how any one particular community interprets these things. This therefore led to local pressure for a community police force, composed of local people—a sort of official vigilante group. It eventually foundered as did all other local attempts to set up such bodies on the fact that any community consists of a number of groups with different attitudes and aims. Unless one group has continual control and widespread acceptance or unless all the major groups as well as the majority of the rest of the community can agree over the limits of the policing then such a force can never have sufficient support to operate successfully. Even though on the Shankill and elsewhere one group would for a period of time have considerable support, such support would often be given because of that group's ability to be able to protect the community from attack and support given for this is not the same thing as support for that group becoming the established local police force. Similarly agreement between the different groups usually only occurred when the community was under attack.

Therefore because of vandalism and the need to be seen to be doing something about it, neighbourhood became a valid concept. While through social planning it was possible to suggest ways that some sense of belonging to a neighbourhood could be built up it was quite clear that there was no possibility of recreating an exact replica of the neighbourhood that used to exist.

THE REDEVELOPMENT PROCESS

The destruction of the old communities was hastened by the whole way the redevelopment process was handled. Redevelopment in Belfast started with the 1956 Housing Act which required all local authorities in Northern Ireland to submit reports on how they were going to tackle unfit houses in their area. On October 24th 1958 the Medical Officer of Health, in a report to Belfast Council, estimated that of 114,955 dwellings in the city, 18,440 were unfit, and of these, 14,240 were suitable for redevelopment. It was not until 1960 however, 2 years late, that the Corporation produced proposals for dealing with these unfit houses. They grouped them into 30 areas which would take in total 20 years to clear. It was then of course that blight started as landlords realised that it was no longer worth their while spending money on houses which were eventually to be pulled down.

A start had already been made on the first redevelopment scheme, Area A at the foot of the Shankill. The public inquiry to vest this land was held in February 1960, some 2¼ years after the Housing Committee had instructed its officers "to submit preliminary proposals for the clearing and redevelopment of the area."[68] However further delays ensued:

"During discussion the Town Clerk reminded the Committee that until appropriate legislation was passed enabling the Committee to deal with licensed premises in the area the scheme could not be proceeded with as the effect of a Vesting Order made before the legislation was passed would be to close all the licensed premises in the area."[69]

The actual vesting order was not granted until December 1962.

Area C in the Shankill was declared a proposed redevelopment area on the 4th January 1967 and formerly designated as such in February but the vesting order inquiry was not held until June 1968 and the vesting order did not become operative until 21st October 1968.

In the meantime Building Design Partnership had taken a look at the whole question of redevelopment and had found that over "90 per cent of houses in redevelopment areas have no fixed bath, inside toilet or hot water system."[70] In 1966 the City Surveyor had prepared a detailed redevelopment programme which listed 42 areas, covering 750.3 acres and 93,060 people living in 26,888 houses. Building Design Partnership using this programme as a base went on to establish housing and population density standards for these areas after redevelopment.

Back on the Shankill, Belfast Corporation announced its intention of declaring the south side of the Shankill road (areas 12/13) as a redevelopment area in June 1971. The vesting order inquiry was held in May 1972 and became operative in June 1973. The public inquiry for the final

94

Shankill redevelopment areas, 11/33 was held in March 1973 and became operative in January 1974.

Therefore it took 14 years from the time the areas were first designated as potential redevelopment areas until they were all formerly vested. During this time the people had to sit and watch the gradual decline and destruction of the area:

"This area was always a pleasant neighbourhood to live in. There was no such thing as strangers. Everyone knew everyone else. Then a hint of redevelopment and people began to move out and new people moved in. More hint of redevelopment and people began to get uneasy wondering when this was going to take place. The opposite side of the Shankill Road and Peters Hill were vested and houses pulled down. Against the wishes of the people high flats were built. Then disaster struck—riots began and deterioration set in. More people left the district, there was more talk of redevelopment and then houses became empty. Vandalism became rampant and generally the area has become what I would call a slum. Landlords will not do repairs, however urgent. When a house goes empty there is a long period before it is blocked up and the house becomes a wreck. People living beside such houses have discovered that rats, mice, fleas, cockroaches and snails are very prevalent in their own homes and are impossible to get rid of. For the last three years vesting has been just around the corner. Now approximately half of each street is empty and more are going each week. Soon there will be no one."[71]

As we saw earlier in the chapter one of the factors at work in persuading people to leave was the need for skilled workers to move to growth centres outside Belfast.

A more general reason why people of all ages moved was to be near friends. Though in the redevelopment areas "the longer they had been there, and the closer their social ties, the more they were inclined"[72] to remain, once their friends had moved, a conflict developed between their ties to the area and their desire to preserve their social links with friends. For example the phase one survey in areas 12/13 found that of 22 families who wanted to move, 13 gave the reason that they wanted to be near friends and relatives. This was not a conflict that people wanted. As Building Design Partnership again quite accurately point out:

"separation of family groups is dreaded. Because of the close family groups which are characteristic of the area the imminent dispersal causes anxieties especially to those who have looked forward to the support of nearby children in their declining years."[73]

But despite Building Design Partnership's regret, the plans were that people must move and the old communities be destroyed. For those who remained the crucial battle was to obtain a new house (a detailed description of one person's battle to do this is given in the appendix to this chapter).

This was made difficult because of the shortage of new housing, especially in areas where people wanted to go. On the Shankill while over a six month period in 1973, 5,500 occupied houses were vested, only 486 new houses were completed[74] in the year 1972/3 on the popular

95

Lower Shankill and Glencairn estates. The shortage of housing was made worse by outbreaks of squatting and the allocation itself was complicated by cases of maladministration and by the reluctance of people to accept flats.

The effect of this was to create intense competition between local residents for any houses that were finished. This not only led to the spread of rumours and much ill feeling but effectively destroyed the last remnants of group solidarity that would have been necessary if a redevelopment group were to continue to function effectively. It also gave the Housing Executive the opportunity to remove troublesome people such as leaders of redevelopment groups, from the area by offering them houses elsewhere.

Allocation also effectively put the finishing touches to any hope of transferring community links from the old Shankill to new housing estates. This was because housing officials only took individual needs into account when offering accommodation. There was no attempt to find out whom people would like to be rehoused next to. This was partly because of overwork and more importantly because social considerations were not seen to be of much importance.

While all of this was happening the Shankill was continuing to decay. By 1973 most of the lower end of the Shankill road had already been destroyed, the shops were gone, and replaced on the north side by 4 storey blocks of maisonettes. There were empty houses everywhere and as one local resident commented:

"in my opinion the Shankill is slowly disappearing. The once so close community is now split up. As for the lower end of the Shankill the houses remind me of a camp. They have not got the feeling of a real home."

Another screw in the death of the old community was the large scale way in which redevelopment was handled. In theory it could be argued that if the size of the phase to be cleared was equivalent to a neighbourhood and as each neighbourhood was cleared, a group of new houses were waiting for the people to move into, then neighbourhoods would not have had to be broken up. The Housing Executive paid lip service to this and in its discussion of how it was to handle areas 12/13 it said that:

"the scheme can be completed in 8 phases, containing approximately 150-250 dwellings each at yearly intervals commencing with the highest density area so that leap frog relocation of families can be employed as soon as sufficient accommodation is available to make this possible."[75]

Nice sounding but totally unrealistic. Even the figures don't make sense. There were 2,845 dwellings in the area so dividing them into 8 phases would produce an average of 350 dwellings per phase which would mean an area much bigger than a neighbourhood. It was unrealistic because the result of 14 years of blight was that as soon as vesting came and people were entitled to compensation, they wanted out. People didn't want to spend another 3-8 years sitting in their slum conditions waiting to be rehoused as a neighbourhood. As people had moved out long before vesting occurred the idea was dead before it was put into print.

96

CONCLUSION

But as we have seen the death of the community had little to do with practical issues of housing policy. These simply provided the finishing touches. It had to do with a society changing into a modern industrial state where the needs of workers are subordinate to the needs of large corporations. With the influx of the large firm and the multiple shopping store, with the need for a mobile labour force the old community was gone and buried. Planners understood what was happening in places like the Shankill but were powerless to do anything about it.

The last word should probably be left to the local residents:

"It was a great road to live on. In fact it was one of the best roads for shopping and kindness and people were so friendly and happy. What a pity to watch it just dying away fast. It would break your heart because we loved this road. To me the old Shankill was heaven."

and

"I can see all the changes taking place but I just can't believe it. To me the Shankill will still be the Shankill. The only difference is all our old shops and friendly people have moved away; just thrown about from pillar to post. The changes are drastic. I think they stink."

and finally

"You people who never lived on it, have no feelings about how we feel, so go to hell and build your sloppy homes."

The story of one woman's attempt to get a new house

"I live in a 2 bedroom house off the Shankill Road and there are 7 of us altogether, 4 children working and one boy aged 7 still at school. When all this first started about new houses being built I applied for one. I had an Inspector visit me and he said I would get a 3 bedroom house right away as I was overcrowded and had a mixed family of 2 daughters and 3 sons. That was 7 years ago and I am still waiting. The Housing Executive took over at Westmoreland Street (1972) and I kept going every chance I got and in July 1973 they offered me a 4 bedroom house in the lower Shankill. I refused it because it was too small. That is hard to believe but it was built like a match box and back to front and I honestly wouldn't take a gift of it rent free.

Since then I have been running to Townsend Street, for that's where the housing office is now. I still go there 3 days per week out of 4 and still they say 'nothing for you yet'. I got a telephone number from a good friend of mine which I phoned and kept phoning until they sent out a pest inspector and he said the house was in an awful state. He put powder all round the house. I then phoned again and again until I got the sanitary man out and he said the same. In the meantime I was still going to the Housing Executive and they had the cheek to tell me that I shouldn't let inspectors into my house without showing their credentials first. I told them that I would let them come and look at the house if I thought it would do any good.

I have a letter from my doctor stating that my nerves are bad and the rats don't help. I also have a letter, stating that my boy of 7 was in

97

Purdysburn Hospital for 5 weeks with jaundice and this was due to the rats. The lady in the Housing Executive had the cheek to ask me whether I caught any rats and laughed at the idea of it. I got furious with her and told her I wasn't paid to catch rats and that was why we paid rent to get repairs done or to get a house qucikly.

Now we are in 1974 and I wonder how long it will take them to get on with their work and give me a house, as all the area is nearly blocked up except for a few people who didn't want to move. I will keep on at the Housing Executive, though they tell me they don't hand the houses out but I wish they would tell me who does. They also tell me they can't help it if people with one or 2 children just walk into a 3 bedroom house and get away with it. I only wish I had their job anyway. Two and a half hours every day for 4 days a week. I think I would be a bit more civil to people. After all it's people like me who keep them there doing nothing.

My husband went down and they were cheeky with him. He was furious and said it was a bloody disgrace and walked out. I have come to the conclusion its not what you know but who you know that counts. I can't understand it. Everybody has condemned the house. The repair men said if they were to touch my landing the house would cave in. So what am I to do?

Chapter 5

THE PLUNDER OF THE SHANKILL

This chapter is concerned with examining who lost and who gained financially from redevelopment. As chapter two indicated, redevelopment occurred when there was no longer any economic gain to be made from the houses in the redevelopment areas in their present use as slum dwellings. According to evidence given by the Medical Officer of Health at the public inquiry in March 1973 into the vesting of areas 11/33, 95 per cent of the houses were unfit. In describing the area he said:

"the dwelling houses in this area were built between 1852 and 1887. There was a state of general decay, disrepair, general dampness and instability. Many houses had no secondary means of access necessitating the delivery of fuel and the removal of house refuse through the dwelling. Amenities for personal hygiene were almost non-existent and very few houses have internal w.c.'s. There was inadequate provision for the preparation and cooking of foods and in many cases, improvised sculleries had enclosed the drains and obstructed lighting and ventitation . . .
Detailed inspection of individual houses showed the following defects . . . walls etc.—brickwork scaling or disintegrating, or pointing defective so as to permit the penetration of dampness . . . floors—boards broken or worn so thin as to be unsafe or affected by dry rot or wet rot, or so infested with insects e.g. woodworm, as to constitute a danger to the occupants of the house. Tiles or solid floors so broken, cracked or sunken that a risk of personal injury is present and proper cleaning of the floor rendered very difficult . . .
A large number of the houses lack proper scullery accommodation, some being as small as 20 sq. feet, a few have only a water tap in the yard, others have old, worn and unhygenic sinks with the waste-pipe discharging directly to the drain without a trap: this is also unsatisfactory. Smells and tiny insects can be blown up from the drain into the sink and room."

The final owners of the majority of these houses were the small shopkeepers and others who had bought them as an investment, some seventy or more years ago. Before them the houses were owned by the small builders, the estate agents, the mill-owners etc. who had originally built them. Before them the land had been owned by farmers and before them by the Donegal family. By the 1950's there was no longer any money to be made by renting out cheap houses such as these. Profits in property were made elsewhere and the days of the small scale landlord were over.

This did not mean that the people who actually lived in the houses wanted to move. Many were prepared to put up with the poor living conditions because of the sense of community that the area had. But move, as we have seen, they had to. In a purely physical sense, the majority benefited. This was hardly surprising given what they left. Lawrence found that on the new Shankill Estate, 5/6th of the people she interviewed liked their new homes. Typical comments were: "it's a good bit different from what we're used to" and "the working kitchen is so nice that it's really a pleasure cooking."

People on some other estates were not so lucky. On the Springmartin estate for example, which had only been started in 1968 a survey carried out in 1973

"showed that 90 per cent of 137 people complained that repairs were needed to their houses or flats . . . the complaints about the flats are serious ones requiring drastic action i.e. dampness, structural faults in walls and ceilings, drains etc. The residents of the flats are those complaining most highly of health hazards, especially smells from drains and problems of waste . . ."[1]

Further out of Belfast, in one of the new towns, Craigavon, the same problems were also present:

"People are moving out of Craigavon faster than they're moving in . . . Alliance Councillor Sean Hagan blamed some of Craigavon's problems on badly designed houses . . . 'nearly all the unoccupied houses are in the new city. One estate in particular, at Rathmore is practically uninhabitable because the houses are so badly designed' he said."[2]

However, for most people the forced move meant improved housing conditions in terms of the size of the house, the provision of internal facilities such as a w.c. and increased ease in keeping the house clean. In many cases it also meant an improvement in environmental health conditions. The inner city redevelopment areas, had according to a study[3], the highest incidence rates of bronchitis, a disease according to the report which "is closely related to the environmental quality of the area." In comparison, the report concludes "the areas of lowest incidence are in the suburbs" where the new housing estates are.

THE COSTS OF REDEVELOPMENT

These benefits however, came at considerable financial cost. The Shankill was a mainly poor working class area. Of the heads of household 36 per cent were classified as semi-skilled and unskilled manual workers compared to 16 per cent in the predominately lower middle class Ormeau Road are of the city and nil per cent in the upper class Malone Road area. In 1971 the male unemployment rate in the lower Shankill was 9 per cent, the average rate for Northern Ireland, compared to 20 per cent in the Lower Falls, a Catholic working class area.[5]

According to Building Design Partnership[6] in 1966, 67 per cent of heads of household in Shankill Redevelopment Area 12, had a net income of less than £13 per week, at a time when average weekly earnings for manual workers was £17.06 per week.[7] Most families were therefore not prepared for any increased costs that redevelopment might bring.

Compensation

In theory few families should have suffered, because under different housing acts, most tenants and owner-occupiers were entitled to receive compensation to cover the financial costs that ensued from moving house.

Until October 1973, when new legislation came into force, the main compensation that people in redevelopment areas received was an £85 resettlement grant which was given towards:

"(i) expenditure which is or may be incurred by that person in removing to or furnishing other accommodation;

(ii) the cost of purchase or the payment of rent of that other accommodation;

(iii) any other expenditure which, in the opinion of the local authority, has been or may be incurred by that person as a result of a dispossession."[8]

Instead of people being given the £85 in cash to spend as they thought most appropriate, they received a voucher which could then be exchanged in furniture shops for goods. This opened the way for some shopkeepers to indulge in a number of sharp practices, ranging from increasing the price of goods to offering £60 in cash for the voucher.

The biggest obstacle in getting the £85 was that a person had to be resident in an area at the time the vesting order became operative in order to be able to qualify for the resettlement grant. However, as has already been shown, because of the blight, many people were forced to leave prior to vesting. In areas 11/33, between 1966 and the public inquiry in February 1973, almost half the people left the area. The two years prior to vesting, when the cumulative effects of 12 years of blight were really beginning to show, saw the sharpest outflow. In 1970/71 the Medical Officer of Health found[9] that there were 1,488 occupied dwelling units, containing 4,240 people, in the area. A survey carried out by the Housing Management division of the Housing Executive[10] in February 1973 found that there were 1,181 occupied dwellings, containing 2,829 people, in the area i.e. a loss in 2 years of 307 families. Given that the vesting orders didn't become operative for a further 10 months, another 150 families could have been expected to have left in that time making a total of 450 families who, under the terms of the existing legislation, would, because of the effects of blight, have been forced to surrender their claim to compensation. But this is an underestimate as some of the families who left between 1966 and 1971 would also have been forced out by blight, i.e. would not have left the area, if it were not for the deterioration caused by the impending redevelopment. Let us presume that half of these families could be put in this category. This would then give a grand total of 550 families, or approximately one third of the original population of the area who would have been deprived of their £85 grant: i.e. a collective total of £46,750. Now if the same one third proportion held for the Shankill redevelopment areas (excluding A) then the sum involved would amount to about £150,000.

The compensation situation changed and became much more complex with the implementation of the Land Acquisition and Compensation Act (N.I.) in November 1973. This did away with the resettlement grant and replaced it with two new grants. There was firstly to be a home loss payment, to compensate a family for the loss of their home provided they had lived in it for the previous five years, amounting to twenty times

101

the rateable value of the house with a minimum payment of £150 and a maximum of £1,500. The second grant was called a disturbance payment and was given to cover reasonable removal expenses.

Though this act came into operation nearly a year after the almost identical English act, the Ministry of Development and the Housing Executive were totally unprepared for its introduction. There were no leaflets explaining how it was to be interpreted circulating within government departments, let alone being released for the general public.

The part of the Act which created a lot of difficulty regarding Home Loss Payments was Paragraph 30(3) which ran as follows:

"For the purposes of this Article a person shall be deemed to have been displaced from a dwelling in consequence of the compulsory acquisition of an interest therein or the making of a housing order in relation thereto if, after the notice of application for, or the notice of intention to make, a vesting order in respect of that interest has been published or after the making of the housing order as the case may be but before such an order becomes operative, he gives up occupation of the dwelling by arrangement with the Housing Executive or with the authority proposing to acquire the dwelling compulsorily."

Little wonder that there was some problem over interpretation. However, after numerous conversations with the responsible Ministry officials, it appeared that what the paragraph meant was that anybody who left a redevelopment area by arrangement with Housing Executive from the time when the notice of the intention to make a vesting order was published was entitled to a home loss payment. The point about this is that the notice of intention normally comes at least a year before vesting orders finally become operative. Therefore anyone who moved within that year would be entitled to claim. Difficulties however, arose because when the Act first came into force the Housing Executive claimed, that as with resettlement grants, people were only entitled to home loss payments, if they were still resident at the time vesting orders became operative. The local housing office for a period of time refused to hand out claim forms to other people and as late as January 1974, the Housing Executive's Belfast Regional Information Officer was still arguing:

"that Home Loss Payment will only be made to someone who has moved after a vesting order has become operative and that a person who moves before this will not be entitled to the payment."[11]

only to correct himself a week later:

"if the other conditions are satisfied, a Home Loss Payment will be made to anyone who has left a proposed redevelopment area by arrangement with the Housing Executive on or after the date on which a Notice of Application for the Vesting Order for that area has been published."[12]

As late as June though, there was still no agreement as to what by "arrangement with the Housing Executive" actually meant. This bureaucratic inefficiency was a further way then that local people were denied compensation that was their due.

A further factor which resulted in many people losing out on compensation was that the new act was backdated to October 1972. This meant that anyone in areas 11/33/12/13 who had been in their house for five years and had then moved after October was entitled to a Home Loss Payment even if they already had received a resettlement grant. In the case of areas 11/33 this would have involved some 200 families who would each have received at least £150. The problem was that the Housing Executive had no record of those people who moved before vesting and had no way of contacting them except by newspaper and T.V. advertisements. However, if the take-up of rent rebates and well maintained payments is anything to go by these will have been largely ineffective.

Similar problems occurred with the disturbance payments. According to guidance notes put out by the Housing Executive:

"The Disturbance Payment is based on the reasonable expenses incurred by the claimant in removing from his former address . . . The Claim Form should be signed in the presence of a Justice of the Peace or a clergyman or school teacher or a member of the Royal Ulster Constabulary of a rank not lower than Sergeant and witnessed accordingly.

Claim forms when received, properly completed will be forwarded to the Commissioner of Valuation of the Valuation Section of the Ministry of Finance who will negotiate the amount payable. If you employ a professional advisor his fees may also be paid. Payment will be made by the Northern Ireland Housing Executive after agreement has been reached as to the amount payable."

Difficulties arose on a number of points. What for example were 'reasonable expenses'? Community Action[13] when translating this phrase in terms of the identical English legislation said that in addition to removal expenses:

"It is also reasonable to claim for the costs of remaking or refitting curtains and carpets for the extra areas as long as they are of the same quality as you would normally buy . . . if you buy new carpets or curtains and free fitting is offered in the price then ask for separate bills for the item and the fitting costs.

If your existing items will not fit your new dwelling i.e. they are either too big or too small, then you can claim the loss on full sale of these items. This is the difference between what you get for a quick sale and the current second hand value . . . This can only be claimed if you do not sell the items before you move."

But subtle interpretations such as this did little to help people know what they could claim for. Another difficulty arose because of the need to be able to show receipts for all expenses claimed when many activities were simply done by friends. The result was that there were enormous variations in the sums being claimed for similar removal problems. They ranged from £2 by old age pensioners to some of over £300 by wide-eyed boys working the Act to its limits. This was leading to delays in paying out the claims as each claim had to be checked individually. Furthermore the valuation office faced by a shortage of staff and inundated with claims arising from the "troubles" was already over stretched. The valuation office therefore came up with the idea of making standard payments related to the rateable value of the house. A valuation of under £12 for example, entitled the claimant to a disturbance payment of £85. This decision which was at first given verbally, took a long term to become accepted policy with the result that 3 weeks after the scheme was in operation, local housing officials were still refusing to accept disturbance claim forms unless they fulfilled all the old, and now redundant, conditions. A further difficulty with the disturbance payments was that they were only paid out some 2-6 weeks after a person had moved. This put tremendous difficulties in the way of lower income households who had no savings by which they could finance their move. Even though over the phone the valuation officer agreed that he could see no reason why, if given sufficient notification disturbance payments in these cases couldn't be paid out the day people moved, this proved impossible to arrange.

Because of these bureaucratic delays and other problems in the paying out of home loss and disturbance payments, more local people lost money to which they were entitled. It is impossible to put a precise figure on this, but conservatively one could add a further £50,000 to the earlier figure making a total of £200,000. This might not seem much, but it is equivalent to £35 for each house in the Shankill redevelopment area (excluding Area A). Given that there are 26,888 houses in all the Belfast redevelopment areas and assuming that the same conditions apply as to handling compensation claims as in the Shankill then the collective loss suffered by working class people in these areas would be in the region of £1 million.

Compensation problems, however, didn't end here. A further payment that some people in redevelopment areas were entitled to was what was called 'a well-maintained' payment. These payments are for tenants and owners of tenanted property which is classified as "unfit and incapable of being made fit at reasonable cost" to cover any maintenance work that has been done to the property in the 5 years before vesting. This seems all fairly clear.

However the actual form that was sent out to people read:

"Notification to a person to whom Section 2 of the Act of 1961 may apply

If you consider that any house included in the above scheme has been well-maintained, either internally or externally and that such good maintenance is attributable to a material extent to work carried out by you or at your expense, you should make a representation to the Secretary, Ministry of Development, before the 23rd February 1974. Representation may be made in respect of internal good maintenance or external good maintenance or both."

In addition scattered amongst the Housing Executive blurb sent out to tenants at the time of vesting was an additional relevant sentence:

"The Well Maintained Claim is intended for owners of **tenanted** unfit property and the **tenants** of unfit property who have maintained their property in good condition before the date of vesting."

As might be expected the result was nobody understood what it was all about. How did you know whether your house qualified? In theory such notification should have happened when the notice of the intention

104

to make a vesting order was first published. But even if people had received such notification then and even if they had understood what it meant, it would have long since disappeared because there was no real storage room in Shankill houses. But who knew what 'maintained' meant, let alone what a 'representation' was?

Having been round a few houses it became clear no-one was putting in a claim for a well-maintained payment. I telephoned the Housing Executive and asked them for a list of all the houses in areas 11/33 that qualified for well-maintained payments. They sent the list but couldn't understand why it was needed as everybody had been notified.

According to the list in areas 11/33, tenants of 349 houses (as well as the owners) were entitled to submit a claim. As this is one in 5 of all dwellings in the area, it gives some idea of how run down the area was. Of the 349 houses, 186 were already empty (53 per cent). Of the remainder, residents in seven didn't qualify as they turned out to be owner-occupiers, in a further three, tenants hadn't been there for five years and in another 15 cases tenants had done no maintenance for the past 5 years. In a further 74 dwellings there was no one at home, though in 21 cases it was possible to leave information on how to claim with neighbours. Of the 64 people interviewed, who were entitled to claim, 35 had read the notice but didn't think it applied to them, 14 hadn't read it, six had lost the form, five couldn't read, three had misplaced all their Housing Executive papers and one person couldn't understand what all this compensation was about.

The amount of money that people in areas 11/33 were entitled to claim for was at least £60. The actual maintenance work that had been done ranged from £5 to £300 at an average of about £20. Therefore given that there were 138 eligible families, the total amount involved was in the region of £2,750. Unless some families, in houses where no one was in, had submitted claims, not a penny of this would have been handed out, unless this survey had been carried out.

It is clear therefore by the way that notices were written and the administration of the claims handled that the intention was to make sure that housing bodies fulfilled the letter of the law. Whether people actually got what they were entitled to was beside the point. The authorities themselves undertook no research to see how many people received the compensation they were entitled to.

A further group of people who got 'done' at vesting were the owner occupiers. According to the law they were entitled to receive as compensation the market value of their house. However, market value was affected by the condition of the surrounding area and as blight spread, the market value fell until at the time of vesting many owner occupiers were being offered less for their houses than they had paid ten years ago. One such person was offered £625 in 1974 for a house that had cost her £750 in 1962. This problem was compounded by the fact that there was a variation by as much as 15 per cent between what valuers in different parts of the city were prepared to offer. Though in theory it was possible to appeal to the Land Tribunal if one was not satisfied, this was difficult to do because: it took up to six months to get a hearing; there was no legal aid; if one lost then all costs could be awarded against one and finally it was possible to lose by precedent i.e. if other owner-occupiers in similar houses had already accepted the amount being offered then this could be used to show that it was a reasonable offer. Therefore success at a tribunal would have depended on a degree of unanimity among occupiers that was difficult to achieve.

Owner occupiers also suffered at the hands of estate agents and lawyers. For example, many people who had bought their house in the early 1960's, when the Shankill area had already been classified as a future redevelopment area, were not told of this. Later at the time of compensation, few estate agents explained to their clients that the rule of the game was that it was possible to refuse the first two offers made by the valuer and that only the third offer was an unconditional one. Many people, not knowing this, accepted the first offer made to them.

The Lawyers who actually handled the negotiations between the Housing Executive and the owner occupiers at the time of vesting were not above a bit of sharp practice.

The Housing Executive paid all legal fees:

"The Executive will be responsible for proper legal costs and agent's fees according to the appropriate scale of the professional bodies concerned."[14]

but lawyers still tried on occasions to claim that they had a right to withold a fee for their services from the compensation paid. For example, one owner occupier received the following letter from her solicitor:

"As we pointed out in our recent communication to you there was approximately the sum of £50 held pending determination of responsibility for payment of Agents fees . . . as far as Agents Commission is concerned the Northern Ireland Housing Executive have never accepted to us responsibility for the payment of Agents Commission . . . you will receive from us in due course a fully itemised Bill of Costs and Statement, which statement could not be prepared until your responsibility for the payment of Agents Commission could be cleared up."

According to the local Citizen Advice Bureau this was by no means an isolated case. Nor were these problems restricted to Belfast. In St. Mary's, Oldham, a report[15] found that many residents:

"felt that the legal and administrative procedure under which their homes were compulsorily purchased and their compensation assessed was not only bewilderingly complicated but, in some cases, unfair."

The story of compensation then is of a people having to fight at all stages to receive money that they were entitled to by law. The crucial villian was the blight which forced people out and reduced property values. The blight also meant that even after vesting, when the Housing Executive became the overall landlord for the area, those people who didn't leave immediately were forced to remain living in deplorable conditions. These were so bad that most people said 'they ought to pay us to remain in these houses'.

The next chapter on the repair question catalogues the social costs that people had to bear under the reign of the Housing Executive.

Rent Increases

As we saw at the beginning of this chapter, when people finally did move, their new homes were usually a vast improvement on what they had left. But it came at a price and part of this price was the increase in rent:

Year	Average Weekly Shankill Rent	Average weekly household income in Northern Ireland	Shankill redevelopment or Shankill new estate area	Rent as % of income
1967	70p[17]	£23.98[16]	Redevelopment	3%
1972	82p[19]	£36.25[18]	”	2%
”	£4.00[20]	”	New Estate	11%

Therefore as the table shows, in the new estate, rent accounted for approximately 11 per cent of household income compared to 3 per cent previously. Lawrence reported[21] that on the new estate most people found it expensive compared to where they lived before. This replicated the results of a survey[22] done two years before on the same estate, just after people had first moved in, which found that "the disadvantages expressed were mainly to do with the cost of living in their new accommodation. Nearly everyone commented on the rent charge and to half of the families it was causing very considerable concern."

Rents have gone up for a number of reasons. Firstly there has been the increase in building costs. Between 1968 and 1974 the cost of wages went up by 100 per cent, the cost of materials by 121 per cent and overall building costs by 119%[23]. Coupled with increases in the price of land, the result is that a 3 bedroom house which cost £3,745 to build in 1971[24], cost £5,500 in 1973[25] and £7,500[26] in 1974. Increased costs and an expanding building programme means that the housing authorities have to borrow more money. In addition interest rates have gone up from 8½ per cent in 1971 to over 10 per cent in 1973 which means that on the 1971 house, loan charges amounted to £6 per week while on the 1973 house loan charges had risen to over £11 per week.

Both the Housing Trust and the Housing Executive have always paid out more in loan charges than they have received in rents. In the financial year to the 31st March 1973 the Housing Executive for example[27] paid out £21.1m in loan charges while its income from rents amount to only £14.7m. The difference was made up by subsidies received from the government. This subsidy amounted to £3.5 per week for a 3 bedroom house in

1971 and had risen to £6 per week in 1973. The increase in subsidy however never quite matches the increase in costs and interest rates which is why the rent for a 3 bedroom house rented from the Housing Trust in 1971 was £3 a week and from the Housing Executive in 1973 was £4 a week. This can be seen from the following table:

	1971[29]	1973[29]	% increase
Costs of a new 3 bedroomed house ...	3,745	5,500	47
Loan repayment per annum	320	572	79
Government subsidy per house per annum	184	310	68
Rents per annum	159	210[30]	32

In addition to rent increases tenants on the new Shankill estate had to pay a heating charge. This is because a district central heating scheme serviced all the dwellings on the estate. This not only meant that there were no coal fires, which had provided a central focus in the old sitting rooms, but people had to pay a heating charge which according to the Belfast Housing Manager[31] amounted in a 3 bedroom house to about £2 per week. This is 39 per cent more than households with incomes between £20 and £25 per week spent on coal and manufactured fuels per week in 1972[32].

Other Costs

These were not the only costs which went up. As we saw in previous chapters the number of corner shops was being reduced and the rents for those remaining had more than doubled. Therefore even before the shops in the new Shankill estate had been built a report prepared for the Belfast City Planning Department had hypothesized that:

"artificially low numbers of local corner shops based on extremely rigid standards may have the effect of either creating monopolisitic standards with consequent high prices . . ."[33]

When the shops actually became operational, Lawrence[34] found in her survey that the estate shops were "far too expensive for everyday shopping by many people. They are more often used when just a few items are wanted."

In parts of areas 12/13, in addition to corner shops it was planned to have two small parades of shops. Now though this might have been expected to have brought in an element of competition and therefore kept prices down, this is unlikely to happen. This is because where such parades have been built previously, as on the Highfield estate, instead of permitting competition

"we restricted the types of trade to one in each shop. In other words, one butcher, one grocer and so on, and that gave that particular trade pretty well a monopoly in the area. Of course, it had a resultant effect on rents offered. I think in doing that we were not in any way exploiting the tenants of the particular estate."[35]

108

There is therefore a consistent policy as regards shopping. With redevelopment the total number of shops is reduced, with the result that those left are in a monopoly position. The rents that can be charged are therefore beyond the range of most local shop keepers who go out of business to be replaced by branches of chain stores. Where a monopoly is not guaranteed initially, allocation policy by housing officials makes sure that planning policy creates one. The new district shopping centre is at the apex of the new shopping hierarchy where rents for a shop are likely to be in the region of £1,600[36] compared to an average of £327[37] at present. Even though the overall reduction in the number of shops in the Shankill virtually assures the commercial success of most of the shops which will eventually move into the centre, Greer warns that:

"development of the centre by private finance may mean over representation in the centre by national multiples and a resultant price war with existing traders, the elimination of the latter and the inevitable price rises by the former."[38]

It is no doubt correct to argue that with increased rents, the larger stores are likely to be cheaper because they can buy in bulk but this is not to say that they will necessarily be cheaper either than local shops were before redevelopment forced up the rents or would be if they continued to operate at low rentals.

The effect however of a shopping policy which consists of building a small number of district centres and a restricted number of outlying corner shops coupled with an increase in rents will be to increase the amount that a family has to spend on food each week, completely irrespective of other inflationary pressures which are forcing up the price of food.

As chapter 3 showed, people in redevelopment areas were also faced with increased transportation costs. This was because firstly of the cities' transportation policy which meant that bus fares were to go up. To quote Travers Morgan:

"we recognise that a policy which results in a bus service the costs of which are greater than is absolutely essential may cause some hardship to the poorest section of the community . . . fares are likely to double today's fares (relative to the cost of living)."[39]

A second reason for increased transportation costs was that as redevelopment meant that half the families had to move away from the inner city areas this entailed longer, and more expensive, journeys to and from work. Thirdly the centralization of shopping and community facilities meant in many cases a bus ride rather than a walk to get to them. Finally the cumulative effect of the above changes was to persuade some people, who would not otherwise have done so, to purchase cars. According to the Family Expenditure Survey of households with a weekly income of between £20 and £30, of those who owned a car, 17 per cent of their weekly expenditure went on transport, compared to 4 per cent in families which didn't own a car.[40]

A further cost related to the centralization of facilities will be in terms of the new leisure centre for the area. While such centres provide

109

modern and extensive facilities they are expensive to build and operate and

"if one allows for inflation this means that by the time the Belfast centres open, running costs will be in the region of £100,000 p.a. with interest payments amounting to perhaps a further £20,000. Assuming 24,000 people use the centre a month (BDP's estimated figure) this would mean that each user would have to spend 42p per visit on admission hire charges, snacks etc. if the centre were to break even."[41]

Therefore either the centres will need to be subsidised, which means that rates will go up, or local families will have to find the money from their income to allow the children to use the centre.

Coping with the increased costs

One way of meeting these increased costs is by more members of the household going out to work. Lawrence[42] therefore found that "several women who were not working before now work." However, this is dependent upon the availability of jobs. Now before redevelopment there were:

"600 small businesses in the Shankill Redevelopment Areas which, between them, employ about 2,000 persons, almost all of whom reside locally. Although half of these employed are 'family labour' the net result is still a large number of very local jobs for Shankill residents. This can provide part time work for married women or an easy transition from school to work."[43]

After redevelopment, instead of 600 small businesses there will be about 90 with a consequent loss in the number of jobs. The effect of this on the employment situation was recognised at the 1967 Public Inquiry into the vesting of area C:

Q . . . Mr. Booth (representing Belfast Corporation), that if these small businesses are going to be vested and demolished, that then there will be quite a serious effect on the unemployment situation?

A Well the Council have recognised the situation of the small businesses and have decided to take positive steps to do something about it . . .

Q Would you agree that no matter how vigorous the methods be that are taken they will not completely counteract the unemployment position that will arise.

A Yes, I think this is so."[44]

Not only was it therefore more difficult to find jobs locally but having found one, new problems arose. Lawrence discovered that "some of the women who have started work are worried about their children coming home from school to an empty house."[45] Now this problem would not have been so bad in the old Shankill because the child would have been welcomed in many houses in the neighbourhood. But with the neighbourhood gone, this child caring role has also disappeared. Therefore instead of the community being able to look after those in need, in this case children, a whole variety of state run groups are required— pre-school playgroups, day nurseries, playground supervisors and so on.

It was not of course only the wife who was under pressure to increase the family income. The husband also faced similar pressures. In fact Young and Willmott[46] in their London study of people moving from Bethnal Green to Greenleigh found that as regards finances:

"the main sacrifice was made by the husbands. They had to increase their housekeeping allowances as well as meet the extra fares and the like, and to do this they had, unless they were able to earn more by a great deal of overtime, to economise on other things which they used to spend their money on before they moved. Many of the husbands gave up drinking, a change made all the easier by the absence of pubs."[47]

An additional financial cost to do with new jobs occurred for those families who moved out of Belfast. Even though the majority of people wanted to be rehoused on the Shankill or on estates closeby, a small percentage of people left the Belfast Urban Area (BUA) altogether and moved to new towns. In addition to the expected problems of increased transport costs, remote shopping facilities and so on there was one additional factor that was often overlooked. This was, that in the old Shankill, family income was closely related to the number of people within that household who were in employment. According to Building Design Partnership[48] in 1966 in area 12 of the Shankill while only 5.3 per cent of heads of households had net incomes of over £19 per week, 33.5 per cent of families had net incomes over this amount. When families moved to new towns, while there was normally work available for the head of household, there were not necessarily positions available for other members, particularly the wife, and thus families were faced with a reduction in income just at the time they were having to meet increased costs.

Therefore husbands were faced either with working longer hours or with finding a new and better paid job or by cutting down their expenditure. There was no way to avoid these increased costs whether they lived in the city or in a new town. Just to make it worse all the costs mentioned so far themselves lead on to further costs. For example one of the functions that corner shops used to serve was that they were the neighbourhood fridge—a place where throughout the day and night, local people could send their kids to get ¼lb butter or a piece of cheese. However, with their being fewer corner shops, and those that did exist keeping more regular hours, the neighbourhood fridge went.

On top of that with more cases of both husband and wife working the move is towards a once a week shop. However this requires increased storage space and in particular a separate fridge for each house. This helps boost demand in the refrigerator business but becomes another necessary expense for the household. The same holds with television sets. With the old neighbourhoods gone, where people used to pop in and out of each other's houses, the television becomes an essential standby for lonely housewives during the day and the isolated family in the evening. It is hardly surprising that families become more concerned with 'things' than people and the means, 'money' to purchase the things. Take again Young and Willmott's findings:

"The first essential is money for material possessions. When people

111

move to Greenleigh the standard of life, measured by the quality of housing, is at once raised. They attempt to bring the level in other respects up to the same standard. Furniture and carpets have to be bought . . . this understandable urge to acquisition can easily become competitive. People struggle to raise their all-round standards to those of the home, and in the course of doing so they look for guidance to their neighbours . . . all being under the same pressure for material advance, they naturally mark each other's progress . . . in a life now house-centred instead of kinship centred, competition for status takes the form of a struggle for material acquisition . . . people think that they are judged, and judge others, by the material standards which are the outward and visible mark of respectability."[49]

Therefore Young and Willmott found that in addition to the increased costs occasioned by the move, money, and what it could buy, became a replacement for the old kinship system. The same thing happened on the Shankill where, according to Lawrence

"many people said that they and their husband or wife, and sometimes children, were now much more interested in keeping the inside of the home looking nice and putting money into it."[50]

With the neighbourhood gone people were forced to spend more time at home with occasional forays to the district centre. Therefore through redevelopment the social fabric of a way of life was destroyed. The new life was more home centred, more expensive, less friendly and with the extended family and neighbourhood gone, families became more isolated and more dependant on state agencies to help them with their problems. But at least the homes were new. The ideal compromise for most people would have been the new house in the old social setting.

THOSE WHO BENEFITED

Among those who gained directly from redevelopment were people who held an interest in either the houses or the land. At the time of vesting the Housing Executive was forced to buy out the interests of all those who had ever owned the land on a leasehold basis i.e. received ground rent right back to the heirs of the Chichester family who stole the land in 1603.

Thus, if a tenant farmer had leased the land from the Donegal family he would have paid ground rent to them. If in the 1850's he had leased the land to a builder then the builder would have paid ground rent to the farmer who would still be paying ground rent to the Donegals or their heirs. If the builder put up 20 houses on the land, then sold the houses, the house owners would then have paid ground rent to the builder.

The cost of buying out the ground rent is determined by the net rent times years purchase (Y.P.). The net rent is the difference between what the owner of the land receives in ground rent and what he pays out in ground rent. The years purchase is the number of years required to reach a set return on investment and reflects current interest rates.

Therefore if we take the case of the builder with 20 houses and assume that he receives a ground rent of £2 per house and pays out a ground rent of £10 to the farmer's heirs, then the relevant figures would be:

Income:	£2 × 20 houses	=	£40
minus	rent payable		£10
		net rent	£30
			×
Y.P. (at 10% interest rates)			10
			£300

i.e. in this hypothetical case it would have cost the Housing Executive £300 to buy out the builders' interest in the land.

Therefore in addition to having received ground rent for, in some cases, hundreds of years, all owners of the land received a lump sum at vesting which could then be reinvested elsewhere.

A second group who had a direct interest were the landlords. In Shankill Redevelopment Areas 12/13, 71 per cent of the houses were rented from landlords.[51] If we take a typical example of an original investment of £75 in 1894 to buy a house at an annual rent of £8.45, rising to £26 by 1919 when most rents were frozen, then by 1954 the landlord would have received approximately £1,250 in rent. If one subtracts ground rent (£1.75 per year) and maintenance (at £3 per year) and the original purchase cost, this leaves a profit of around about £900 per house. But as houses were usually sold in blocks of 4 or more, a typical profit over the 60 years might have been in the region of £3,500.

As we have seen, by the end of the second world war, these houses were no longer profitable—income didn't match outgoings and landlords wanted to be rid of them. Redevelopment was for most of them a godsend. Those who didn't do so well were those whose houses were classified as unfit and incapable of being made fit at reasonable cost (about one third of the houses). Here the landlord only received site value. However in all other cases the landlord received the market value of the property, which in the Shankill worked out between £200—£800 depending on the size, location etc. of the property. Therefore redevelopment enabled these landlords to get rid of what had become liabilities at a small profit.

However, no one could say that these landlords were making vast profits. Their interests had not been looked after in the last 30 years and they were bought out cheaply. The total cost of acquiring all the property in areas 12/13 worked out on 1972 prices at £2,320,000[52] or £815 per house (this is a slight over-estimate as the area included dwellings other than houses). In contrast the cost of building a new house was £5,500. Of this, allowing a minimum profit rate of 10 per cent, £550 went to the builder. But the main money was not involved in the building but in the financing of new houses. House building was financed over a 60 year period. According to Housing Executive figures on a 1972 £5,500[53] house the loan charges were £11 per week bringing the total cost of the new houses over 60 years to £34,320. Equivalent 1975 figures were £9,000 per house at 17½ per cent interest making a total cost over 60 years in the region of £90,000. While in Northern Ireland the majority of this money is loaned by the Government, in Great Britain over 50 per cent of local authorities' borrowing is done from non-government sources and in 1970 the interest on these loans, of which two thirds were for housing, came to £696 million.[54]

These changes, in terms of who made money out of housing, reflect the growing importance of finance capital, held by banks, insurance companies etc. in the national economy. At a local, Northern Ireland level, it indicated the decline in importance of the old land-owners and the small landlords. Redevelopment was therefore one element in the changing economic base in the province which destroyed the petty bourgeoise.

It was the new industrialists and financiers who supplanted the small businessmen who gained indirectly from redevelopment as the land was turned over to motorway and to direct centres. The intention was that the 12 district centres should be built by property developers in collaboration with central government. As far as could be calculated the developer could expect to make £½m profit on an original £1m investment over a seven year period. In addition those who gained included the multiple stores who would dominate the centres, the estate agents and lawyers who would service all of the deals and the rate payers by the increase in the rateable value of the city.

The middle classes in general benefited from the changes. They had the cars to use the motorways, the nasty eye-sore slums had gone and the time and money to make most use of the new leisure centre. A study of five sports centres in England and Wales found that:

"nearly half the users were in Socio Economic Groups 5 and 6, the group of intermediate and junior non-manual workers. A further 20 per cent of users were in professional or managerial occupations. Non-manual workers outnumbered those in manual occupations by approximately 2 to 1."[55]

CONCLUSION

The role of the state is to serve the dominant interests within society. From the 1940's onwards these changed from those of the Orange system to the new English industrialists who dominated the economy. It was this changing power base which enabled the different elements of the Orange system to be bought out so cheaply. The interests of the Protestant working class, petty bourgeoise and land-holders that the Orange system protected clashed with the need to modernise the state. It was for this reason that the Protestant working class were treated so badly, not that the Unionist party had ever treated them well, as the Civil Rights campaign eventually showed them. The plunder had little to do with bureaucratic inefficiency, it had a lot to do with relative power positions and whose interests the state saw itself serving.

Eventually the Shankill realised what was happening. The next chapter chronicles their attempt to do something about one aspect of this betrayal— getting repairs done to their houses. But by the time this happened the Shankill had been raped and then plundered and reborn as isolated families struggling to buy and find the goods and services they needed to replace the life they had lost.

114

Chapter 6

THE REPAIRS THAT NEVER GET DONE

This chapter chronicles the attempt by the Hammer Redevelopment Association (HRA) to get repairs done to houses in the Hammer community on the Shankill. The story starts in January 1973. Houses in the area were in a poor state of repair. According to the Medical Officer of Health[1], 95 per cent of them were unfit. A door to door survey carried out by the HRA found that 45 per cent of the houses had 4 or more problems. The most common problems were:

Type of Problem	Percentage of houses reporting the problem
Damp	80
Snails	51
Something wrong with the roof	49
General state of disrepair	32
Defective lavatory	28
Rats	24
Cockroaches	24
Faulty drains	22
Mice	16

The reasons for houses being in this condition have been described in earlier chapters. They include Unionist housing policy in the inter-war period when there was no redevelopment of existing slums and few working class dwellings were built. Then there was the effect of rent control legislation where rents were fixed at 1914 levels with landlords only permitted to make minimum increases. The result was that from the 1950's onwards many landlords claimed that it was no longer economic to do repairs to their houses:

"Representation has been made that many of the older properties in the City, which are let at low rents because of Rent Restriction control over the years, are in some cases in considerable debt. The agent in one particular case alleges that he is out of pocket several hundred pounds in connection with the administration of one lot of houses, and had little chance of recouping his loss."[2]

On the other hand it is clear that many landlords did not even carry out the minimum repairs necessary to keep the houses habitable. The Minister for Housing in the Northern Ireland Assembly claimed in March 1974, describing the repair problem in the Shankill that[3] "I understand that many of the problems which arose during a recent flooding would have been avoided if the former owners had made adequate arrangements to ensure that the houses were in a habitable state."

115

A third reason for the poor condition of the houses lay in the blight caused by the delay in between when the Hammer (which was in redevelopment areas 11/33) was first designated a redevelopment area in 1960 and when it was finally vested in January 1974. During this period landlords stopped doing most repairs as they realised they would not receive any return on money so invested.

The HRA decided that its main tactic would be to push for the vesting orders for 11/33 to be confirmed as possible. This was because of the difficulty of getting landlords to do repairs and it was thought to be easier to get repairs done if only one body, the Housing Executive, owned all the houses. At present with houses being owned by scores of small landlords it meant a separate action had to be prepared against each of them. The second reason for adopting this tactic was that the blight was forcing people to leave the area and thus lose their £85 settlement grant. As people had then to be resident when vesting was confirmed to qualify for the grant, the sooner it was confirmed the fewer the number of families who would lose out.

The public inquiry into the vesting of areas 11/33 was held in March 1973. The crucial question was how long it would take from then until the vesting orders was confirmed. The HRA was worried that on the other side of the Shankill, redevelopment areas 12/13, it had taken 13 months for the confirmation to come through. The Association therefore, on the 28th March wrote to Mr. Whitelaw, the Secretary of State, pointing out how bad the living conditions in the area were and asking for vesting to be carried out as quickly as possible. The reply stated[4]:

"The Secretary of State . . . agrees fully that pending redevelopment, living conditions in a designated area should not be allowed to fall below normally accepted standards . . . Mr. Whitelaw appreciates your anxiety that the length of time taken to deal with Redevelopment Areas 12 and 13 should not be repeated in Areas 11 and 33."

and in reply to a further letter from the HRA it was repeated that[5]:

"as regards the vesting of areas 11 and 33, the Ministry will try to ensure that there is no undue delay in coming to a decision on this matter."

The inquiry took place in March. The Inspector's report was handed in to the Ministry of Development on 27th June. By October the HRA had heard nothing more. It was difficult to know what was causing the delay. There had only been a handful of objectors at the inquiry and the major part of the inquiry was concerned with the type and location of dwellings to be erected in the area after redevelopment. These were obviously matters requiring serious consideration but it was still difficult to see how this took more than seven months. The HRA unable to get a satisfactory reply from the Ministry on how much longer they would have to wait, turned to the press to see if they could find this out while at the same time applying a bit of public pressure. On the 20th October the Newsletter reported that:

"A spokesman for the Ministry of Development said last night a decision on the issue was 'imminent'. "It's possible there has been a longer delay than normal in reaching a decision on this but loose ends had to be tied up and legal technicalities sorted out," he said."

On the 3rd November the Newsletter said:

"The dispute over slum homes on a Belfast site earmarked for re-development will be settled "very soon". A spokesman for the Ministry of Development confirmed last night that vesting orders will be served on 1,596 houses on Shankill Road "inside the next few weeks."

He was correct. They were announced at the end of the month and became operational on 5th January 1974.

Overall then, in 11/33 the vesting process took 3 months less time than in 12/13. Community pressure probably played a small part in this. Even so the effects of a ten month wait were disastrous for the Hammer community. People moved out and lost their rights to compensation; the repair situation got worse, as did the rats, and more and more houses were left dirty and empty, attracting vermin and further blighting the property on either side of them.

While waiting for the vesting orders to be confirmed the HRA attempted to tackle these problems. On the question of resettlement grants it tried to persuade the Medical Officer of Health to put closing orders on houses which were unfit and incapable of being made fit at reasonable cost, as tenants would then be entitled to claim compensation when they left. However the Medical Officer of Health wrote to say that:

"only in the most exceptional circumstances, where public health is in danger, would an individual Closing Order be considered in an Area already subject to redevelopment."

Later research showed that the reason for this statement lay in an earlier decision by Belfast City Council[6], where, because of the size of the redevelopment programme, the Medical Officer of Health should be instructed to make Closing Orders only in the most urgent cases.

On the rat problem the HRA wrote to the Ministry of Health and Social Services and to the Medical Officer of Health requesting action. Getting little satisfaction the HRA finally sent a delegation down town to see him and when he refused to meet them, they threatened to call in the T.V. so that they could record this example of council participation. The Medical Officer of Health saw them, and the rodent control team came to the area. There was however a catch to this service which was that the Ministry charged local people for rat catching done inside houses:

The HRA wrote to the Ministry of Health and Social Services[7]:

"We understand . . . you have refused to completely waive charges for rodent control in our area and other redevelopment areas of Belfast. We fail to understand why it is that authorities can allow housing conditions to deteriorate to the extent that rats infest our area, and then insist it is our fault and our responsibility to do something about it."

The reply three weeks later was[8]:

"The position . . . is that the Rats and Mice Destruction Act 1919 clearly lays the onus on the occupier of the land to destroy rats and mice on the land and to prevent it from becoming infested. I would be misleading you were I to suggest that I personally could alter this law."

In the meantime the rat catchers had come and gone. They couldn't remain long as there was only one Mobile Rodent Control Unit (as the rat exterminators were called) for the whole city and the Shankill was not the only redevelopment area with rats. The result was that the Unit only remained in an area for a week or so before moving off elsewhere. The problem was soon as bad as before.

Empty houses left by people moving out of the community were a particularly difficult problem to deal with. As soon as they were empty, the houses were raided by vandals who stripped them of lead and copper and left gas leaking and water pouring into the premises. The younger children then used them as play areas. This led to accidents and disease— there was for example a hepatitis outbreak in the area. Empty houses also tended to make those on either side of them that much worse as the damp and smell from rotting garbage spread. The HRA therefore tried to persuade the City Surveyor to speed up the rate at which his department blocked up the empty houses. But[9]:

"Dear Mr. Regan;
      A deputation from the Hammer Redevelopment Group met with you at 11.30 a.m. on Monday 7th May. During that meeting it was agreed (a) that by the end of the week you would send us details of what had been done about the empty houses we had reported to you and (b) that arrangements would be made for the local inspector responsible for the area to call with us every ten days or so. As nothing had been heard by the end of the week, I phoned you the following Tuesday and you said that you had a list of the details that had been given to you the previous Thursday and we agreed that you would put them in the post.

Neither the list nor the local inspector from your department has yet arrived. This is regrettable because such a lack of response makes people disillusioned with discussion as a means of getting anything done.

Instead of sending you notification of individual houses requiring blocking up, we have carried out a quick survey of redevelopment areas 11 and 13 and found 209 empty houses, a list of which are enclosed. Many of these houses have rubble, broken glass, in some cases live electric wires and therefore in terms of what you said about interpreting the terms 'in dangerous condition' require immediate blocking up. Some with offensive matter required immediate clearing out and a copy of this letter has therefore been sent to the City Health Dept. Some houses have been blocked up with corrugated iron but as the state of houses in Fortingale Street shows, this presents few obstacles to children and these houses therefore also need to be breeze-blocked."

Even the blocking up of houses presented problems. In theory houses were meant to be cleared out first of any offensive matter, such as old food, but as this was the responsibility of the cleansing department while block-ing up was the responsibility of the surveyor's department, communication lines often got crossed. The result was that often the 'blockers up' arrived before the 'cleaners out' and went ahead and did their job. Thus houses got blocked up with rotting debris still in them which only encouraged the rats.

On the question of repairs, for reasons outlined before, the HRA found it difficult to get landlords to do anything which made any notice-able difference. A half hearted rent strike was started by some tenants.

The result was that a couple of landlords caved in immediately and sent a repairman around. Others sent summonses. Summonses always came to the old age pensioners who were least able to handle them and for whom the house was their only security. Many were also reluctant to break the law. Therefore even though there was little risk of them being evicted, it would have been unlikely that a court would have ordered an eviction and even if it had, there was no way it could have been enforced on the Shankill at that time; it was necessary to pay up to save the old people from further anxiety. The HRA considered calling an all out rent strike but decided against it, as at that time it didn't have the organisation capable of collecting all the money due and holding it until the strike was over. The HRA knew from experience elsewhere that if this was not done then many tenants would simply spend the money and be in trouble later, when once the repairs had been done, they would have been liable for back rent.

Given that the HRA's strategy was aimed at speeding up vesting so that the Housing Executive would become the sole landlord for all the houses in the area, the Association was concerned to make sure that the Housing Executive had an adequate repairs programme ready for when it assumed control.

As early as April 1973 the Belfast Area Housing Manager had warned[10] the HRA that "after vesting, the Housing Executive will under-take the minimum repairs which are necessary to keep property windproof and watertight." The HRA was not satisfied with this approach and at a meeting on the 12th April 1973, eight months before vesting at which the district housing manager was present, point 4c on the agenda was:

"what plans does the Housing Executive have for phases other than the first phase when vesting occurs? Will there be a repairs squad in the area? Will houses be kept in reasonable condition so that people in the first or second phase who do not want to move out of the area can be rehoused in the empty houses in later phases."

The points were noted.

The HRA's fears about the Housing Executive's ability to carry out adequate repairs were further reinforced by what was happening in areas 12/13 on the other side of the Shankill Road. The area was vested in June 1973. In October 1973 the Chairman of the Lower Shankill Re-development Association which represented groups in the lower part of the area, wrote to Simpson, the Director-General of the Housing Executive:

"I am writing this on behalf of the above committee, who, I am sorry to say, are getting frustrated and very annoyed. We have written repeatedly to, and had meetings with representatives from the Housing Executive office at Peters Hill but unfortunately we seem to get nowhere. We have forwarded the addresss of houses which we know to be suffering from damp, leaky roofs, missing guttering, blocked gutters which need cleaning out. We have also complained about the need to block up empty houses more quickly and to stop the dirt being left in those which are blocked up . . . Up to date we have received little satisfaction on any of these matters, although the Peters Hill office has assured us that the complaints have been forwarded through the appropriate channels to the repair contractors. We have asked for a conference with the Housing Inspector, representatives from the contractors and from Peters Hill office to see if anything can be done to speed things up a bit. This letter was written three weeks ago and though the Peters Hill office has acknowledged it, nothing has happened. Surely by this time something could have been arranged. We, as a community, do not ask for more than reasonable comfort until such times as we are rehoused . . . Prior to vesting, we as a committee were assured of full co-operation by the Housing Executive representatives. We have no complaints with reference to Mr. Rogers and Miss Young at the Peters Hill office but they seem to be frustrated through a lack of response from other quarters."

The HRA's worst fears were to be justified. On January 5th the Housing Executive took over responsibility for areas 11/33 and were faced with a backlog of repairs, which, despite the meetings and their experience in areas 12/13, they were totally unprepared for. Even the procedure for reporting repairs was cumbersome.

The only way that repairs could be reported was by going down to the local housing office which opened three mornings a week, and then wait in line with people seeing about compensation and allocation difficulties. This meant that people often had to wait over an hour to hand in a single repair complaint. A note of this complaint was made by the counter staff who then in theory would pass them onto the area maintenance manager sitting back at head office. He would send a slip to the local contractor who would only report back when he had completed the job. The system soon collapsed because: many people didn't have the time to wait; many reported repairs never got done; contractors were not doing the few repairs they did properly and finally because the system had no checks. People could never prove they had sent in a complaint, the area manager never had an up-to-date view of the picture and there was no supervision as to the quality of the repairs. The overall effect was that few repairs got done.

This marked the end of the first phase of the HRA's attempt to get something done. So far the Association had adopted a fairly conventional community development approach. The people got themselves organised, they researched their problem, they took their findings and ideas along to the appropriate authorities and then, using the proper channels, asked for them to be acted on. But the positive results had been minimal and living conditions had continued to deteriorate. It was clear that it was not enough to make the authorities aware of the size of the problem and that they would only act under pressure. The need therefore was for direct action.

The switch to this approach came at the end of January when a series of heavy rainstorms hit Belfast. The houses with leaking roofs soon became unliveable in. Many had buckets everywhere catching water while in other houses families were forced to vacate their upstairs and crowd into one room. In an attempt to provoke some action the HRA, together with the Shankill Community Council decided to hold an all night sit out,

120

outside the local housing office. Leaflets were handed out to all passersby which explained:

"WHY ARE WE SITTING HERE ALL NIGHT?

(i) Because the Housing Executive which now owns all the houses in the redevelopment areas refuses to carry out repairs.

(ii) This means that scores of people, including a lot of old age pensioners, are living in houses where water is coming through the roof.

(iii) We have written to the Housing Executive, we have phoned to the Housing Executive, we have written and phoned the Public Health Inspectors and still nothing gets done.

(iv) So we are sitting here all night to bring home to people that throughout the Shankill there are lots of people who because of the condition of their houses have to sit up every night."

About 60 people took part in the protest. The press, television and local radio came as did senior housing officials. The local housing office staff complained the next morning about the sit out there when the real 'enemy' was situated in the downtown head office. However it was pointed out to them, that as the aim was to reach local people the protest had to be staged on the Shankill. The divisional maintenance manager toured the district and said that he never realised conditions were so bad! The next night heavy winter rains fell again and living conditions in the area deteriorated still more. The people decided on further action[11]:

"Shankill Residents flee floods—
Families Homeless

Forty families from the Hammer district of Belfast's Shankill Road spent last night in Agnes Street Methodist Church Hall after severe flooding in their homes. Earlier yesterday the angry residents confronted Housing Executive officials with their problems. They demanded that repairs to their houses be carried out as quickly as possible and a greater effort made to rehouse them. Mrs. Sally Cummings of the Hammer Redevelopment Association said the houses were severely hit during storms at the beginning of January and in the latest gales the water was pouring into many homes."

This really got some action. The divisional maintenance manager was now calling the area a disaster area and there was talk of spending £500 a house in doing them up. Welfare officials offered blankets and beds, the police community relations offered breakfast, the television cameras were touring the district etc. Peter McLachlan an Assembly representative raised the matter in Stormont and Mr. Currie the Minister responsible said[12]:

"I can inform the Assembly that the Housing Executive has taken the following action to help overcome this problem.

(i) Action to make the houses windproof and waterproof is being accelerated and there are now five contractors working in the area."

And so there were, and they worked all weekend as well. In the meantime the Housing Executive was offering the families in the Hall accommodation either in outlying estates or in flats or maisonettes that no one wanted. So the majority of the people stayed put until their houses were repaired.

The Housing Executive tried to disclaim responsibility for the state of the houses on the ground that they had only owned them for a month. But as a spokeswoman for the HRA said[13]:

"they had warned the local Housing Executive representatives that unless something was done quickly the families were going to squat . . . Said Mrs. Morrison: 'The Housing Executive blame the landlords for the condition of the houses but most of them were condemned about a year ago. The Housing Executive knew the condition of these houses before they took them over and they should have had something prepared."

Though the attempt to get the Hammer designated as a disaster area failed, meetings were held with the housing authorities to see what else could be done. The Minister for Housing met the Shankill Community Council where the Housing Executive, who were also present, agreed to "undertake a complete survey of all houses in the Shankill Road area to determine the quality of the housing stock so that even within the area, families could be rehoused in better accommodation."[14]

The Shankill Community Council took this to mean that the survey would be as they had requested in two parts: Firstly of the Upper Shankill, outside the redevelopment area, to locate empty houses which could be used to rehouse people living in the worst conditions in redevelopment areas. Currie, the Minister of Housing, had announced in the Northern Ireland Assembly that he was giving the Housing Executive permission to buy 100 such houses; and secondly of all houses in areas 11/33 to get a total picture of the repairs that needed doing. This latter point was confirmed in a letter by Currie when he said[15]:

"at the meeting with the Community Council it was agreed that, as part of the normal housing management function, the Executive would carry out a survey of all the houses already owned in areas 11 and 33."

The Housing Executive was later to deny all knowledge of both these surveys which they never did.

There was now increasing concern throughout the whole Shankill redevelopment area about the state of repairs and it was decided to call a public meeting to which Mr. Lazenbatt the Director of Housing Management and Miss Seale, the Belfast Area Manager, would be invited. It was clear by now that many parts of the area, were in just as bad condition as the Hammer. It was therefore decided to hold the meeting on the other side of the Shankill, in areas 12/13, as people there felt that the Hammer was getting too much attention. Among the demands put forward at the meeting were:

(i) That the Housing Executive immediately buy up and renovate all empty houses in the Upper Shankill . . .

(ii) that within the redevelopment area repairs are concentrated on the better houses in later phases . . .

(iii) As there is a shortage of dwellings for old age pensioners, two bedroom flats should be used as temporary accommodation for them and rents subsidized."

The first, second and third points were agreed to in principle, though only the third was ever acted on.

At the time of the meeting there were still half a dozen families living in the Agnes Street Hall as a result of the flooding and there was still a lot of anger against the Housing Executive. People wanted Lazenbatt to tour the area and see the conditions for himself. There was a discussion as to whether he should be held hostage until all the people in the Hall were rehoused but it was decided not to because conditions were such in Belfast at the time that the Housing Executive would probably have used it as a reason to stop participation with all community groups everywhere. The tour still went ahead and after a confrontation between the HRA and Lazenbatt and Seale a commitment to do something urgently about the worst case was won from him.

As a result of this and other meetings a number of further promises were extracted from the housing authorities; the area was to be given priority in terms of repairs; the number of contractors were to be increased; four area repair supervisors were to be appointed; a separate local repair office was to be established; a new card system for recording repairs was to be introduced and a start was to be made in buying up the empty houses in the Upper Shankill.

But by April little had happened other than the contractors and supervisors being appointed. It appeared as if the authorities had responded with just sufficient action to placate the immediate demands of the community but that was as far as they were prepared to go. Frequent meetings were held with Housing Executive staff but little changed on the ground.

No local repair office had been established nor had the card system been introduced. In fact it turned out that this system which the HRA had been led to believe in February 1974 was a new idea, had been discussed at a meeting of the Greater West Belfast Community Association in October 1973 when the GWBCA were told that:

"within 4-6 weeks the Northern Ireland Housing Executive hope to bring in a system where if a tenant comes in with a complaint, it is written down on a form and the tenant gets the duplicate form of the complaint."[16]

The Housing Executive claimed it couldn't begin buying up the empty houses in the Upper Shankill at it was still waiting procedural clarification from the Department of Housing. The surveys still had not been done and many urgent repairs were not carried out. The HRA had one set of 28 urgent repairs which had all been reported at least once by February 28th. By April 28th only half of them had been done despite a Housing Executive pledge that urgent repairs would be seen to within 2 days and others within 5 weeks.

A further problem concerned houses which were in such a bad state that they could not be repaired. What happened in such cases, as far as could be ascertained, was that the local maintenance man concerned would report the case to the regional maintenance manager Mr. Murphy, who would tell Mr. Molloy the divisional maintenance manager who would inform Lazenbatt the Director of Housing Management who would tell McCabe the Belfast Area Housing Manager, who would tell Miss Seale, the Belfast Area Housing Manager, who would tell Mrs. Boyd the district housing manager to get them a house. But as there were no suitable houses in the Shankill area where these people wanted to be rehoused, a fact that everyone knew from the beginning, Mrs. Boyd had no option but to pass the case back to the local maintenance man for his attention.

Finally nothing further had been heard of a document ("Policy for Maintenance of Dwellings in Redevelopment Areas") that the Shankill Community Council had been shown in February. It had been prepared by the Divisional Maintenance Unit of the Housing Executive and for the first time outlined the need for more extensive repairs to be done to houses in later clearance phases of redevelopment areas

The HRA and the Shankill Commuunity Council drawing upon past experience, decided that more direct action was needed.

"Yesterday there was a protest in the Shankill area outside the Housing Executive's Office in Peter's Hill. Pieces of paper which stated that the Housing Executive must be forced to act now were handed out. They were headed 'the repairs that never got done!. The proper channels get nowhere.' I have examined some of these cases. I have examined the history. I have met the people who are concerned. I have seen some of these so-called repairs and they are a disgrace. What standard of repairs are supposed to be done I have no idea, but it is atrocious that cloths have to be stuffed into ceilings, that rooms are beginning to come down, and that wallpaper peels off as soon as it is put on because of dampness. These are intolerable conditions.'[27]

One of the two cases that the protest gave publicity to was:

SEENAN—32, RICHMOND STREET. (PHASE 2)—MOTHER—TWO CHILDREN

Property vested by Housing Executive 5th January 1974. The following complaints for repairs were reported two weeks later—overall dampness; slates off back and front; large hole in toilet pot; inside front door won't close. No one came out to do them. During the heavy rain 29th January—1st February, the damp got worse, repair men working in the street but 32 wasn't on their list so they wouldn't repair it. Shortly after, the next door neighbours moved out, the damp got even worse. The little boy had been admitted to hospital 3 times because of asthma as a direct result of the dampness. Rats began coming into the house from those bricked up either side. The complaints were reported a further 3 times to the local repairs office, and eventually to Mr. Molloy (Divisional Maintenance Manager) on 28th February. On the 19th March repair men arrived to fix the toilet. They removed the old pot, left a new one in the yard without installing, and left an open sewer, more rats came up it. All this time the Housing Executive refused to give Mrs. Seenan a rent book, since they couldn't establish whether or not she was a legal tenant. On Good Friday, accompanied by a Community worker, Mrs. Seenan went again to the Townsend Street office. They explained that it would cost a lot to fix the toilet and the house wasn't really worth it, but couldn't offer suitable alternative accommodation. By a simple phone call to C. Allan, Cliftonpark Avenue her old landlord, they established that she had been a legal tenant, and gave her a rent book. During this past week the slates were fixed. The inside door still won't close, the toilet pot is still lying in the yard, the damp still rises, but they've bought a dog to try and keep the rats out."

The protest was quite small but it got a lot of publicity and resulted in a further series of meetings. They centered on two issues. The first was the buying of the 100 houses in the Upper Shankill area. Even though the Housing Executive now had permission to buy the 100 houses the HRA learnt that: these were to be bought for people in bad housing conditions throughout Northern Ireland and not only on the Shankill; the Shankill would be lucky to get 30 of these houses; anyway the Housing Executive had only permission to purchase 12 houses in the first instance and the Housing Executive had not yet worked out how and where the houses were to be purchased.

The HRA pointed out that even if all the 100 houses had been allocated to the Shankill, this would have been inadequate as there were already more than 100 families looking for accommodation in the Upper Shankill area. There were more than enough empty houses in the area. As the Housing Executive still refused to carry out the survey of empty houses, the Shankill Community Council had asked the local girls' secondary school to do it. They found 277 empty houses. The Housing Executive claimed that this whole argument was unrealistic as with existing resources they would be lucky to buy the 12 houses by the end of the year.

The second issue concerned the number of outstanding repairs in the Hammer and other Shankill communities. The Housing Executive had still not carried out its survey of the repair situation in areas 11/33 and the local area representatives claimed that the Housing Executive was up-to-date with all its repairs in the area. To prove them wrong the Shankill Community Council carried out a quick survey of one street in the Hammer and found that sixteen out of the twenty occupied houses were in need of repair.

The explanation for the discrepancy between the two claims rests in the fact that local people were no longer reporting repairs. This was both because they no longer expected anything to be done about them and because they feared that getting their house repaired would reduce their chances of getting a new house in the immediate future. Local people no longer trusted the Housing Executive. People were only prepared to accept that something had been achieved when they actually saw houses being repaired. Protestations, excuses and promises didn't count. Local repair supervisors were correct then when they said they were up-to-date on repairs, meaning of those that had been reported. However they knew quite well that many repairs were not being brought officially to their notice but they reported the findings which were most likely to appeal to those above them.

By this time Shankill community workers no longer felt that any further meetings with housing authorities would serve much purpose. Three of those who had been most active in the repairs campaign decided

to boycott further meetings until something concrete had been achieved on the two issues. In an open letter that they wrote to the Housing Executive they claimed: [18]
"The history of these meetings is largely one of broken promises, half fulfilled pledges, miscommunications etc. . . .
We have discovered that there is no point in attending a meeting where Mr. Lazenbatt is not present as no one else within his department is prepared to make any decision which might affect policy. There is little point in attending meetings where he is present as what we get are promises instead of action."
Justification for this stand came from a survey carried out under the auspices of the Shankill Community Council in July/August 1974 into the state of house repairs in the Shankill redevelopment areas. In January 1973 when the repairs campaign began, local community surveys found that 90 per cent of houses in the Hammer and 71 per cent in the first phase of areas 12/13, needed repairs. Twenty months later, the 1974 survey, which took one street at random from each of the 12 clearance phases, found that 70 per cent of occupied houses needed repairs. On top of this it needs to be remembered that many people had left during this period so that some of the worst houses were no longer occupied. The survey found that 50 per cent of the repairs had been reported
"via the proper channels, to the (Housing) Executive, but either the job had been inadequately done or, as was mainly the case, there had been no response from the Executive . . .
Some of the houses, in all phases, were in an unrepairable condition. Gaping roof holes, caved in ceilings, houses with only one or two rooms usuable, and excessive rising damp were not uncommon. Some reported severe health problems as a direct result of living conditions, and rats in the houses were frequently mentioned."
Therefore even thought the campaign after the first year switched from community development to community action, the results were negligible. The reasons why this was so are tied up with the more general limitations of trying to produce change from the basis of any one community on problems which affect other communities.
Repairs were a city wide problem. Springmartin for example was a new Protestant housing estate, on the hills above the Shankill, that had only been started in 1968. A report on a survey carried out by the local tenants association in November 1973[20] showed that out of 166, 2 room flats, on the estate 127 were unoccupied, the main reason being because of damp. Of the flats which were occupied, 75 per cent needed repairs done to them. Residents in the 176 houses on the estate complained of mice, rats, drains and waste and litter lying about. The local tenant association had been no more successful than the HRA in getting the repairs seen to. It concluded:
"The general position about repairs in the estate is highly unsatisfactory and even complaints which could be dealt with immediately have received no attention. The many number of times people have reported their repairs is 3.1. Only 7 of the 46 complainants with permanent rent books had a reply from the Housing Executive."

Local residents reached similar conclusions to those in the Shankill:[21]
" . . . the Northern Ireland Housing Executive appears to have forgotten about the damp altogether. Presumably they reason that, if they forget about the problems for long enough the people, and therefore the problem will go away! The only conclusions that can be drawn from the above account can be that:

(i) Allowing inspections of damp flats has only been an inconvenience for the residents and a waste of time for all concerned.

(ii) Preparing reports for the Housing Executive merely accentuates the paper shortage.

(iii) It does not matter that people have to live in damp flats with water streaming down the walls and clothes and food being ruined, as long as the officials concerned have peace and comfort.
We would like to allege that the Northern Ireland Housing Executive have, by their attitude and lack of concern and action concerning the damp flats in Springmartin, been guilty of both severe negligence and maladministration. We further ask that some *action be taken immediately* to rectify this deplorable situation. We can now understand the attitude of those who claim that *violence is the only way to achieve results.*"
One of the main problems in trying to solve these repair problems from the basis of any one community is that resources are limited. According to the 1974 Housing Condition Survey[22] for Northern Ireland, the Housing Executive owned 13,380 dwellings which required an average of £610 in repairs i.e. £8.2 million. In the year ending 31st March 1974[23] the Housing Executive had only £3.9 million to spend on repairs. Given that too little money was allocated to solve the problem, success by any one community could only be achieved by another community's loss. Furthermore localised action simply meant community groups competing against each other with the one protesting loudest gaining a temporary advantage as resources (contractors, rodent control units etc.) were rushed in to dampen the community agitation.
Even within this community based framework redevelopment associations were not always a good base from which to put pressure on the housing authorities. The Hammer Redevelopment Association for example was centered around the leading personalities in one of the neighbourhoods which made up the Hammer community. Because of rivalry other neighbourhoods were reluctant to give their full support to the HRA. The Lower Shankill Redevelopment Association attempted to overcome this problem by having a representative from each street on its main committee. Though this widened the focus of the group there was wide variation in the commitment of different representatives. A fundamental weakness of both groups was a loss of membership after vesting as people left the area. Furthermore as people left, the groups found themselves increasingly involved in the day-to-day problems of the many elderly people who remained. This left them with little time to concentrate on longer term aspects of the repairs campaign.

As both groups basically remained isolated from other groups—political parties, para-military organizations, trade unions etc.—this also limited the amount of pressure they could put on housing authorities. Also as housing was mainly seen as woman's work, the job of getting repairs done was largely left to the woman which again cut out much mass support.

The groups were further weakened by the fact that it took some time for them to analyse properly the role of the state as regards the question of repairs. At the beginning there was a belief that once the full extent of the problem was brought to the notice of the authorities they would take appropriate action. But as we saw, this hypothesis didn't hold up in practise.

Next it was believed that housing authorities had to be goaded into action. But with limited community backing all that direct action achieved were a few short term palliatives and countless meetings.

Then it was argued that what was wrong was the way that the Housing Executive was administered. There was no doubt that the Housing Executive had problems, especially in the Housing Management division. Decisions made at upper levels rarely filtered down to local staff who complained that they could never get decisions from those above them. Important documents such as the "Policy for Maintenance of Dwellings in Redevelopment Areas" seemed to disappear in the labyrinth. Representatives of the Shankill Community Council saw a copy of the document in February 1974 but in May the Belfast Housing and Maintenance Managers said that they had never heard of the document.

But inefficiency is not a sufficient explanation to account for the continuing repair problem that existed in the Shankill and other areas. Furthermore it doesn't explain the lack of overall consideration shown to tenants such as the broken promises and the need to wait outside for an hour in winter to hand in a complaint about repairs. It was not only the Housing Executive who had these attitudes; a Ministry valuation officer told a community worker, preparing an information leaflet on people's rights to compensation, that 'he hoped it wasn't one of those leaflets which would encourage people to complain.'

These attitudes could not have existed if housing officials saw themselves as representing the interests of the tenants. But this was not the case. They administered a housing policy which was subordinated to the economic needs of the state. These determined not only when and where new houses should be built but also how much money would be available for different aspects of housing policy. There was little that the Housing Executive could do when out of an income of £25 million, £20 million went on repaying the interest on previous loans. To put these figures into perspective the actual cost on 1974[24] prices of repairing, improving and renewing existing houses in Northern Ireland, which required some action, was £286 million. On top of this are the 15,000 new houses needed annually at an average cost each of £9,000. In the year 1973/4 public expenditure in Northern Ireland on housing amounted to £61 million. There is little that locally based community action programmes can do to effect repairs until there is a change in the way housing is financed.

On the Shankill what they knew was that[25]:

"it was a cold bitter night and as I lay in my bed I could smell the damp and wet and I could see a clock (cockroach) climb down the ceiling. I lay there listening to the rain beating against my window. It sent a sharp shiver up my back and the slates sliding off the roof. I lay there in the middle of the mattress with a blanket twined over me. I live with my mother in a little house with two rooms . . .I am taking a touch of the flu. My mother is 48. But if you looked at her, you would have thought she was sixty."

Chapter 7

PARTICIPATION OR NEGOTIATION?

The previous chapter showed the limited success that the Hammer Redevelopment Association had in its dealings with housing authorities to get repairs done to houses in their community. This chapter will put the whole question of participation into a wider context and examine in detail two other participation exercises in which the Shankill was involved.

The Skeffington Commission which was set up by Westminster in 1968 to look at the question of participation in the making of development plans such as the Belfast plans, produced by Building Design Partnership and Travers Morgan defined it as:

"the act of sharing in the formulation of policies and proposals . . . Participation involves doing as well as talking and there will be full participation only where the public are able to take an active part throughout the plan-making process."[1]

Before the production of the mid 1960 development plans for Belfast, there had been few attempts to involve communities in the planning process. The reason for this lies in the way the province was run. As earlier chapters have shown the dominant forces were those which made up the Orange system—the local capitalists and small businessmen and it was these interests which determined the form of the political system—the decentralised political structure with power vested in local authorities who then, through the controlled allocation of resources via patronage, protected the position of the Protestant labour aristocracy. Therefore as far as the majority of the Protestant working class was concerned the system was being run in their interests and they saw little need to question any decisions being taken by those who claimed to represent them.

As far as the Catholic population was concerned, they had little effective voice at either city or province level and much of the efforts of their political representatives were directed to making sure that their position was not further weakened. The main Catholic party, the Nationalists, known as the Green Tories, were dominated by Church and small business interests. The poor showing of the Northern Ireland Labour Party and its eventual inability to bridge the sectarian divide adequately reflected the number of people who put class issues first.

During the 1960's the situation changed rapidly. The crucial battle was taking place within the Unionist party between those who supported the economic changes taking place in the province and wanted to alter the way the state was organised to facilitate the entry of, and control by, new industries and those in the Orange system who stood to lose from these changes. On the Catholic side as the possibility of unification became more remote, Catholics became more concerned about their position within the Northern Ireland state. What had started off as a largely middle class concern about discrimination expressed through pressure groups such as 'National Unity' and the Campaign for Social Justice ended up as the civil rights campaign. The issues raised by this campaign made the Protestant working class realise that their living conditions were little better than those of the Catholics. At the same time the progressive wing of the Unionist party, which temporarily gained the ascendancy, started making concessions to Catholic agitation and initiated a series of meetings with Dublin. The Protestant working class began to realise that the price of economic progress was to be the end of their protected employment position and the beginning of a short path to domination by the Catholic south. They came to see their short-term interests as lying with the other elements of the Orange system, the petty bourgeoise and local capitalists and landowners, who were losing out, and this coalition of interest formed the basis of what came to be known as the United Ulster Unionist Coalition. With the realisation of how the Faulknerite Unionist party was betraying them, the Protestant working class was freed for the first time to attack Unionist policies without such tactics being branded as disloyal.

These political changes coincided with the first stages of the implementation of the Belfast development plans. These themselves had been produced with the minimum of public participation. What there was consisted largely of social surveys. But participation does not amount to much when a sample of individuals are asked a few questions by an interviewer employed by a team of foreign consultants working to a brief drawn up on behalf of industrial interests. Therefore in the case of the Travers Morgan transportation plan, it was part of the consultant's brief that an urban motorway would be part of their recommended solution. To ask people how they want to travel then becomes a largely irrelevant exercise. Moreover to ask the question in an historical context is to bias the answer. If there has been a deliberate attempt to run down the quality of public transport over a number of years and there appears to be no perceivable change in this policy, then few people are likely to opt to use public transport if they have any choice. However, if people were told that past policies were to be reversed and that it was possible to run a cheap, frequent and city wide bus service, then the choice they made would probably be very different.

People quite naturally recognised this form of participation as a sham. In the Shankill for example an attempt was made to find out which of three different district shopping centre alternatives people wanted. People were not asked whether they wanted the shopping centre, nor were they informed of what its costs would be. They were simply given a marginal choice as to its location. Some 10,000 badly designed leaflets were sent out asking for opinions, less than 10 were returned.

The most tangible sign to many community groups of what the new Belfast was to be like was Divis Towers—a 15 storey block of flats erected in the Lower Falls. In addition houses were being cleared to make way for the motorway and blight was beginning to spread its tentacles of decay. The new towns had their development commissions, factories were being set up there and the skilled workers began to move out.

Then from 1969 onwards with the beginning of violence, people in the communities became actively involved on a daily basis in politics. The different para-military groups on both sides emerged and became involved by necessity in the problems of redevelopment as well as law and order and defensive and offensive actions. In addition numerous community groups, tenants associations and redevelopment groups were set up. By 1973 there were over 300 such groups in Belfast. They were supported by the Community Relations Commission which was set up in 1969 as part of the Callaghan reform package to save the province. The Commission decided to base its work on a community development strategy and its field staff were sent out to help local groups to establish themselves.

Participation and the Shankill

Building Design Partnership produced a district plan for the redevelopment of the Shankill in 1968[2]. By then work had already started in building Unity Flats at the bottom of the Shankill and detailed recommendations had been submitted for area C. These plans were all approved by Belfast Council and for the reasons outlined earlier, there was little discussion with, or opposition from, the Shankill community over the plans.

The first major opposition started in 1969 with the election of two Protestant Unionist councillors for the Upper Shankill to Belfast City Council. They campaigned on a dual programme. They firstly attacked the Unionist party for disbanding the B specials—part of the betrayal by the Unionist party of the Protestant working class—and secondly at a local level for not doing enough on housing and social issues for Shankill people. Not only had the civil rights campaign made the Shankill people realise that in terms of houses they were little better off, if any, from those on the Lower Falls, but the attempts by the Unionist party to meet some of the civil rights demands made Protestants feel that it was they who were by now being discriminated against.

Shortly after this the Shankill Redevelopment Association was set up with the express purpose of fighting Building Design Partnership's plans. The main aims of the Association were to speed up redevelopment and to get rid of the high rise flats. In the original plans for area C, 16 per cent of the new dwellings were to be in three, 15 storey point blocks and it was these the Shankill Redevelopment Associated planned to get rid off. They were also opposed to the 6 storey 'noise barrier' blocks being built in the Lower Shankill along the line of the motorway and were the first to give them the name of the 'Weetabix' blocks.

In its campaign on the tower blocks, the Shankill Redevelopment Association persuaded local councillors to head deputations, and a number of meetings were held with Ministry and Council members and staff. Eventually the Council was persuaded that the people would not accept the tower blocks and they were scrapped. The final bargaining point, according to one of the Association's members, was their threat to gelignite any foundations that were laid. As was to be proved time and time again effective opposition depended on having sufficient power to at least thwart unwanted plans.

Having achieved this victory the Association began to fade in importance. Its members became more involved in the political events that were taking place. In the last analysis it was always the wider political

132

issues which determined what was possible on the Shankill Road by way of agitation on social issues.

The next issue on which local people fought the authorities was control of housing allocation. The violence in Belfast following the introduction of internment in 1971 was instrumental in the setting up of the Ulster Defence Association. The Association was established through the coming together, with some tacit British Army support, of the different local vigilante groups which had been set up to protect their areas.

With the establishment of Protestant no-go areas in 1972, the UDA became the most important political force in the area. Even the Army collaborated with it at a time when the army was virtually running the state under martial law—licences, which in Northern Ireland contain a photo, functioned as general identity cards and in specific areas surveys plus a policy of frequent and widespread arrests enabled a check to be kept on the movements of most inividuals. Internment enabled the military to lock up suspected trouble-makers. Helicopters patrolled the city night and day and at night used search lights to illuminate different streets.

As the UDA strengthened its hold, normal government services were either withdrawn from the Shankill or became irrelevant. Thus law and order passed from the hands of the police to the UDA and no other agencies were able to operate without its approval. Therefore local people continually turned to the UDA to help them solve social problems.

Foremost amongst these was squatting. Squatting in Northern Ireland had its roots in intimidation. During a 3 month period in 1971 over 2,000 families were forced to move because of 'the troubles'. As a consequence mixed areas became segregated and houses in border zones were vacated. Many people took the opportunity to change their dwellings and move from undesirable flats to highly prized houses. In March 1973 according to the Northern Ireland Housing Executive over 5,000 houses were illegally occupied.

Housing thus became a free for all where the strongest won and paramilitary groups made sure that members of their organizations were looked after. However, those who had legitimate rights to new houses soon began to complain to the UDA which had to do something if it wanted to retain popular support. Support which was given willingly when outside attack seemed imminent, fell away when the immediate danger was past.

The UDA started on its own initiative to tackle the problems but soon found that it required the support of other para-military bodies because without this support, it had no mandate to stop members of other organizations squatting. A meeting was therefore called in December 1972 to which representatives from all para-military groups on the Shankill Road were invited. On the basis of this, and one subsequent meeting, it was decided to set up the West Belfast Housing Association (WBHA) on which all organizations would have a member on the committee. The WBHA invited councillors to work with them on the understanding that the councillors would be responsible to the Association.

The first step was to send around a leaflet setting an arbitary date, 22nd January 1973 when all squatting had to stop. Anyone found unjustifiably

133

squatting after that date would be given 24 hours to leave or would be evicted. An advice centre, dealing with housing problems, especially those to do with allocation, was set up by the Association. Two or more members of the committee listened to the complaints, and up to 200 people attended each time: and then each Sunday the committee met and went through all the forms. Emergency cases were extracted and one of the councillors would then take their forms to the Housing Executive to get these people allocated houses.

For a period of time the Housing Executive collaborated with the Association. It is easy to hypothesize why. Firstly, the Association was the only group which could control squatting. Unless squatting stopped, the Housing Executive had no control over allocation. With no control over allocation, it was difficult to clear people from redevelopment areas. Secondly, as the Association could control vandalism, the damaged houses which existed on many estates could be rebuilt Thirdly, the Housing Executive was having difficulty in filling vacancies which existed in unpopular dwellings and estates. Any help the Association could give in persuading people to move to these places was therefore appreciated.

Therefore the deal that was set up was, that in return for control of squatting and vandalism by the WBHA the Housing Executive would; stop issuing squatters' rent books to people who squatted in the area, give preference to emergency housing cases and would give the Association a say in the allocation of dwellings on unfavourable sites. The deal lasted for about six months before collapsing. According to the WBHA it was the Housing Executive who broke the deal by again giving out rent books to squatters thus legitimising their presence and undermining the ability of the Association to evict them. According to one of the councillors who worked with the WBHA:

"Neither the police nor the military were able to do what we did. But we have not got the backing of the Housing Executive and no action was taken by them against squatting. Now there appears to be an increase in squatting again."

So why did the Housing Executive change policy? Again it is only possible to guess at the reasons. There can be no doubt that the Housing Executive's need to get things moving had always to be balanced against the risks, as far as it was concerned, of giving power to community groups. These risks were twofold: firstly, there were risks in dealing with an Association which could well be classified as having sectional interests—something that a 'neutral, non-sectarian body' such as the Housing Executive could not do, without damaging its credibility—secondly, because the whole rationale of the Housing Executive rested on the assumption that only centralised control could solve Northern Ireland's housing problem

While Housing Executive support was crucial for the WBHA's existence there were other factors leading to its downfall. In the second half of 1973, the political situation quietened and, as normality returned, people found that a direct approach to the Housing Executive was often as likely to work as going through a para-military organization.

But probably the most crucial factor was that at this time the para-military organizations saw no role for themselves beyond a military one. The aim was to defeat the IRA to enable a return to 'normal politics'. But normal politics,, as some were beginning to realise, meant the exploitation of the working class. There were always isolated individuals and groups, such as the Ulster Citizens Army, within the Protestant community who put forward this viewpoint, and usually ended up getting shot. As far as the majority were concerned it was better to be an exploited labour aristocracy than simply to be exploited. This meant a coalition with the remnants of the Orange system. Any talks of a socialist solution not only threatened this coalition but implied an accommodation with the Republican movement which was pledged to destroy what remained of the Orange state. In practical terms it meant that on somewhere such as the Shankill it was okay to advocate policies which stressed the need for the Protestant working class to get a better deal as long as these were not identified as 'socialist' or 'communist'. In other words the reforms that were demanded by the Protestant working class were not revolutionary but social-democratic in that they asked for greater equality within the existing system.

Therefore though the UDA at this time had the power to push for community control on most social issues, something that Westminster would only have been too happy to have supported since it would have made the UDA reponsible members of the community; there was no theoretical basis for such actions.

The next stage of the fight over redevelopment reverted back to the plans for the Shankill area. A basically petty bourgeoise grouping of councillors, redevelopment associations, concerned community workers etc. came together on the premise that given the changes planned for the Shankill the best thing that could be done was to attempt to negotiate, from as strong a base as possible, the maximum number of alterations to the plans.

All the parties to this grouping were basically social-democratic in so far as they believed that state institutions and policies were reformable by action, protest, influence etc. through the appropriate channels. Some believed in a consensus view of politics, that different classes and groups had basically similar goals and values. Others took a pluralist view where different interest groups were seen to compete between each other for resources and what was therefore required was for the Protestant working class to put their case more strongly than in the past.

Within the pluralist standpoint there were those who thought that it was sufficient to simply participate more effectively using the accepted channels. These and the consensus politicians therefore emphasized the need for negotiation and a rational discussion of the facts. Then it was up to those vested with authority by the state—politicians, planners etc. to listen to the arguments put forward by different interest groups, discuss alternatives with them on the basis of the available facts and from this produce a 'best fit' solution. This was the position taken by the Housing Executive which, when it eventually moved from a policy of public relations to one of participation, saw this as involving discussions with community groups of how, within given limitations, the best plans could be produced.

135

There were others who operated within a pluralist framework who argued that as all groups did not start off with either equal resources or access and influence with decision makers, it was not sufficient for working class groups to use the normal channels to bring about a change in the way resources were distributed. What was needed instead was direct action even if it lead to conflict.

In the United Kingdom as a whole this latter model best fits the growth of community action and in particular the activities of the squatters. In Belfast the struggle described in the last chapter by local groups to get houses repaired is a good example of a progression from a consensus to a conflict model reflecting a shift in thinking about the housing authorities from 'people on our side doing their best in difficult circumstances' to 'them who are out to exploit us'

Of the parties who made up this grouping the two who clearly supported the consensus model were the Churches and the Shankill Community Council. Given the delayed introduction of monopoly capital into Northern Ireland, traditional values, reflecting the almost feudal social relations which went with the Orange system, remained strong. While some fundamentalists were opposed to the increasing materialism, recognising quite correctly that it would destroy their power base, the majority of churchmen believed as always that it was the job of the church to adapt itself to the dominant set of values in the state They were therefore in favour of collaborating with the state and consequently were always one of the first community bodies that the state courted when it went participating. Church bodies never raised more than token opposition to the fates destined for their parishoners.

The Shankill Community Council was set up in 1971 by voluntary and full-time workers in community organizations in the Shankill area. Its position was clear cut. It saw its task as "helping the community and the statutory authorities to come together to make something better out of this redevelopment." The reason why it adopted this approach can be clearly seen in the make-up of the Council's executive committee and officers Of these, six were full-time youth or community workers and of the four others, two were clergymen, one was an accountant and only one person was a local working class person. As all of the people on the Council, with one exception, saw their job as being to help the state work better, they readily adopted a consensus model and hence were also to the forefront of the list of suitable courting partners for the state.

But the Shankill Community Council didn't speak for anyone. Of the thirteen people concerned with its running only three actually lived on the Shankill itself. Executive members were elected from the votes of 50-100 people who were in no way representative of the Shankill Road people. The Council itself was dominated by three of the many social welfare organizations on the road and these three were often bickering between themselves For a long time it had no contact with any of the para-military groups even though these were the local groups with the widest following.

Two of the other parties to this grouping adopted mixed approaches. The first of these were the local shopkeepers, whom as Chapter 4 showed were threatened with annihilation if the plans went through. Shopkeepers not surprisingly therefore played an important role in setting up the UDA and establishing links between it and other Protestant bodies opposed to the economic changes. As far as the local plans were concerned the local traders association had had in the early 1970's a series of discussions with the then chief planner for Belfast who told them that their interests would be protected and he would keep them informed of any developments: that was the last they heard from him. In the meantime the City Council quietly forgot the pledges it had made to protect their interests.

These pledges were:

As far as the letting of new shops went the Committee decided that

"existing shopkeepers should, in the first instance be asked to tender for the new shops and if their offers were considered reasonable by the Committee . . . allocation would be made accordingly. Offers would then be invited by public advertisement for any shops not so allocated"[3] and again, Building Design Partnership recommended

"(i) the continuation of the policy of acquisition in appropriate cases of property affected by redevelopment and road proposals in advance of clearance date and the short period of lease of their property to the owners of tenants at reasonable rent until such time as they could move.

(ii) the establishment of an office accessible to the public, adequately staffed to deal with possibly 2,000 business relocation problems in the next 10 years . . .

(iii) a policy of acquisition of suitable property unaffected by redevelopment which at low cost could be converted to accommodate at economic rents those businesses displaced by public action, for both temporary and permanent use. Such properties might be factories or warehouses . . .

After discussion . . . the Committee accepted the report in principle, subject to the Corporation obtaining such legal powers as might be necessary to give effect thereto."[4]

The fact that the second and third of these recommendations were never acted on, is yet another indication of how the petty bourgeoise interests were losing out. The vesting order inquiries went ahead for the new Shankill shopping centre without the traders being fully aware of what was going on. By the time they woke up it was virtually too late.

The traders found themselves split five ways. A few had argued that the best way to protect their interests was on the political level and had put their energies into either one of the para-military bodies such as the UDA or one of the recognised parliamentary parties such as the DUP. Their intention was to fight for a return to pre-1968 conditions where the Orange system controlled the state and their interests were at least in part protected. A second lot of traders, the more profitable ones, felt they had a chance of making it in the new centre and were not therefore opposed to it being built. The next lot, those who were doing okay and were alert as to what was happening, had taken sites further up the road just outside the redevelopment area. Then a further group of smaller shopkeepers,

137

particularly those near retiring age, decided to call it a day. This then left a small and ever dwindling number of shopkeepers who weren't quite sure what to do. They were prepared to offer lukewarm support to any action aimed at saving the Shankill Road but, because of their past experience, they had little expectation that it would amount to much. They were prepared to lend their name to fighting the public inquiry but were more dubious about supporting more direct action. They were caught between realising that some such action was required if their shops were to be preserved but not wanting to be party to illegal actions which would at a future date count against them, when and if, normal political relations returned.

The next party were the local councillors. By 1973 these had split into three groups. The traditional middle class Unionists who showed no real concern for local issues unless there was money to be made and who were therefore on the side of the different state authorities. The Alliance and NILP councillors who at local level would take a middle of the road Labour party stand i.e. community involvement but only to the extent of modifying plans, not altering them to reflect different interests; and finally the various 'Loyalist' councillors who all were in slightly different ways allied to the old orange system and derived their power from being able to make the system work for them. They basically believed that it was possible to do the same with the new centralised bodies such as the Housing Executive without realising that they owed allegiance to a totally different set of interests.

Therefore in general the Loyalist councillors preferred to meet with authorities to negotiate 'deals'. They tended though to oscillate between such deals and going along with the more direct action approach of the WBHA. This was because they were caught between trying to strengthen their position at the base of the government system by making deals favourable to their clients and realising that the system as they knew it was under attack and that more direct action was needed if it was to survive.

The final parties were the redevelopment associations. There were three of these in the Shankill area. The original attempt was to have one association for each of the redevelopment areas and they were set up around a key person in one of the local neighbourhoods which made up the communities in which they were based. Even though attempts were made, as the last chapter showed, to broaden the operating base of the groups, the rivalry between different neighbourhoods meant that it was difficult for any other neighbourhood to give the association more than partial support.

The redevelopment associations had many weaknesses in addition to their limited neighbourhood base. First of all they were only formed after blight had started when many people had already left the area. Therefore a large proportion of their membership came from the elderly. Secondly the associations were set up to tackle immediate problems and the demands these made upon their resources meant that they had little time, energy or interest in combating the longer term plans for the area. Throughout the attempts to save the Shankill, one of the greatest difficulties was that local people became bogged down in immediate problems which required action. There were many reasons for this: the sheer quantity of hardship cases requiring assistance; the lack of time that over-committed people had in which to do the necessary thinking and research; that political credibility was assessed in terms of actions where everyone could see the results (who could assess the significance of moving a couple of lines on a plan?) and perhaps most important of all, a lack of a theoretical perspective enabling them to understand how and why the changes were occurring and what could be done to stop them.

A further problem with the redevelopment associations was that people were always leaving the area especially after vesting was confirmed. The leaders were often among the first to go. It is difficult to know to what extent they were offered houses because they tended to be the most pushy or how far it was a deliberate tactic on the part of the housing authorities to break up the associations.

During 1973/4 the grouping representing these parties was involved in two major participatory exercises. The first was the public inquiry into the vesting of area 11 and 33 which was held in March 1973, the second a series of negotiations over the detailed plans drawn up by the Development division of the Housing Executive as to how the Shankill would look after redevelopment.

Though the public inquiry is the only stage in the redevelopment process where those affected by the plans have a statutory right to participate, many local people felt that it was a waste of time to do so because, 'they would never listen to us'. There was no question of opposing the inquiry. With 95 per cent of the houses unfit people wanted vesting to take place as quickly as possible so that they were at least entitled to compensation when blight forced them to leave. To some extent people were correct to be sceptical as to the value of such inquiries. At the inquiry into the vesting of Area A in 1960 the local people appeared and asked for; rehabilitation and not redevelopment; if redevelopment then community renewal street by street and the retention of shops along the front of Peters Hill and houses instead of flats. They got widespread redevelopment, no shops on Peters Hill and flats.

Part of the reason for this is that the main purpose of the public inquiry under the then redevelopment legislation was to show that houses in the area were so unfit that comprehensive redevelopment was required. Where the existing housing was concerned all the authorities were required to do was to provide an action area plan showing proposed land use and containing a statement of aims on how the area was to be redeveloped. Hence detailed discussions as to the type of new housing were not officially part of the proceedings. But housing types was one of the main areas of concern that local people had.

A further problem was that three of the major land uses in the action area plan were also outside the scope of the inquiry. The first of these was the road system. Areas 11 and 33 were affected by the Travers Morgan transportation plan. The Shankill on the Southern side of the area was to be busier. Agnes Street was to become a district distributor cutting the area in two, while on the northern boundary the Crumlin Road was due to become a six lane primary distributor. In addition because of the projected increase in car ownership, more land was having to be reserved for car parking.

The second was the district shopping centre which was going to replace the shops along the front of the Shankill Road and the third was a new school. The amount of land required by the roads, the district centre and a new secondary school meant that the land available for housing was reduced from 58 per cent of the total to 44 per cent.

Now the roads and district centres were part of the BDP and Travers Morgan development plans for Belfast and as such had already been subjected to a public inquiry. Since the Housing Executive was bound by the development plan the only land use which was part of the inquiry was that devoted to housing.

The result was that the issues which most concerned local people had been ruled out of court before the inquiry started. The Hammer Redevelopment Association carried out a 50 per cent door to door survey of the area. The survey showed that 68 per cent of the people in the area wanted to be rehoused where they were. Therefore the amount of land available for housing was crucial. The survey, reflecting the high proportion of elderly people left in the area, found that two of the items they were most concerned about were the distances they would have to walk to get to the shops and to see the doctor. Hence the centralization of facilities was important.

As regards the type of housing that people wanted the survey showed that of those who wanted to be rehoused in the area, half wanted only terraced housing, a quarter were prepared to live in ground floor flats and one in ten in upper floors of three storey blocks. But according to the Housing Executive's aim for housing in the area presented at the inquiry which were based on Building Design Partnership's plans it:

"recommends the establishment of a density standard for public housing in the Redevelopment Areas of 115 habitable rooms per acre, i.e. 125 persons per acre net including 15 per cent to 20 per cent high rise accommodation dwelling units (above four to five stories) and 80 per cent to 85 per cent in two to four storey dwellings."

Because of the earlier protests the City Council had decided that there were not going to be any tower blocks. The statement of aims therefore lamely concludes; in mid sentence:

"It is, however, clear that residents of the Shankill are not prepared to accept any "point block" development and are therefore, depending on the detailed layouts produced by the Northern Ireland Housing Executive,"

But detailed housing layouts did not have to be presented at the inquiry. Therefore the community did not know what was going to be suggested instead—all it could do was say what it would like to see.

Given all of these difficulties, what were the reasons for going ahead and participating? The first was that there was nothing to lose and as it was up to the inspector conducting the inquiry to decide what was or was not permissible evidence there seemed a good chance of the community

140

being able to put its points across. At least then it would be on record that these objections existed and this might make it more difficult for the Housing Executive to rail-road unwanted plans through. Secondly it would give the community the chance to cross-examine the Housing Executive and therefore probe weaknesses in their position which could be used later. The only risk that the Hammer Redevelopment Association could see was that by participating in the inquiry, they might delay the whole procedure when people wanted vesting to be confirmed as soon as possible. But it didn't seem as if dragging out the inquiry for another day would matter that much.

The Hammer Redevelopment which was the main body involved in the inquiry decided to base its case around: the type of new housing that people wanted and how the shopping centre was to be developed. In the case of housing the Hammer Redevelopment Association's argument was that the housing design which would best tie in with the people's wishes was low rise, high density housing with nothing over 4 stories in height. In the case of the shopping centre the argument was that if it had to exist then it ought to be built by the state rather than property developers and all the space within it reserved for local traders at subsidised rents.

The Hammer Redevelopment Association got active support from some of the local councillors and the passive support of the Shankill Traders Association. The actual case and the cross-examination was handled by a leading solicitor who agreed to do it for minimum costs. The witnesses consisted of the Professor of Planning at Queen's University, a community worker and three local residents.

The inquiry took place in March 1973, the Inspector reported in June and the next the local people heard about it was in December when it was announced that the vesting order had been granted. The actual Inspector's report is not made public but according to informed sources his recommendations were that: replacement housing should not exceed four stories in height; the quality and size of the shopping provision and the rental arrangements for the new shops should be related as far as possible to the needs of the area; the area should be planned to minimise the distances from homes to shops and doctors' surgeries and that adequate provision should be made for elderly people.

Therefore most of the points that were made seemed to have been taken. The crucial test though would lie in what the detailed plans contained. According to the November 1973 plans for the area produced by the Housing Executive none of the dwellings were to be above 4 stories in height. However, the key argument had been that people wanted to live in houses rather than flats or maisonettes. Yet according to the plans only 40 per cent of the dwellings were to be houses, 34 per cent flats and 26 per cent maisonettes. The plan had nothing to say on the shopping centre as such but in the meantime the Ministry had endorsed the concept of the district centre without announcing any changes in how they were built or financed. As regards the decentralization of shopping there was only one corner shop and one small parade of shops outside the district centre planned for the area.

So was it worth participating in the inquiry? The actual gains in terms of what the area would look like after redevelopment were minimal. Neither was there much increased local awareness as a result of participating in the inquiry. The number of people actively involved in the public inquiry was minimal. Though people in the area were informed of what was happening through public meetings and leaflets the inquiry didn't mean much. Firstly people were much more concerned with immediate problems such as getting repairs done. Secondly it was difficult for people to see what the fuss was about given that the houses hadn't even been vested. Anyway public inquiries weren't anything that concerned them—it was either: irrelevant; or what would be, would be, irrespective of what they did; or fighting the inquiry was what their councillors were elected for. As we shall see later much more was achieved once local people decided to take their objections outside the correct channels.

Even for those more actively involved the inquiry had little value.

This was due firstly to the way the inquiry was handled. The inspector, the housing authorities and the solicitors all sat around tables at the front of the room, everyone else sat in chairs at the back cut off from what was happening. Secondly the language was often technical, there were no photos or models to make the plans more real and there was little drama to excite interest. Thirdly it was probably a mistake employing a lawyer—the extra skill that he brought was not worth the effect of having someone else imposing themselves between the people and what was going on. Finally the nine months delay in between when the inquiry was held and anything was seen to happen meant that even those involved could see no relationship between the inquiry and any subsequent plans.

The grouping of interests that participated in the inquiry never really functioned as a group—they all simply leant support to the case being made by the Hammer Redevelopment Association. In the next participation exercise a core group did develop around the councillors. The background to this exercise was that from early 1973 onwards, the Housing Executive achitect responsible for the area began to produce detailed plans for the new Shankill.

The first plans for areas 12/13 produced in March 1973 contained 18 blocks of flats/maisonettes, five to six stories high. Altogether excluding old age pensioner dwellings, 73 per cent of the new dwellings were to be flats or maisonettes. But most people wanted to live in terraced housing. Therefore if these plans were not to go ahead as they were, there needed to be a group representing Shankill interests to oppose them. The first group set up was centred on the three redevelopment associations but this didn't really work as they were too involved with short term problems such as repairs. It was therefore decided to widen the group to include local councillors, the redevelopment associations and the Shankill Community Council.

A preliminary meeting was held to thrash out a common approach which was that

"the best solution therefore seems to be to demand that the plans for areas 12 and 13 are redrawn so that at least 65 per cent of the dwellings are houses and that no buildings are more than 4 stories high even if this means that fewer people are going to get back."

At the first full meeting held at the City Hall in November 1973, 10 members of the local group, one of whom was chairman, met with 4 members of the Housing Executive. The result of the meeting, according to a summary that I prepared, and which the chairman agreed was a fair report was that:

"It was therefore agreed that

(a) around about 65 per cent of the dwellings in areas 12 and 13 should be houses . . .

(b) if the Belfast transportation and shopping policies were not changed and noise barriers were necessary then alternative methods to six storey blocks of flats should be looked at . . .

(c) no flats where possible should be over 4 stories high . . ."

Therefore it appeared, in the face of all one's doubts, that the participation had been a success. However, on the 16th November I received a letter from the Acting Director of Development, who had been present at the meeting, which said:

"I cannot accept as a statement of fact, the numbers and percentages stated in (3a) and (3b). Moreover I cannot guarantee that my architect will achieve these estimates with low rise development. Nevertheless I am willing to guarantee that they will try to house as many families 'on ground' as possible."

But why the climb down?

It couldn't really have been that the 4 Housing Executive members heard something from the ten members of the local group. Much more likely that it was simply a negotiating strategy—to make verbal agreements at meetings in order to buy off the opposition which could then be refuted at leisure if the deal no longer proved to be feasible.

The redevelopment groups had also run into the same sort of problem before with the architect for the Shankill area who had also been present at the above meeting. This had concerned arrangements for the earlier set of meetings between him and the redevelopment groups.

On the 29th May he had written to me that:

"You will appreciate, however, I will be unable to attend at regular fortnightly meetings but I will be available on occasions . . ."

But as my reply pointed out:

"Have just received your letter of the 29th May. It is both Mr. Stevens (the CRC field officer for the area) and my recollection of our meeting with you that what we had agreed was that what we would start with were fortnightly meetings but if there wasn't sufficient material to discuss then the meetings would become less frequent as nobody wanted to waste time on unproductive sessions."

But to return to the correspondence arising from the November meeting. I replied to the Acting Director of Development that·

"I doubt whether from the communities' point of view it is more 'useful' to talk in terms of 'ground access' and 'off ground dwellings'. There is a clear preference for a particular type of dwelling, i.e. houses over both flats and maisonettes and this difference is blurred if the former way of referring to dwellings is used . . .

While one agrees that it is not possible to commit the Executive to precise figures, it is our recollection of the meeting that it was agreed by all parties that in the region of two thirds of the proposed dwellings would be houses and that this was possible to achieve with low rise development especially as densities would be reduced to about 95-105 ppa/net."

And just to finish the tale, on the 11th December the reply from him stated that:

"I regret that I still cannot bind the Housing Executive to precise figures or even estimated figures at this stage except to say that generally speaking at 95-105 ppa (net) it is possible to obtain the proportion of houses that you state. However there are other factors such as parking provision, access roads and adjoining land use which effect this."

There were another couple of meetings which looked at the plans for the first phase of areas 12/13. The group agreed that these could go ahead because over 60 per cent of the dwellings were houses. But approval was conditional on all plans for further phases being similarly approved.

The meetings faded out early in 1974. There were a number of reasons for this. Firstly, the group felt that it had made good progress i.e. that the participation had produced meaningful changes in the plans presented to them and that there was not much point in meeting again until there were new plans to be looked at. But though there were changes towards more houses and fewer flats being built, overall the changes did not amount to that much. No firm commitment existed that plans would attempt to get everyone back in low rise housing if this were technically possible. Secondly, there had been no progress on saving the Shankill Road as a shopping street or, if they proved necessary, on alternative 'barrier blocks' to flats. There had been little discussion on piece-meal redevelopment nor on the relationship between new physical structures such as high rise flats and possible resultant social patterns such as the isolation of housewives—there was little attempt to learn from what was going wrong with the new Shankill estate.

Among the reasons why these points were never raised was the fact that the group was always working from the existing plans drawn up by the housing authorities according to their ideas and regulations about what people wanted or ought to have. This development occurred because the grouping believed from the beginning in compromise and this meant that the meetings became technical discussions i.e. in what ways is it possible to adapt these plans, rather than debates on principle, i.e. who has the right to deny people the type of housing that they want. As soon as it became a technical discussion the group could never hope to achieve much because they could always be out manoeuvred in terms of both knowledge and regulations. This was further emphasised by the way some group members got seduced. In meetings with the group, the community worker had attempted to expain to them something about the way plans were drawn up. The effect was that people who previously would have either accepted or rejected a plan on very simple criteria were now inclined to enter into discussion over different aspects of the plan. Because they now had some knowledge, they no longer felt it was possible to reject plans unless there were technical reasons for doing so. Nor did they find it easy to admit that they didn't know what the planners were sometimes on about. Having been initiated into the planner's world they were forced to recognise that the planners knew more than they did, while at the same time they recognised a certain comradeship with the planners which tended to cut them off from their electorate.

The second reason why the meetings faded out was the changing political climate. During the reign of the short-lived Assembly in the first part of 1974 there was intense opposition in the Protestant community against the arrangement, especially the Irish dimension. This tended to push other problems into the background. The opposition eventually culminated in the Ulster Workers' Strike. Though the political parties soon regained control, those local politicians who had participated in the running of the state were now, during the period of increased working class consciousness, looked at suspiciously as it was felt that they had let the people down. Thus the councillors were no longer felt to represent people's interests.

The only effective opposition to what was happening to the Shankill could now come from the Protestant para-military groups and the Ulster Workers Council (UWC). At the end of 1974 these groups came together, along with members from the UUUC (the United Ulster Unionist Coalition), the Shankill Community Council and the churches to form the Save the Shankill Campaign.

STS could only hope to succeed to the extent that the para-military groups and the UWC dominated it. Both the Churches and the Shankill Community Council were likely to go for a compromise. But more than that was now needed. Though in the past as a result of the councillor led campaign, the maximum height of dwellings had been reduced to 4 stories, in the latest plans for areas 12/13, 59 per cent of the dwellings were still going to be flats or maisonettes.

The coalition of interests at a local level between the para-military groups, the UWC and the UUUC reflected what was happening at a province wide level. Here the coalition was based on the groups all being united together politically in wanting to see a solution which protected different Protestant interests. These included: old Protestant capital represented largely by Vanguard; agricultural interests represented by Harry West's Unionist Party; petty bourgeoise interests represented by the Democratic Unionist Party and that of the Protestant labour aristocracy by the Ulster Workers Council.

It was therefore a rearguard action being fought by those whose economic position was threatened by the changing industrial base. This was reinforced by the political changes being forced on the province by Westminster together with the IRA guerilla campaign which looked like forcing Protestants into a Catholic dominated state. At the local level it was now recognised that traditional Unionism aided by the British government was prepared to destroy the Shankill and it was up to local people to save it as no one else would.

As regards the redevelopment areas the STS had two main aims—to get rid of all flats and maisonettes from the plans and to retain what was left of the Shankill as a shopping street. After a number of preliminary meetings the STS campaign really got under way when the Housing Executive changed the phasing plans for areas 12/13, placing the front of the road in the next phase. This meant the destruction of the remainder of the lower Shankill as a shopping street and the end of the Shankill Road as a community centre.

The STS switched to the attack and in two months, by the end of March 1975, had achieved both of its main aims. There were to be no more flats or maisonettes built on the Shankill and no buildings more than 2 stories high. The phasing order for the Lower Shankill had been reversed, all existing shops were to be given 5 year leases and the same offer was to apply to anyone re-opening a bricked up shop or erecting a temporary store on a site where existing shops had been demolished on that part of the Shankill Road.

So why did the STS succeed where earlier campaigns had largely failed? The main reason was that the STS had sufficient power to thwart the housing authorities. When the Housing Executive announced its intention of knocking down the rest of the shops on the Lower Shankill, the STS retaliated by 'blacking' all demolition work on the Shankill. They made it clear that any bulldozer that came onto the Road without the permission of the STS would be destroyed. The STS were thus in the position of being able to stop not only the shops being knocked down but also to control the speed of the housing clearance programme. In the short term this put the STS in a very strong position as the Housing Executive was under pressure to do something about its poor building record. In the longer term though the Housing Executive could turn the tactic against them by appealing directly to the Shankill people on the grounds that the STS were stopping them getting new houses.

The STS's power stemmed firstly from the UWC which was the body which actually blacked the demolition work. The strength derived from the June 1974 strike which brought down the Northern Ireland Assembly and made people aware of the potential strength of the Protestant working class community. This power was backed by that of the para-military groups who were able to operate only because of the British government's desire to avoid direct confrontation with the Protestants. Thus the power the STS had and their ability to use it was a direct consequence of the struggle taking place at the provincial level.

A second power lever that the STS possessed was that one councillor, Hughie Smyth, who acted as a spokesman for one of the para-military groups, was prepared to regard himself as operating, on the question of the planning of the Shankill, under the direction of the STS. He also happened to be vice-chairman of the Committee concerned with planning on Belfast council. Though, since re-organization this committee only had advisory powers, it still saw all the plans and it would have been unlikely that the Ministry would have approved a plan that the Council planning

146

committee had rejected. Therefore any time the Housing Executive attempted to force through a plan which was not to the liking of the STS, the STS arranged for the Committee to reject it or at least postpone a decision on it.

Therefore for the first time the Shankill was in a position to bargain from strength. The STS could stop the plans and their implementation. The obvious Housing Executive response was to set up meetings.

The second reason that the STS won was that it changed the basis of the meetings. From the beginning the STS were clear what they wanted the plans to contain. This was what all surveys had shown the majority of Shankill people wanted—two storey terrace housing designed around a neighbourhod unit. The STS arranged for alternative plans, incorporating this idea, to be drawn up by sympathetic academic planners who were prepared to take the people's demands as their guidelines. Armed with these plans the STS were now in a position to change the argument from one about technicalities i.e. we can't change X because of Y, to one about why people of the Shankill can't have the plans they want. It then became clear that the only reason was that the authorities were not prepared to accept that participation meant that communities had the right to design for themselves the types of houses they wanted. But given the power the STS had, there was little the Housing Executive could do about it and their plans got redrawn.

The success of the STS campaign can be seen from the following table:

Plans for areas 12/13	Maximum planned height of dwellings	% of dwellings which were to be flats/maisonettes excluding A.P.D.'s
1. BDP: Redevelopment of the Shankill 1968	15 stories	60% +
2. Draft NIHE Plans after the success of the Shankill Redevelopment Association 1972	6 stories	76%
3. Draft NIHE Plans March 1973	6 stories	73%
4. 1974 Draft NIHE Plans after the councillor led protests	4 stories	59%
5. February 1974 Draft Plans for Phase 1	3 stories	37%
6. February 1975 Draft plans for Phase 1 after the STS campaign	2 stories	0
7. March 1975 Agreement reached between Housing Executive and the STS for the rest of the Shankill still to be redeveloped	2 stories	0

It is now time to move on and take a more general view of the whole question of participation and who benefits from it.

The first question that needs asking is why does the state decide to set up participation exercises? The usual reason advanced is that people should have a right to have a say in the plans which affect their life. Agreed, but that doesn't explain why the housing authorities in Northern Ireland became interested in the idea in 1972 while before, generally speaking, people got what the planners designed for them and that was that. The answer is that in Northern Ireland as across the water, participation became fashionable when local authorities, wanting to proceed with unpopular measures, found that there was strong local opposition to them.

Participation then became an attempt to buy the opposition off. This was made very clear at one meeting held between the Belfast Urban Study Group and Travers Morgan when local groups were preventing the motorway going ahead. The Travers Morgan representatives congratulated BUS on the work they were doing providing information for community groups on the transportation plan and said that if BUS hadn't been doing this, then they would have had to consider employing people to do similar work. The reason for this was that as the local groups were strong enough to stop the motorway and as the local council had supported their position, an attempt had to be made to win them over. This could only be done if the groups had some knowledge of the subject. Hence BUS, which at that time still believed that logically demolishing the case against the motorway was necessary to have it stopped, was unwittingly lending support to those who were for it. The Minister, acting for these interests, wanted the level of argument changed from one where locals perceived the motorway as a road being imposed on them to one where it was seen as a necessary evil and the efforts of local groups would be appreciated in helping to mitigate its worst effects.

Similarly in the housing field, the need for the housing authorities to participate was related to the break-up of the orange system. Previously under the rule of the monolithic Unionist party, participation as such tended to be through local councillors who, because of their powers of patronage, were key people in the community. But when the para-military and other community groups were set up and with the disbandment of Stormont, the break-up of the Unionist party and the re-organisation of local government, city councillors could no longer deliver the goods. As far as the authorities were concerned they could no longer guarantee the compliance of local people and as far as the local people were concerned they were unable to deliver the services such as houses, jobs etc. which the Orange system enabled them to do. In order therefore to get the communities' agreement to the planned changes for Belfast, that few of them wanted, it was necessary to deal directly with them. Thus according to the Housing Executive:

"the active co-operation of tenants and communities is also essential, and the Executive will do all that it can to encourage responsible and enlightened attitudes by stimulating an informed dialogue with tenants associations."[5]

But exactly what are 'responsible and enlightened attitudes'? A clue comes in a statement made by the ex-Director of Development, Rae Evans in an interview:[6]

"We are one step nearer the reality of having to deal all day with the public and politicians (who may indeed have unrealistic expectations, stimulated by some third-rate planners and/or academics)"

Therefore the Housing Executive was prepared to participate but preferred it to be with groups who agreed with them. This explains why they were so quick to drop the West Belfast Housing Association and so eager to embrace bodies such as the Shankill Community Council.

Even when the Housing Executive was forced to negotiate with the Shankill as a result of the STS campaign, they tried first of all to set up meetings with the local councillors whom they knew would approve the Housing Executive's modified plans. The STS overcame this manoeuvre both by calling a public meeting and march to show that they, and not the councillors, commanded the main body of support and by pointing out that most of the councillors, that the Housing Executive was meeting with, represented wards in parts of the Shankill outside the redevelopment areas.

As part of the same participation process, the need for neighbourhood councils is now stressed in England as an important part of an effective local democracy. But there is little point in voting people onto a body unless it has power to do something. The motivation for neighbourhood councils comes from the 'powers to be' who realise that with the reorganization of local government that a power vacuum exists at the level below district councils and if they don't fill it then it could become the domain of radical groupings. The advantage of an elected neighbourhood council is that it is likely to attract petty bourgeoise elements onto it. Broady[7] for example quotes studies of Halifax and Glasgow where white collar workers held a disproportionate percentage of leadership positions in community organizations. These people will see their job as being to collaborate with the system. The authorities can then legitimately claim that they can only feed resources into the area and negotiate with the elected representatives thus forcing more radical groupings to collaborate with the neighbourhood council if they want to get anything done.

Participation therefore is little more than one further strategy in the state's armoury to persuade people to do things which aren't in their interst —though the whole point of the participation exercise is to convince them otherwise. In order to persuade community groups to participate the state employs community workers. The biggest showpiece effort so far in Britain are the Home Office Comunity Development Projects which were originally conceived

"as a modest attempt at action research into the better understanding and more comprehensive tackling of social needs, especially in local communities within the older urban areas, through closer co-ordination of control and local official and unofficial effort, informed and stimulated by citizen initiative and involvement."[8]

Northern Ireland had its own Community Relations Commission with its community development approach. At first its Chairman and Director believed that it would be possible to use this approach to produce significant change but by 1972 they had both learnt better and resigned. The new Director saw the situation differently

"the Commission's first responsibility is to advise the Administration on strategies which may help community relations. Its second responsibility is to the community itself . . ."[9]

But despite the efforts by the Commission to make sure the field staff restricted their activities to working with reformist groups, many of the staff were actively working with the para-military groups. During the short reign of the Assembly these workers became such a threat, that in April 1974 the then Minister of Community Relations, Ivan Cooper, announced that the Commission would be wound up.

The state, where possible, prefers to employ its community workers directly so that it can keep a tighter control of them. Already some of the English CDP projects have gone 'left'. Therefore community workers are normally employed by local authority housing, planning, education and social service departments. In Northern Ireland in addition to these agencies, there was a Ministry of Community Relations; whose task was

"to secure acceptance of the Government by the people. Given that a significant minority of the population is distrustful and suspicious of Government it is particularly important that there should be a direct means of communication between Government and people."[10]

which also employed community workers. As the Community Relations Commission's field staff became more radical, the Ministry cut down the funds available to them, built up its own staff and gave them access to moneys made available under the Social Needs Act (Northern Ireland's equivalent to the Urban Aid programme). The Ministry's field staff were usually therefore in a position to bid for community groups' allegiances by promising them more resources than other workers could offer.

Under 'normal' political conditions the state is in a position to persuade most groups to participate in some way with it. This changes if the situation becomes more polarised. Then the same field workers whose job was to help community groups work with the state, are now told in effect to spy on those groups who no longer co-operate. They thus become agents of direct rather than indirect state control. This can be seen in Northern Ireland with the Ministry of Community Relations field staff. The idea for them to exist:

"lies not with the Ministry but with the Army. It is reliably believed that the inspiration for, what were then called, Civilian Liaison Officers came from Brigadier Kitson."[11]

According to one such official:
"the purpose of these appointments is that whenever anybody comes to the Army with any complaint whatsoever they will be immediately referred to the Civilian Liaison Officer . . . in fact I suspect that this idea of providing a feedback on conditions and attitudes and so on through these Officers to Mr. X (a civil servant) in the Cabinet Office may be the primary reason for these appointments."[12]

In addition both the police and the army had their own community relations field staff who were continually popping up at community meetings. At one small meeting on the Shankill, according to one community worker, three of the six people present were non local people in civilian clothes, one she recognised as a police community relations officer, while two she had never seen before. Half way through the meeting a senior ranked Army Officer walked in and the two strangers stood up. It appeared that one of them was the departing community relations officer of the local army regiment and the other was his replacement. The army, police and ministry community officers all had regular joint meetings at which they exchanged information.

The second big question is what is there to participate about. In Belfast the crucial factors affecting people on the Shankill were related to changes in the economic base of the province which had been taking place since the turn of the century. The actual plans they opposed were devised to suit the needs of monopoly capital interests and put into effect by political parties and bureaucracies who represented these interests. But there had been no local participation in producing these plans. Participation only was permitted at the level of detail. Hence it was possible to talk about the line of a road but not whether the road was needed. It was alright to argue over whether people should be rehoused in flats or houses— no dominant interests were threatened here. All that was at stake was bureaucratic efficiency and professional pride. It was not alright to dispute the need for district centres where large commercial interests were at stake.

As a general rule, the more important an issue is to the needs of the ruling interests the less participation there is for those who might be opposed to it. For example with development and structural plans where crucial land use decisions for a city or region are made, participation is limited. One way this is done is by arguing that the public does not have sufficient knowledge to make a worthwhile contribution at this level. This argument was used by the Inspector at the 1972 public inquiry into the Belfast Urban Area Plan:

"There is room for argument over assumptions and predictions and only the lapse of time can prove them right or wrong but these appear to have been made by experts using the best available techniques . . . there is a limit to participation if anything is ever to be finalised. The Public, as many of them admitted, are not experts in general nor can they be expected to always grasp the full consequence of their points of view on the Plan as a whole but the tremendous value of their contribution lies in the fact that they speak from experience in their own environment . . . no plan will ever be wholly acceptable to an entire community and to place fully prepared and documented alternatives before the public would involve much time, money and resources and could result in a disadvantageous slowing down of all development . . . It was suggested that the public could not reasonably expect to have access to all the detailed processes of evaluation leading to the formulation of a plan and must of necessity rely to a large extent upon the skill and integrity of the consultants.'[13]

A more direct method of control of participation happens with reference to the new structure plans where the Secretary of State has reserved the right to decide not only what matters will be discussed at the public examination of the plan but also who will be allowed to participate.

Thus at this level where crucial land use decisions are made effective participation is restricted to the public inquiry and that is controlled by the state. There will be mock participation exercises e.g. surveys, public meetings, displays of maps and models etc., but unless those who participate have the power to force through the changes they want then such participation can never be more than a sham exercise. To assume otherwise is to believe that the state mediates between a plurality of interests rather than that it represents industrial interests.

It is therefore argued that the role of the state is to force through changes beneficial to ruling class interests. Participation is simply one tactic used by various state bodies to persuade opposition groups to go along with these changes. Any participation beyond the minimum laid down by law is dependent at least on the ability to prevent something from happening such as happened with the first phase of the Belfast Urban motorway. But it then no longer makes sense to talk of participation. Participation implies a willingness of both sides to meet, underlying at some level a perceived communality of values. But where it is a conflict, where people are fighting to prevent a set of values being forced upon them, it makes much more sense to talk of negotiation which is simply one tactic that sides use at a particular stage of a conflict when they perceive that they might gain from using it.

Ultimately the state has access to the law which can be used to jail strikers and ban picketing and the state can use the police to harass people

"Peaceful picketing in the street is illegal unless done in the course of a trade dispute, Mr. Justice Forbes ruled in High Court chambers yesterday . . . This is the first court ruling in modern times on the legality of non-industrial picketing . . . there was no right to use the street or pavement for political demonstrations . . . Mr. Justice Forbes said . . . nevertheless the arrangement to picket was a conspiracy to use the highway unlawfully and a public nuisance against which an injunction would be granted."[14]

But normally the state doesn't have to resort to such methods—a little bit of divide and rule, such as the way the government persuaded the Belfast City Council to change its stand on the motorway, and a lot of buying off—titles, pensions, status, the right to allocate a few houses—it's simple enough while you have the resources and control the socialization process which gives them their value as reinforcers.

153

Chapter 8

WHAT'S IT ALL ABOUT

The previous chapter looked at the success the Save the Shankill (STS) camgaign had had in determining the future layout of the Shankill. This chapter looks briefly at the further demands that the STS might make before it draws together the main themes in the book.

Save the Shankill Demands

The demands that the Save the Shankill campaign can make are limited in terms of their class demands by the need to preserve their links with the UUUC in the fight to maintain their economic position and the Protestant way of life. Within this limitation some further demands that the STS could make, in addition to those successfully fought for already, are firstly that the Belfast Travers Morgan transportation plan be scrapped in totality. As chapter 3 showed the costs of a car based transportation plan—in terms of finance, mobility, pollution, loss of land etc.—fall disproportionately heavily on the working classes. Therefore in place of the existing plan there ought to be one based on public transport. In Belfast such a system would involve: an outer ring road to connect the M1 and M2 motorways, which would also serve as a traffic collar controlling the number of cars entering Belfast as well as providing the basis for a park and ride scheme; policies discouraging people bringing cars into the inner city area such as a reduction in the number of long term parking spaces and a frequent, cheap and comprehensive bus service. This service would include express buses operating on radial and ring roads; dial-a-bus services, that exist for example in Stevenage, and which in Belfast could be based on the existing 'people's taxi services', operating around and between housing estates and connecting with the express buses; the building of bus shelters and the subsidisation of bus fares. More controversial might be schemes to communalise car ownership with cars either being owned by the city, such as was tried in Montpelier in France, where metered cars could be picked up and left at designated parking places or alternatively cars could be owned by community associations and rented out to members. This could be based on the community transport schemes which already exist in cities such as Liverpool.

A second set of demands that the STS could make would be in relation to shopping. It could demand that: the district centre be scrapped and the Shankill retained as a shopping street for existing traders; more corner shops be built and let at subsidised rents to existing shopholders thus recognising the social function that such shops have and that shopkeepers on the Shankill itself, who want to rehabilitate their shops, be entitled to improvement grants.

A third set of demands relate to redevelopment. The STS has already demanded that a neighbourhood base be built into the new housing area plans. But if the aim of the neighbourhood is to enable functional relationships to be created between people with different needs—old people being guardians of the street in return for having errands run for them—then households of different sizes need to live near each other. There are a number of ways that this can be done. The simplest is for houses of different sizes to be built next to each other ie. a two bed, two storey house next to one bed flats suitable for o.p.d.'s etc. While this is in theory possible, few building firms would be prepared to build in this way as they are geared up to produce most economically rows of identical dwellings. Another way would be to have a standard house suitable for nearly all household sizes. The Northern Ireland Housing Executive was thinking at one time of adopting the 3 bed house as its basic design. This was based on the idea of the house the young married couple could move into and which would have sufficient room for all future additions to the family. However, this totally ignores the increasing percentage of the population which requires one bed, accommodation and the overall decrease in family size. It also means that many families will end up with a spare room for much of the time. According to the architect this would be an advantage but many local people simply saw themselves having to pay extra rent for a room they wouldn't need.

It would make much more sense to adopt the 2 bed house as a basic unit. This would make it possible for single people, couples and family units to live beside each other. In order to cope with families who had more than 2 children or 2 children of different sexes, additional bedrooms could be added to the house. There are already a number of different methods in existence to do this. One way is to add a new room to the rear (if terraced) or side (if semi-detached). Another is to leave a large loft space which can be turned into a third bedroom. Yet another is to put all the basic amenities; kitchen; bathroom, etc.; on the ground floor and then have moveable walls on the first storey so that the layout can be adopted to contain 1, 2 or 3 bedrooms. Finally there could be a spare room linking two houses whcih could be blocked off at either end so that it could be used by whichever household needed it. The problem with both the first and last alternatives is that people will be reluctant to give up space (Parkinson's law) once they have got used to it. This applies in the first case where the rooms added on are not permanent, but temporary additions.

The final demands relate to the Upper Shankill area which as long ago as 1968 Building Design Partnership recommended should be an improvement area. While there is an obvious need in Northern Ireland for recent English legislation regarding housing action areas, priority neighbourhoods etc. to be implemented, such measures should only be used within the context of a district plan for the whole area. Without such a plan which takes into account both physical—overcrowding, condition of houses etc.—and social—community and neighbourhood networks—factors; it is impossible to decide what to do with individual groups of streets. One needs first to know what facilities exist or are needed at neighbourhood and community level and whether networks are restricted to one or two streets or are more widespread.

All of the above demands could be made without seriously threatening the coalition with the UUUC. However if the STS were to go and demand that all local shops should where possible be taken over by tenants and run as co-operatives, this would cause splits with the UUUC whose members would see their interests threatened. It is here that the limits of community based social action are reached. Firstly in terms of where the dominant needs of that community are opposed to those of the ruling interests and secondly where demands are put forward which no longer command majority support within the community.

Summary

When the Northern Ireland state came into being in 1921 its economic base lay in the linen, shipbuilding and engineering industries. These industries, for political, geographical and economic reasons were concentrated in the Belfast area. Because of: lack of transportation; low wages and long working hours workers' dwellings were located close to the factories.

As industries remained fairly stable in terms of the skills they required and where they were located, there was little movement of population within cities from one district to another. This enabled close-knit communities to develop over generations in places such as the Shankill which were centred on the extended family and the neighbourhood. Communal living was important as a means of coping with the poverty that existed.

Local government was decentralised reflecting the needs of the orange system—the coalition of landowners, local industrialists, small shopkeepers and landlords—in whose interests the Northern Ireland state was run. The Protestant working class who dominated the labour market joined with the coalition in return for a disproportionate share of jobs, houses and other services the state controlled. These resources tended to be distributed through the community where local councillors and others could influence where jobs and houses went.

From the 1940's onwards this all began to change. The depression in local industries led to foreign capital being invited to invest in the province. In order to make Northern Ireland an attractive site for investment the necessary infrastructure had to be built. In particular this led to the Belfast transportation plan. The new, mainly capital intensive industries which came to the province required green field sites with a lot of space for expansion. This was one factor which led to the stop line around Belfast and the growth town policy. This meant that workers had to be encouraged to move and this policy of labour mobility meant the end of the extended family and the neighbourhood as the bases of community life. In addition the new industries demanded financial assistance, the provision of a skilled workforce and an attractive environment if they were to be persuaded to come. This led to the increased need for central government control and the development of physical and economic plans and resulted finally in the reorganization of local government with the centralization of all important decisions.

The increasing domination of the economy by foreign capital and the reshaping of the province to meet its needs could only be done at the expense of the small shopkeeper, local industrialists etc. who made up the orange coalition. This led to the conflict within the Protestant camp from the 1940's onwards between those classes in the economy who were losing out and those who represented and allied themselves to the new industrial interests. Gradually the latter gained the upper hand and during the 1960's the O'Neill Unionists were able to force through many of the necessary structural changes in the way the province was run. These same changes were important in raising Catholic demands for a right to participate in the running of the state and for a fairer distribution of services which led to the civil rights campaign.

At a localised level these changes necessitated the end of the close-knit community as both an important social unit and as a base for the distribution of resources. In the former labour mobility combined with the promised material benefits that industrial development would bring, led to younger families moving out to the growth towns. Large scale redevelopment further decimated remaining family and friendship networks.

In their place new communities were built whose structure was determined by the needs of the monopoly capitalist firms who now dominated the economy. Thus communities became defined in terms of the number of people necessary to provide a profitable catchment area for district centre/community hall/primary school etc. Economic criteria replaced the need to placate individual communities in determining the type and location of community facilities. This resulted in the centralisation of leisure and social centres. This centralisation together with an expected increase in economic wealth led to the end of the community as an idea tied to a specific geographical base and its replacement by a community based on shared activities.

As the importance of the classes represented in the orange coalition declined so did the structure through which they exerted their influence. With the centralisation of government functions, local authorities were left with little power. The centralised bodies with their appointed and elected members did not necessarily depend on any one community for their support. As the old communities were broken up they lost their position as a base through which resources could or needed to be distributed

None of these changes took place without a whole series of inter-related conflicts developing at national and local level. On the Shankill itself the small shopkeepers through redevelopment and the need to create monopolies for the large retail stores, were threatened with extinction. The working class elements were split in a number of ways. There were the minority who moved to the new towns in search of a better way of life. For many, as evidenced by their return to the Shankill, this turned out to be a mirage. The effect of the 'troubles' and the general international economic recession meant that the planned employment growth did not materialise. The planners' vision of an affluent working class commuting to and from growth centres along the motorways and primary distributors while their wives used the district distributors to go to the local district centre, turned distinctly sour.

Another section of the working class came to realise that the changes in terms of redevelopment, employment opportunities etc., which were held ot be developments taking place to benefit them, were in practice an attack on their living standards as well as being part of a policy aimed to destroy their position as a labour aristocracy and forcing them into a Catholic dominated united Ireland. They saw that the increased financial (rents, retail prices, bus fares etc.) costs and social (loss of community, high rise flats etc.) costs associated with the redevelopment of the Shankill did not lead to any noticeable increase in their well being.

Finally there were those who from the beginning saw that the loss of community that redevelopment entailed could never be replaced. These included the old age pensioners who lost their last remaining social usefulness and those in low paid unskilled jobs who had no way of compensating for the increased costs.

It is in the light of these objections that the Save the Shankill's campaign can best be understood. The demands to retain as much of the Shankill as possible, especially the Shankill as a shopping road, and to replicate what had been destroyed—terraced housing built around a neighbourhood base, reflected a common awareness that the planned changes were not in their economic and social interests. It is working out what these interests are which is now the task facing the Protestant working class.

Postscript

THE SAVE THE SHANKILL CAMPAIGN - SIX YEARS ON

This postscript is an attempt to outline the major developments on the Shankill during the past six years during which the Save The Shankill Campaign has been in existence. It neither necessarily reflects the analysis or views of Ron Wiener, nor those of the Save The Shankill Campaign, but is an attempt by Jackie Redpath, who has been centrally involved in the Campaign and who lives locally, to understand what has been happening, and to point some ways forward for the Shankill.

By March 1977 the Save The Shankill Campaign believed that the process of destruction of the Shankill, begun unwittingly under post-war Unionist Governments, had been seized on by the Northern Ireland Office and British Army, after the imposition of direct rule, as a means of solving the sectarian strife in Belfast. Redevelopment was to be used to effect a division of the city into Protestant East and Catholic West, separated by the commercial city centre and connected only by three bridges across the river Lagan.

Until this point, it had seemed that the Save The Shankill Campaign was well on its way to achieving most of its objectives. Guarantees had been given that no more dwellings would be built on the Shankill above two storeys, and two-storey terraced houses had already replaced blocks of flats at Percy Street. Plans for the multi-national district centre for shopping had been abandoned and the Campaign was involved in detailed negotiations about the future of ribbon shopping, which it wanted to retain; the Department of Environment had scrapped the grandiose ringroad proposals for Belfast and was setting up a further public inquiry into the city's transportation needs. In the Upper Shankill, above the redevelopment area (soon to be named "Middle Shankill" by the planners) the Save The Shankill Campaign had persuaded the Northern Ireland Housing Executive to carry out a pilot rehabilitation scheme on a small number of derelict houses, and had itself formed the Woodvale and Shankill Housing Association Ltd. to engage in rehabilitation work. The troubles, which discouraged significant economic investment, the economic recession, and not least, community opposition and pressure, were all factors which had helped to destroy the "grand schemes" of the Belfast Urban Area Plan.

However, the significance of two crucial factors was not fully realised by the Save The Shankill Campaign at this stage. Firstly, while vetoing unacceptable plans was important, forcing the implementation of acceptable alternative plans was much more difficult; and in the meantime the rate of demolition in the redevelopment area was far out-pacing the rebuilding. The exodus from the area from 1973-77 was at a rate of 2000 people per year leaving an increasingly ageing population and an unbalanced and untenable population structure.

Secondly, central government was not going to lose control of the situation. What appeared to be important concessions won by the Save The Shankill Campaign also involved them in long and detailed negotiations, which suited the government since they had time and resources on their side and the process of decline was accelerating all the time. The Campaign was involved in seven major negotiating meetings over a three years period before a final plan for the future of ribbon shopping was agreed. It is difficult for a local group to maintain support and credibility over such a long period with few obvious achievements.

At the same time the discredited Urban Area Plan was being redrawn in a different fashion. With the renewed national interest in the problems of the inner-city, the role of the Belfast Development Office (B.D.O.), was switched from depopulating inner Belfast by the growth centre policy, to revitalising the inner city. For Belfast this meant piecing together a new plan for the future of the city. Significantly, the B.D.O. staffing was increased by the addition of the Civilian Liaison Officers, formerly based in British Army Barracks. (See page 151) The new Development Officer for the Shankill had been based with the Army in Crossmaglen for the previous five years. A new dimension had been added to the redevelopment process.

THE SHANKILL PLOT

In March 1977 the Save The Shankill Campaign issued a leaflet, alleging that a plan existed at Northern Ireland Office level to completely wipe out the Shankill using redevelopment as the means. Since November 1976, five main pieces of evidence had come into the Campaign's possession which led it to this conclusion. Firstly, while plans for the district centre for shopping had been scrapped, no long term leases had been given to the remaining vested shops, now managed by the Housing Executive. Instead the Save The Shankill Campaign documented evidence of ten shops, which when they had become idle had been bricked-up, in spite of the fact that new traders were anxious to open businesses in them. Secondly, in November 1976 the Ladybird Clothing Factory was closed following a multi-national takeover of the firm and 200 jobs were lost. The Department of Commerce refused to intervene despite evidence showing that the factory unit was viable and profitable.

Most significantly in January 1977, a confidential document was presented to the Board of the Housing Executive, prepared by a Northern Ireland Office working party, on the future of West Belfast. (The report was leaked to the press by a Board member, after which all members were forced to sign the Official Secrets Act). In relation to the Shankill, the report recommended a curtailment, if not complete abandonment of further house building on the Shankill. At the same time the Campaign came into possession of a plan produced by the B.D.O., about the future of Shankill shopping, of which even the Housing Executive planners were unaware, which showed the moving of the redevelopment line from Crimea Street to Tennent Street at the top of the Shankill. These latter two proposals, if implemented, would have destroyed virtually the last remaining populated part of the old Shankill and left acres of dereliction in the original redevelopment areas, 11/33 and 12/13. The 109 new houses built in the Percy Street area were all that would replace the original 3000 houses on the south side of the Shankill.

Finally, in early March 1977 it was confirmed by the Department of

Plan to wipe out Shankill!

WITHIN THE PAST WEEK THE SAVE THE SHANKILL CAMPAIGN
HAS RECEIVED STARTLING INFORMATION THAT THE GOVERNMENT
IS NOW DELIBERATELY ATTEMPTING TO WIPE OUT THE SHANKILL.

SECRET GOVERNMENT DOCUMENT

A secret N.I.Office Report has already gone before the
Board of the Housing Executive (in January) which
recommends the complete abandoning of plans to build
any more new houses on the Shankill. The area above
Malvern Street is to be turned into one big playing
field.

DEMOLITION LINE EXTENDED

A plan has been recently drawn which moves the redevelopment
line up to Tennent Street - because of this the Shankill
Mission have been ordered to stop opening bricked-up houses
in an area above Crimea Street. The houses above Tennent
Street are to be demolished to make way for a major 6
lane road.

SCHOOLS SCRAPPED AND RUNDOWN

The Dept. of Education has just taken a decision to scrap
a big new Community School in the Lower Shankill. One
headmaster has been instructed to reduce his staff due
to an expected reduction of population in the Upper Shankill
area.

JOBS LOST

Within the past 2 years 4000 jobs have been lost in the
area. The N.I.Office deliberately allowed the Ladybird
Factory to close when they had information that it could
have continued as an economically viable unit - 200 jobs
were lost.

Support the

The SAVE THE SHANKILL CAMPAIGN
accuses the N.I.Office of
deliberately trying to wipe out
the Shankill and its people.

We call on all the people on the
Shankill to be aware of this plot
and to organise and fight!

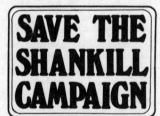

STAND TOGETHER AND WIN TOGETHER!

*Signed: U.W.C./U.D.A./O.V./U.V.F./Shankill Unionist Assoc./Some
Local Clergy/Womens Action/Shankill Community Council.*

Leaflet issued by the Save The Shankill Campaign in March 1977

SAVE THE SHANKILL CAMPAIGN | What has been achieved:

1. NO MORE FLATS will be built on the Shankill. Instead the Shankill will be developed in a series of small neighbourhoods, on a street pattern, with TERRACED HOUSING –
look at the houses in Percy Street then compare them with the flats in the Lower Shankill.

Terraced housing at Percy Street development:–
A Victory for the Save the Shankill Campaign.

2. The Campaign has stopped the building of a massive international chain store monopoly at Agnes Street which would have destroyed shopping on the Shankill as we knew it.

3. The Campaign has stopped the demolition of a whole section of shops on the Shankill, between Townsend Street – Percy Street and Spiers Place – Conway Street.

4. The Campaign has stopped the building of a heating plant on the Falls Road to heat the South side of the Shankill. Instead the Heating Plant will be built on the Shankill.

5. The Campaign has had police patrols stepped up on the Shankill at night to stop the break-ins on shops.

6. The Campaign has convinced the City Council to buy the Stadium and turn it into a Recreation Centre for young people.

7. The Campaign has succeeded in stopping Malvern/Forster Street and Blaney Street – Glenfarne Street from being knocked down. Instead the houses will be improved and have bathrooms built on.

8. The Campaign has worked with Shankill Road Mission in having bricked-up houses opened in Ulverston Street, Sugarfield Street, Ohio Street and Mountcashel Street.

9. The Campaign has set up the Woodvale and Shankill Housing Association which will open 30 bricked-up houses in the next two years.

Leaflet issued by the Save The Shankill Campaign in March 1977

Education that the plans to build a new community school in the heart of the redevelopment area, for 1100 pupils, had been shelved.[1]Other primary school principals in the area were told to reduce their staff due to expected population decline in the Upper Shankill area. The result was a huge question mark over the very future of the Shankill.

Ultimately this situation had its roots in the long term economic and industrial policies followed by successive Unionist Governments, which stripped areas like the Shankill of the economically active section of its community, for relocation in growth centres. Unquestionably it also resulted from mismanagement of the redevelopment process by the Belfast Corporation and subsequently the Northern Ireland Housing Executive, in which no street by street, or leap-frog renewal took place, but instead the pace of demolition far exceeded the rebuilding process.

However, the Save The Shankill Campaign had also come to believe that the Northern Ireland Office and British Army, reacting to a spate of sectarian murders in 1976, were, by late 1976, actively hastening the demise of the Shankill. The elimination of Protestant areas from North and West Belfast would alleviate territorial conflicts and equally importantly, free land which could eventually be used to rehouse overcrowded families in Catholic West Belfast. At this time the Chairman and Secretary of the Save The Shankill Campaign were privately told by an official of the B.D.O. that the real plans for the Shankill were in Army Headquarters in Lisburn. Because the Campaign feared leaving itself open to accusations of sectarianism it never made these allegations public; but there is little question that it saw its role as no longer simply negotiating for the quality of life in a future Shankill, but for actual future of the Shankill itself.

At a hastily arranged meeting in Stormont Castle on 13th April 1977, Lord Melchett the Minister of State responsible for a Belfast Areas of Need Programme, while denying that a plot existed to wipe out the Shankill, admitted to Campaign representatives that the future of the area above the redevelopment line (Mid-Shankill) was uncertain and that the planned community school on the Shankill had been shelved until the future population structure of the area became clearer. In reply to the allegation of the secret document at the January Housing Executive Board meeting, recommending the curtailment if not complete abandonment of new house building on the Shankill, the Minister stated, "I am not aware of such a report, I have not seen it." [2] But he could not guarantee that the land originally set aside for housing in the redevelopment area, would now be used for that purpose.

THE CARTER DOCUMENT

Events now moved swiftly. On 7th August 1977, with no consultation of any nature with the community concerned, Ray Carter, Under-Secretary of State responsible for the Department of Environment, issued a document "Housing Proposals in the Shankill Area of Belfast".[3] This outlined the Government's revised view of the future of the Shankill. One month was allowed for reply (Carter refused to extend the deadline) and on the 6th October 1977, Ray Carter accompanied by seven top D.O.E. and Housing Executive officials, including his assistant Permanent-Secretary, the Chief Belfast Planning Officer

163

and the Chairman and Director of Development of the Housing Executive won support for the document at a special Town Planning Committee meeting attended by eight councillor members. According to the City Council minutes of this meeting,[4] Carter stated that he was prepared to meet the Save The Shankill Campaign representatives (as demanded by Councillor H. Smyth) but he considered that the local councillors were the true representatives of the people of the area and he therefore wanted their agreement. By the end of the meeting it had "been moved, seconded and carried that the members agree in principle with the proposals as submitted". This was a bitter blow to the Campaign, especially since the same committee had pledged their support for the Save The Shankill Campaign three nights earlier at a private hearing. Subsequently, Carter stated in a letter he would meet Campaign representatives only, "in the context of my decision to proceed with the Shankill Housing Proposals as set out in the Department's Statement". Since this closed the door on any meaningful participation or negotiation the offer was not taken up.

The Carter blueprint for the future of the area confirmed the worst fears and allegations of the Save The Shankill Campaign. The acres of dereliction in the redevelopment areas, 11/33 and 12/13 would only be rebuilt "when there is clear evidence that there is sufficient demand within the Shankill area to justify this net addition to the housing stock in the Shankill". [5] The document also indicated that further redevelopment areas were to be declared above the present redevelopment line at Crimea Street, to be called Middle Shankill. The strategy outlined quite simply failed to grapple with the basic problem, of an ageing population, which could not sustain the fundamentals of community life, such as schools, shops, industry and which would in fact result in the eventual demise of the area.

THE HOUSING EXECUTIVE DOCUMENT

Ray Carter, having received City Council consent to his strategy instructed Northern Ireland Housing Executive planners to draw up detailed proposals for the redevelopment of Mid-Shankill. Four months later a document, "Shankill–Crimea Street/Tennent Street: A Development Strategy" was published by the Housing Executive.[6] It was launched to the people of the Shankill through the press and media in a major publicity effort. Once again, no consultation at any stage of its production had taken place with any group in the area. The document fully accepted the principles of Carter's proposals but was a masterpiece in public relations. It recommended the declaration of 6 new phases of redevelopment in Mid-Shankill, involving 1000 homes, with the displaced population moving in a carefully managed operation to new housing built on the derelict land in the existing redevelopment areas (11/33, 12/13). It emphasised, "no-one will have to leave the Shankill because of our plans".

The Save The Shankill Campaign soon however came into possession of an internal and unpublished document to which the Housing Executive were working. This differed from the public document considerably. It included the following reason for more demolition on the Shankill: "The proposed area for redevelopment is defined by the following criteria – the area of housing necessary to provide sufficient families to complete redevelopment in R.D.A.s. 11/33 and 12/13." This had been deleted from the public document. Also deleted was the zoning of areas as "white lands" based on "the expected continued decline of population in the area" which would result in these "white lands" becoming open space.[7] In other words, further redevelopment of the Shankill was being introduced not primarily because of poor housing, but as a means of covering past failures which had led to the population exodus. Far from the strategy revitalising the area, it was now accepted that the Shankill would decline further.

Even where the Executive document recommended the declaration of four Housing Action Areas within the remainder of Mid-Shankill, their action plan required the demolition of a further 600 houses within these areas. Beyond this the public document also failed to state that both short and long-term rehabilitation would be carried out in these Housing Action Areas allowing for the development of "core areas into which residents would be moved – to concentrate vacancies which could then be programmed for redevelopment". In view of this sort of duplicity and the increasingly overtly political nature of the redevelopment proposals, some community workers on the Shankill found it difficult to resist drawing parallels with South African government bulldozer action against black African townships.

THE SAVE THE SHANKILL CAMPAIGN RESPONSE

In response the Campaign demanded that the acres of derelict land within the existing redevelopment areas should be rebuilt with high quality family housing, to be allocated to young couples and those with families wishing to return to the area. This they claimed would help restore some population balance to the area.

Until existing redevelopment areas (11/33, 12/13) were completed Save The Shankill Campaign stated its opposition to the declaration of further redevelopment areas. Regarding Mid-Shankill, the Campaign recognised that a two-fold problem existed; an ageing population and poor housing conditions. In this context it argued that is was senseless to rebuild on the derelict redevelopment land for these residents, as recommended by the Housing Executive, since this would merely move the problem of the ageing population. Instead the Campaign proposed that the housing problem should be dealt with within the Mid-Shankill area by the declaration of a series of Housing Action Areas, with an emphasis on rehabilitation of the existing housing stock, but allowing for infill of new housing where required.

Subsequently, an independent study by Queen's University Department of Town and Country Planning confirmed that 88% of the residents of Mid-Shankill wished to remain in their area and concluded that, "a redevelopment programme would break up an existing community and never replace it". The Campaign also called for the establishment of a Shankill Development Agency which could adopt a comprehensive approach to shopping, employment, education and community facilities, as well as housing. However the Housing Executive has claimed that it can only discuss the future of the area within the limits of Ray Carter's document and deadlock has resulted. In January 1980 the Save The Shankill Campaign issued a press statement in which it claimed, "the 1970's have been the worst decade in the Shankill's history. The advent of the 1980's should be seized on as an opportunity for correcting past wrongs and building a future for

165

the Shankill." The statement concluded by calling on the D.O.E. and Housing Executive "to enter into full hearted and open-minded negotiations about the future of the area."[9]

CONCLUSION

So far the main lesson for those involved has been that popular community acion can exert only a negative, arresting force. The Save The Shankill Campaign has had significant practical achievements. Among these the district centre for shopping has been abandoned and ribbon shopping on the Shankill has been revitalised, with shopkeepers being given 20-25 year leases, new shops being built and older properties renovated. This has followed five years of negotiations between the Belfast Development Office and Save The Shankill Campaign. All attempts to build more flats have been abandoned and the disastrous 'Weetabix' blocks in the lower Shankill are to be demolished. Instead, several excellent phases of housing development have been built on a terraced street pattern mixing house types for old and young, which has almost eliminated vandalism and led to a high degree of satisfaction among the tenants. Community facilities in the area have also been improved resulting in a better quality of life for many people. The existence of the Campaign and its actions have focused the Governments attention on the area. The Campaign's strength lay in the popular support for the issues it fought, its ability to organise militant action; the maintenance of alliances with key councillors in the area; the paramilitary backing which could be called on when necessary; the local base of the activists in the Campaign and the availability, especially, early on, of outside planning expertise to draw up alternative plans, and the planning knowledge built up over 6 years by those involved.

A spin-off from the Campaign has been the growth of community self help schemes, resulting in the development of small employment projects and housing associations. However, the ability of these schemes to pass control into the hands of local people is questionable since they are invariably dependent on government assistance and this obviously creates difficulties for those involved in both them and the Campaign. There is nothing like having a housing association rehabilitation scheme awaiting registration at the Department of Environment, or submitting an application to set up a Y.O.P. employment scheme, to make you think twice about setting up barricades to stop redevelopment bulldozers.

In broader terms, at a time of public expenditure cuts and recession in traditional heavy industries, the area will come to match with ever greater approximation the employment conditions of Catholic West Belfast. Where approximately one quarter of the Shankill's employed population works in shipbuilding and engineering industries, as in the 1930s, a "sump" of unemployment, unparalleled anywhere else in the U.K. will be created. The absence of any coherent working class movement or opposition to this is likely to lead to increased confusion and general demoralisation, if it cannot be rectified. In such a situation the prospects of "local self-help" as an economic life-line are slimmer than ever, and local makeshifts become less and less satisfactory expedients to meet the recessionary pressures.

166

However against all this, those involved in the Save The Shankill Campaign will point to their firm belief that if it had not been for the Campaign's existence, it is questionable if the Shankill would exist at all today as a community.

Clearly the main weakness of the Campaign has been its inability to effectively tackle the Shankill's central problem, the restoration of its population balance, requiring the creation of jobs and the building of family houses in sufficient quantities. The resources to do this are held by central government and short of a major change in the control of those resources, community action on the Shankill, as elsewhere, can only hope to marginally influence their allocation.

A broader base from which the Campaign may be judged is whether it has brought about increased political awareness or a change of attitudes locally towards the power structure in our society. There are those within the Campaign and the community who see it purely as a form of defence against an expanding Catholic community in West Belfast. Others in the community, particularly those among the Churches and established political parties, continue to believe that the planners are "well-meaning folks" who make mistakes but who, with reasonable and intelligent persuasion are prepared to rectify them. These people see their own interests as synonymous with the status quo. However, there is a significant group of people within the Campaign, community workers and other groups within the community, who have recognised that what has happened in the Shankill over the past ten years has been against the social and economic interests of the Shankill community at large. These people are searching for a base through which their views and analysis can be expressed and developed. They recognise the need for a structure that is strong enough to develop in the face of sectarianism, and seek to implement a coherent political education programme.

All this is taking place against the background of continuing violence and uncertainty about British intentions on the political future of Northern Ireland. A growing lobby in Britain for the withdrawal of the constitutional guarantee to the majority will help to drive Protestants to a more extreme position. Locally, an increasingly economically depressed community sees its very existence within North and West Belfast threatened. Clearly, the Save The Shankill Campaign, while having an essentially utalitarian function, is not the vehicle for launching such a long term and positive programme.

Its strength as a veto body is it weakness as an "achieving" body and its history clearly illustrates the contradictions and difficulties which exist in N. Ireland for those who wish to see political and economic advance at a local level. The only long-term hope is the emergence of a politically conscious group with a strong base in the community who will recognise the need for wider working-class links and will be strong enough to make and maintain them.

Bibliography

CHAPTER ONE

1. E. Green: 'Economic History' in *Belfast in its regional setting: A Scientific Survey*: British Association for the Advancement of Science, 1952.
2. A. W. Hutton (ed.) *Arthur Young's Tour in Ireland (1776-1779)* London, George Bell & Sons, 1892; vol. II p. 209.
3. ibid Vol. II page 214
4. ibid Vol. II page 65
5. I. Budge & C. O'Leary: *Belfast: Approach to Crisis*: McMillan London 1973
6. A. W. Hutton (ed.): op.cit. Vol. I page 144
7. Budge & O'Leary: op.cit. page 18
8. A. W. Hutton (ed.): op.cit. Vol. II page 56
9. J. Moore M.D.: 'On the influence of Flax Spinning on the Health of the Mill Workers of Belfast in *Problems of a growing city: Belfast 1780-1870*: Public Record Office of Northern Ireland 1972.
10. ibid.
11. 'Extracts from the report by Capt. Gilbert on the proposed extension for the boundaries of the borough of Belfast 1852-3' in *Problems of a Growing City* op.cit.
12. Budge & O'Leary op.cit. page 75
13. Paraphrase of the Liberal-Unionist case against Home Rule put by Thomas Sinclair as reported in Budge & O'Leary op.cit. page 107
14. C. Desmond Greaves: *The Irish Crisis*: Lawrence & Wishcart 1972 London
15. I. Isles & N. Cuthbert: *An Economic Survey of Northern Ireland*, HMSO Belfast 1957 page 174
16. *Report of the Joint Working Party on the Economy of Northern Ireland*: Cmnd 446, HMSO Belfast 1962 par 198
17. J. Bayley: '*Northern Ireland 1950-1970: The Economic Base*' Northern Ireland Reasearch Institute, Occasional Paper 1973
18. Quoted in J. Bayley and K. Boehringer. *A Political Economy of Northern Ireland;* Northern Ireland Research Institute Working Paper 1974.
19. ibid.
20. *Problems of a Growing City* op.cit.
21. Quote from an English newspaper, reported in A. Boyd: *Holy War in Belfast* Anvil, Kerry 1969 page 87
22. E. Jones: Belfast: A Survey of the City: in *Belfast in its Regional Setting* op.cit.
23. A. Boyd op.cit. page 44
24. F. Wright: 'Protestant Ideology and Politics in Ulster': *European Journal of Sociology* xiv (1973) 213-280
25. E. McCann: *War and an Irish Town:* Penguin 1974
26. F. Wright op.cit.
27. W. M. Johnston: Belfast Newsletter 15th May 1861. Quoted in F. Wright. ibid.
28. D. Barritt & C. Carter: *The Northern Ireland Problem:* OUP London 1962 page 97.
29. ibid page 67
30. ibid page 108
31. ibid page 68
32. Figures derived from Budge & O'Leary op.cit. and J. Harbinson: *The Ulster Unionist Party* 1882-1973 Blackstaff Press 1973.
33. Liam de Paor: *Divided Ulster* Pelican 1972 page 105
34. R. Lawrence: *The Government of Northern Ireland* Clarendon Press Oxford 1965 page 25

35. A. W. Hutton (ed.) op.cit. vol. 1 page 146
36. Quoted in Budge & O'Leary op.cit. page 156
37. ibid page 82.
38. ibid page 50.
39. *The Elections,* Fortnight March 22, 1974
40. Quoted in Budge & O'Leary op.cit. page 61
41. ibid page 146
42. This section relies heavily on F. F. McKenzie Porter: A study of the urban growth of the Shankill, Falls and Springfield areas of Belfast from 1860-1900. Public Records Office N.I.
43. Extract from A. Malcolm: 'The sanitary state of Belfast with suggestions for its improvement' A paper read before the statistical section of the British Association 1852: Public Records Office N.I.
44. McKenzie Porter op.cit. page 17
45. Budge & O'Leary op.cit. page 55
46. ibid page 110
47. ibid page 111
48. Quoted in McKenzie Porter op.cit
49. Budge & O'Leary op.cit. page 126
50. W. D. Birrell et al.: *Housing in Northern Ireland* Centre for Environmental Studies October 1971 page 53
51. ibid Table 1.19
52. Professor N. J. Gibson in a letter to *The Guardian* 4/6/74.
53. W. Birrell op.cit. page 59
54. Sir. Lucius O'Brien quoted in W. Birrell: ibid page 76
55. ibid: page 68
56. Budge & O'Leary op.cit. page 167
57. R. J. Lawrence op.cit. page 68
58. ibid page 70
59. W. Birrell op. cit. page 82
60. ibid table 3.2
61. ibid page 117
62. ibid page 97
63. Northern Ireland Housing Executive: *Housing Condition Survey:* 1974 Belfast
64. Housing (clearance and redevelopment) Committee Belfast Corporation 27/1/60
65. ibid
66. ibid 24/10/58
67. ibid 30/3/60
68. ibid 2/9/64
69. Ald. Sir Cecil McKee reported in the *Belfast Telegraph* 3/1/64
70. W. Birrell op.cit.
71. Housing Committee Minutes op.cit. 12/2/64
72. W. Birrell op.cit. page 122
73. D. Field: 'Study of unsatisfactory tenants' Quoted in A.E.C.W. Spencer: *Ballymurphy: A Tale of Two Surveys* Queens University 1973

CHAPTER 2

1. *Housing in Northern Ireland:* Interim Report of the Planning Advisory Board Cmd 224 1944 HMSO
2. *Location of Industry in Northern Ireland:* Interim Report of the Planning Advisory Board Cmd 225 1944 HMSO
3. *Planning Proposals for the Belfast Area:* Interim Report of the Planning Commission: 1945 Cmd 227 HMSO
4. *Road Communications in Northern Ireland:* Interim Report of the Planning Commission 1946 Cmd 241

5. *The Second Report on Planning Proposals for the Belfast area* Planning Commission Cmd 302 1951
6. W. R. Davidge: *Preliminary Report on Reconstruction and Planning*: Min. of Home Affairs: Belfast: 1944
7. R. H. Matthew: *Belfast*: *Regional Survey and Plan* 1962 HMSO Belfast 1964
8. *Northern Ireland Development Programme 1970-1975* Belfast HMSO 1970
9. *Report of the Joint Working Party on the Economy of Northern Ireland* Cmd 446 1962
10. C. D. Greaves: *The Irish Crisis* Lawrence and Wishart 1972 p.50
11. Northern Ireland Discussion Paper: *Finance and the economy* HMSO 1974
12. E. McCann: *War and an Irish town* Penguin 1974 p.208
13. Building Design Partnership: *Belfast Urban Area Plan* 1969 vol. 2 p.67
14. Matthew op.cit. Appendix 7
15. 1970-1975 Programme op.cit. para. 68
16. ibid page 140
17. ibid. para. 70
18. BDP op.cit. vol 1. p. 10
19. Matthew op.cit. Appendix 7, table 61
20. BDP op.cit. vol 2. p. 37
21. ibid.
22. R. Wiener *Fortnight* 5/1/73
23. *Re-organisation of Secondary Education in Northern Ireland* Cmd 574 HMSO 1973
24. Education Times 19/10/73
25. Matthew op.cit. para. 176
26. *1970-75 Programme* op.cit. paras. 50/51
27. ibid paras. 55-58
28. Matthew op.cit. para. 173
29. BDP op.cit. vol. 1.
30. *1970-1975 Development Programme* op.cit. page 161
31. *Finance and the economy* op.cit.
32. McCann op.cit. p. 208
33. J. Bayley: *Northern Ireland 1950-1970: The Economic Base:* Northern Ireland Research Institute Occasional Paper Belfast 1973
34. *Review Body on Local Government in Northern Ireland:* Cmd 596 Belfast HMSO
35. BDP op.cit. vol. 2 p. 11
36. ibid. vol. 1 p. 28
37. W. D. Birrell et.al *Labour mobility in Northern Ireland:* New University of Ulster.
38. *Housing in Northern Ireland* op. cit. p. 24
39. Irish Times Friday 29/6/62
40. Newsletter 29/6/62
41. Minutes of Special Belfast City Council Meeting 10/2/64.
42. R. J. McConnell & Co. *The Belfast Property Register* August 1894 Vol. vii No. 1
43. Matthew op.cit. para. 64
44. Minutes of Improvement Committee of Belfast City Council 31/8/64.
45. ibid. 25/8/64.
46. McCann op.cit. p. 208
47. *The BUS Guide to District Centres:* Holy Smoke Press January 1974
48. BDP op.cit. vol. 1. page 86
49. From the Northern Ireland Housing Executive: *First Annual Report* 1972.
50. Figures derived from the Digest of Statistics No. 41. Tables 75/76 March 1974 HMSO Belfast and from Housing Returns for Northern Ireland up to 30th September 1973 Ministry of Development HMSO.
51. *The Report of the Environmental Health Services of the City of Belfast* 1973.
52. ibid.
53. *Housing in Northern Ireland* op.cit.
54. Report of the Ministry of Development 1965/66 Cmd. 504 HMSO Belfast.
55. ibid Cmd. 516

170

CHAPTER 3

1. *Northern Ireland Development Programme 1970-1975:* Belfast HMSO 1970 page 145.
2. Ibid page 147.
3. *Digest of Statistics.* Northern Ireland No. 42 Sept. 1974 Belfast HMSO Table 110.
4. Ibid.
5. *Planning Proposals for the Belfast Area:* Interim Report of the Planning Commission Cmd 227 Belfast HMSO 1945.
6. *Road Communications in Northern Ireland:* Interim Report of the Planning Commission Cmd 241 Belfast HMSO 1946.
7. R. H. Matthew: *Belfast: Regional Survey and Plan* Belfast HMSO 1962 para 867.
8. Ibid para. 689.
9. Ibid para. 703.
10. Ibid para. 705.
11. Minutes of Belfast City Council Improvement Committee 31/8/64.
12. Belfast Telegraph 23/5/73.
13. Ibid.
14. R. Travers Morgan & Partners (N.I.): *Belfast Transportation Plan* Belfast June, 1969 para. 2.06.
15. Ibid. para. 14.04.
16. *Northern Ireland Development Programme* op.cit. p. 157.
17. *Belfast Transportation Plan* op.cit. para. 6.08.
18. *Social Trends* No. 4, 1973 HMSO Table 144.
19. *Digest of Statistics* op.cit. table 97.
20. *Social Trends* op.cit. table 65
21. *Changing Directions:* A Report from the Independent Commission on Transport: Coronet Books London 1974 para. 2.4
22. Ibid table A.
23. Ibid para 2.6.
24. Ibid para. 6.37.
25. *Social Trends* op.cit. table 144.
26. M. Hammer: *Wheels within Wheels: A Study of the Road Lobby* Friends of the Earth 1974.
27. Belfast Telegraph 11/3/73.
28. C.I.S. *British Leyland. The Beginning of the End?* Anti-Report No. 5 1974.
29. W. Plowden: *The Motor Car and Politics in Britain:* Pelican 1973 page 361.
30. *Traffic in Towns: A Study of the long-term problems of traffic in urban areas.* Ministry of Transport HMSO 1963.
31. Ibid.
32. R. M. Rutherford: *Belfast Urban Area Plan Public Inquiry* Belfast HMSO 1973 para. 39.
33. Ibid. para. 41.
34. Second Report from the Expenditure Committee. *Urban Transport Planning Vol. 1. House of Commons* 1972 para 20.
35. *Belfast Transportation Plan* op.cit. para. A.27.
36. R. Overy: Background to the Belfast Transportation Plan: in *Sandy Row at the Public Inquiry:* Sandy Row Redevelopment Association, Belfast 1972.
37. A detailed account of the effect of blight on a community is given in *Roden Street: Death of a Community.* Greater West Belfast Community Association, Belfast 1973.
38. From Minutes of Belfast City Council Housing (Clearance and Redevelopment) Committees.
39. Report by Building Design Partnership to the Belfast City Council Housing (Clearance and Redevelopment) Committee 24/4/65.
40. Belfast Urban Study Group: *The Off-White Elephant.* Belfast March 1974.
41. Department of the Environment: *Fatal Accidents: Record of Fatal Accidents, Fatalities etc. during the* 3 years 1 January 1970 - 31 December 1972 Belfast 1973.
42. M. Hillman, I. Henderson and A. Whalley: *Personal Mobility and Transport Policy* PEP Broadsheet 542. June 1973, page 29.
43. *Belfast Transportation Plan* op.cit. table 5.03.

44. *Urban Transport Planning* op.cit. para. 22 .
45. Quoted in *The BUS Report on the Belfast Urban Motorway* Belfast Urban Study Group, Belfast 1973.
46. *Belfast Urban Area Plan Inquiry* op.cit.
47. Ibid.
48. Why Gun and Bomb may halt Belfast's Urban Motorway *New Civil Engineer* 6/12/73.
49. Cllr. Brand: Belfast Telegraph 1/12/64. Quoted in R. Overy op.cit.
50. *The BUS Report on the Belfast Urban Motorway* op.cit..
51. *The Off-White Elephant* op.cit.
52. *The BUS Report on the Belfast Urban Motorway* op.cit.
53. *Belfast Ring Road.* The Republican Movement 1973.
54. Ibid.
55. *Combat* vol. 1 No. 3 April 1974.
56. Extract from letter by Muriel Pritchard, Alliance Councillor, Belfast Telegraph 10/10/73.
57. Belfast Telegraph 30/4/74.
58. Irish Times 28/3/73.
59. *Urban Transport Planning* op.cit. para. 155
60. Irish News 6/4/74.
61. Quoted in Irish News 7/11/73.
62. Quoted in 'Motorway fight unites Belfast ghettoes' The Observer 14/10/73.
63. Quote from letter by Concannon to Belfast Urban Study Group 7/1/75.

CHAPTER 4

1. The Shorter Oxford English Dictionary: Third Edition Clarendon Press Oxford 1969.
2. A. McKenzie Porter: *A Study of the urban growth of the Shankill, Falls and Springfield areas of Belfast from 1860 to 1900.* N.I. Public Records Office.
3. Ibid.
4. Building Design Partnership: *Redevelopment of the Shankill* 1967.
5. Turf Lodge Development Association: *Report on unemployment survey Nov. 1972.*
6. From evidence given by Dr. Swann, Medical Officer of Health at Area A Public Inquiry, February 1960.
7. Shankill resident.
8. F. Mercer: *Sandy Row—A Study before redevelopment* Dept. of Social Studies, Queen's University, Belfast, Nov. 1971, p. 47.
9. M. Young & P. Willmott: *Family and kinship in East London* Pelican 1972 p. 117.
10. E Bott: *Family and Social Network:* Tavistock 1957.
11. O. Newman and J. Mansfield: Defensible Space: *The Listener* March 8th 1974.
12. F. Mercer op.cit. p. 47.
13. Shankill resident.
14. Ibid.
15. *Redevelopment of the Shankill* op.cit.
16. Shankill resident
17. Ibid.
18. Ibid.
19. Ibid.
20. *Shankill Review* 1969, Howard Publications, Belfast.
21. F. Mercer op.cit. tables 4.8 and 4.10.
22. *Redevelopment of the Shankill* op.cit.
24. W. Birrell et.al.: *Labour Mobility in Northern Ireland:* New University of Ulster.
25. Craigavon New City: *Household Survey for Brownlow* Summer 1969.
26. Phase 1 Shankill Redevelopment Areas 12/13 Redevelopment Group Area Survey January 1973.

172

27. 1966 Census figures in J. Greer: *Progress Report on Redevelopment* Belfast City Planning Dept. 1971.
28. Figures from BDP Redevelopment Area Programme
29. Figures presented by Belfast Area Housing Manager at Public Inquiry into the vesting of areas 11/33 Feb. 1973.
30. Building Design Partnership: *Belfast Urban Area Plan* Vol. 11, p 28.
31. *Shankill Road Redevelopment* Northern Ireland Housing Executive October 1972.
32. Evidence prepared by City Planning Department for areas 11/33 public inquiry Feb. 1973.
33. *Redevelopment of the Shankill* op.cit.
34. *Belfast Urban Area Plan* op.cit. Vol. 1 p. 88.
35. Ibid vol. 2 p. 243.
36. J. Greer op.cit.
37. Mr. Kelly representing local shopkeepers at the Area A Public Inquiry Feb. 1960.
38. These were on the North Side: from Upper Townsend St. to Malvern St. and from Malvern St. to Crimea St. and on the south side from Canmore St. to Northumberland St. and from Northumberland St. to Townsend St.
39. *Shankill Road Redevelopment* op.cit.
40. From Area A Public Inquiry Feb. 1960.
41. P. Lawrence: *Shankill Housing Estate Survey*, University of Surrey/Shankill Community Council, Sept. 1974.
42. for example:
    a) BDP's studies reported in Belfast Urban Area Plan op.cit. vol. 2 p. 27.
    b) Belfast housing department studies reported by McCabe at the Public Inquiry into the vesting of areas 12/13 1972.
    c) Local studies such as that by F. Mercer op.cit. p. 75.
43. Housing (Clearance and Redevelopment) Committee 11/3/70.
44. Statement by the Ministry of Development on the Belfast Urban Area Plan. HMSO Belfast 1973.
45. *Shankill Road redevelopment* op.cit.
46. Ibid.
47. Ibid.
48. P. Lawrence op.cit.
49. Phase 1 op.cit.
50. *Shankill Road Redevelopment* op.cit.
51. Figures derived from latest Housing Executive published plans and figures 1974.
52. Digest of Statistics N.I. No. 39 March 1973 Table 2 HMSO Belfast.
53. *Shankill Road Redevelopment* op.cit.
54. Contained in original plans for Area C.
55. From cross-examination at the public inquiry into the vesting of Area C June 1968.
56. Figures from *The BUS Guide to District Centres* Holy Smoke Press Belfast 1974.
57. *Redevelopment of the Shankill* op.cit.
59. On 1972 Housing Executive plans for areas 12/13.
60. Northern Ireland Family Expenditure Survey Reports for 1968 and 1972.
61. *Shankill Road Redevelopment* op.cit.
62. Housing Executive Phase 1 Draft Plans Areas 12/13 February 1974.
63. P. Lawrence op.cit.
64. See for example S. Keller: *The Urban Neighbourhood* Random House 1968 for an excellent summary of such studies.
65. *Housing in Northern Ireland:* Interim Report of the Planning Advisory Board Cmd 224 1944 HMSO Belfast.
66. From the Report on the *Resident's Association Conference:* Greater West Belfast Area Jan. 1973.
67. H. Frazer: *Study of those areas of the Lower Shankill that have undergone redevelopment.* Shankill Community Council April 1973.
68. Housing (Clearance and Redevelopment) Committee 6/11/57.
69. Ibid 29/11/61
70. Building Design Partnership: *Belfast Urban Area Interim Planning Policy* Sept. 1967.

71. Chairman of the Lower Shankill Redevelopment Association in a foreword to Phase 1 survey op.cit.
72. F. Mercer op.cit. **p. 35.**
73. *Redevelopment of the Shankill* op.cit.
74. Northern Ireland Housing Executive: Second Annual Report 1972/73
75. *Shankill Road Redevelopment* op.cit.

CHAPTER 5

1. Survey of Black Mountain Estate Nov. 1973 in *Blackmountain and Springmartin Estates:* A Report compiled by Ballygomartin Community Group, Springmartin Community Association and Springmartin Action Committee 1974 Belfast.
2. Sunday News 20/1/74. p. 9.
3. F. Boal, P. Doherty and D. Pringle: *The Spatial Distribution of some social problems in the Belfast Urban Area* Northern Ireland Community Relations Commission, Belfast 1974.
4. Figures from table F.04: R. Travers Morgan & Partners: *Belfast Transportation Plan* Belfast 1969: based on 1966 census.
5. Boal et al. op.cit.
6. Building Design Partnership: *Redevelopment of the Shankill* Belfast 1968.
7. *Digest of Statistics No.* 39 March 1973, Belfast HMSO 1973.
8. Housing Act (N.I.) 1961.
9. Information presented at the public inquiry into the vesting of areas 11/33, March 1973.
10. Ibid.
11. Sunday News 13/1/74.
12. Ibid 20/1/74.
13. *Community Action* No. 11 Nov.-Dec. 1973 London.
14. *Shankill Redevelopment* Northern Ireland Housing Executive booklet June 1973.
15. *Moving out of a slum:* MHLG HMSO London 1970.
16. *Northern Ireland Family Expenditure Survey: Report for 1968 and 1969:* HMSO
17. Figure from BDP: *Redevelopment of the Shankill:* Belfast 1967.
18. *Northern Ireland Family Expenditure Survey: Report for 1972:* Belfast HMSO 1974.
19. Figure derived from street surveys in Phase 1 of areas 12/13 and 11/33, 1972/3.
20. Average figure for rent of 3 bedroom house, which is the most typical building on the new Shankill estate, from evidence given by Belfast Housing Manager at vesting order inquiry into areas 11/33 March 1973.
21. P. Lawrence: *A Report on Housing Satisfaction on the New Shankill Estate,* Shankill Community Council 1974.
22. A. Thompson: *Survey of houses occupied in Shankill Redevelopment Area C.* New University of Ulster 1972.
23. Information supplied by the Northern Ireland Housing Executive Belfast Region Information Office, 16/8/74.
24. Northern Ireland Housing Trust *Final Report 1970-71:* 1971 Belfast.
25. Northern Ireland Housing Executive: *2nd Annual Report:* 1st April 1972 to 31st March 1973. Belfast 1974.
26. Minister for Housing, Planning and Local Government: Minutes of the Northern Ireland Assembly 30/4/74.
27. *2nd Annual Report* op.cit.
28. Figures from Northern Ireland Housing Trust *1970-1971 final report.*
29. Figures from Northern Ireland Housing Executive: *2nd Annual Report.*
30. Figure from Belfast Housing Manager.
31. Public Inquiry 11/33 op.cit.
32. *Northern Ireland Family Expenditure Survey: Report for 1972* HMSO Belfast 1974.
33. J. Greer: *Shopping at Shankill District Centre:* Belfast City Planning Dept. March 1972.
34. P. Lawrence op.cit.

174

35. J. Lazenbatt: Belfast Estates Superintendent (now Director of Housing Management: Housing Executive) giving evidence at the Public Inquiry into the vesting of the Upper Library Street Scheme (Area A) February 1960.
36. *The BUS (Belfast Urban Study Group) Guide to the District Centres*: Holy. Smoke Press, Belfast 1974.
37. Evidence from a survey carried out by the Hammer Redevelopment Group and presented at the public inquiry into areas 11/33, March 1973.
38. J. Greer op.cit.
39. *Belfast Transportation Plan* op.cit. para. 22.45.
40. Figures from *NIFES Report for 1972* op.cit. Tables 7/8.
41. *The BUS Guide to District Centres* op.cit.
42. P. Lawrence op.cit.
43. *Redevelopment of the Shankill* op.cit.
44. From the Public Inquiry into the vesting of Area C: 10/6/67.
45. P. Lawrence op.cit.
46. M. Young and P. Willmott: *Family and Kinship in East London* Pelican 1972.
47. Ibid.
48. *Redevelopment of the Shankill* op.cit.
49. *Family and Kinship* in East London op.cit.
50. P. Lawrence op.cit.
51. *Redevelopment of the Shankill* op.cit.
52. N.I.H.E. *Shankill Road Redevelopment* 1972.
53. *2nd Annual Report* op.cit.
54. Islington Research Group: 'Who makes money out of council housing?' *Community Action No. 5* Nov.-Dec. 1972.
55. Sports Council Study: *Indoor Sports Centres* HMSO London 1971.

CHAPTER 6

1. From evidence given at the public inquiry into the vesting of areas 11/33, 12/13th March 1973.
2. Minutes of Belfast City Council (Town Planning and Environmental Health) Committee 14/3/74.
3. Extract from a letter by Currie, Minister of Housing, Local Government and Planning to P. McLachlan, M.A. 12/3/74.
4. Extract from letter by R. Miller, Private Secretary to the Secretary of State to the Secretary, Hammer Redevelopment Group, 24/4/73.
5. Ibid 14/6/73.
6. Belfast City Council Housing (Clearance and Redevelopment) Committee 18/11/64.
7. 26/4/73.
8. 14/5/73.
9. Extract from letter by Hammer Redevelopment Association to the Deputy City Surveyor 23/5/73.
10. Letter from Miss M. Seale 25/4/73.
11. Newsletter 31/1/74.
12. Minutes of the Northern Ireland Assembly 31/1/74.
13. Belfast Telegraph 31/1/74.
14. From Currie to McLachlan op.cit.
15. From letter by Currie to author 30/4/74.
16. Greater West Belfast Community Association: *First Annual Report 1973*.
17. McLachlan: Minutes of Northern Ireland Assembly 30/4/74.
18. Claire Curry, Jackie Redpath, Ron Wiener 9/5/74.
19. P. Mark. *House Repairs in Redevelopment Area, Shankill Road,* Shankill Community Council August 1974.
20. *Blackmountain and Springmartin Estates:* A Report compiled by Ballygomartin Community Group, Springmartin Community Association, Springmartin Action Committee.
21. Ibid.

22. Northern Ireland Housing Executive: *Housing Condition Survey* 1974 Belfast.
23. Northern Ireland Housing Executive: *Third Annual Report* 1st Aprli 1973 to 31st March 1974.
24. Housing Condition Survey op.cit.
25. From an essay by a Shankill schoolgirl.

CHAPTER 7

1. *People and Planning:* Report of the Committee on Public Participation in Planning London HMSO 1969.
2. Building Design Partnership: *Redevelopment of the Shankill* Belfast 1968.
3. Belfast Housing (Clearance and Redevelopment) Committee 31/3/65.
4. Ibid 22/5/68.
5. Northern Ireland Housing Executive: First Annual Report 1971/72.
6. *Built Environment:* 'An Interview with Rae Evans' February 1974.
7. M. Broady: *Planning for People:* Bedford Square Press 1968 p. 55.
8. S. Bailie. et al. *Community Development Project: A First Report* Oldham, July 1973.
9. From letter by Rowlands, Director of Community Relations Commission, to author, 7/4/73.
10. From a Ministry of Community Relations document reported in: H. Griffiths: *Community Development in Northern Ireland: A Case Study in Agency Conflict:* Priorities, New University of Ulster 1974.
11. H. Griffiths ibid.
12. Ibid.
13. *Belfast Urban Area Plan: Public Inquiry* HMSO 1973.
14. The Guardian 9/11/74. 'Judge clamps down on tenant pickets'.

POSTSCRIPT

1. Letter to Save The Shankill Campaign from N.I. Department of Education, March 1977.
2. Save The Shankill Campaign Minutes of a meeting with Lord Melchett, 13/4/1977.
3. *Housing Proposals in the Shankill Area of Belfast.* Department of Environment August 1977.
4. Belfast City Council Minutes, November 1977.
5. Department of Environment, op.cit.
6. *Shankill – Crimea St/Tennent St: A Development Strategy,* Northern Ireland Housing Executive, 1978.
7. cf. Shankill Bulletin No. 1 March 1979.
8. *A Study of the Mid-Shankill Area,* Department of Town and Country Planning, Queen's University, Belfast, 1978. (unpublished)
9. Shankill Bulletin No 11, February 1980.